A Nation of Small Shareholders

STUDIES IN INDUSTRY AND SOCIETY

Philip B. Scranton, Series Editor

*Published with the assistance of
the Hagley Museum and Library*

A Nation of Small Shareholders

Marketing Wall Street after World War II

Janice M. Traflet

The Johns Hopkins University Press
Baltimore

The Johns Hopkins University Press
2715 North Charles Street
Baltimore, Maryland 21218-4363
www.press.jhu.edu

Library of Congress Cataloging-in-Publication Data

Traflet, Janice M., 1970–
    A nation of small shareholders : marketing Wall Street after World War II /
Janice M. Traflet.
        p. cm. — (Studies in industry and society)
    Includes bibliographical references and index.
    ISBN 978-1-4214-0902-3 (hbk. : alk. paper) — ISBN 978-1-4214-0903-0
(electronic) — ISBN 1-4214-0902-X (hbk. : alk. paper) — ISBN 1-4214-0903-8
(electronic)
    1. New York Stock Exchange—History. 2. Stock exchanges—New York
(State)—New York—History. 3. Investments—United States—History—
20th century. 4. Stockholders—United States—History—20th century.
5. Finance—United States—History—20th century. I. Title.
    HG4572.T73 2013
    332.64′27309045—dc23   2012035685

A catalog record for this book is available from the British Library.

Special discounts are available for bulk purchases of this book.
For more information, please contact Special Sales at 410-516-6936 or
specialsales@press.jhu.edu.

The Johns Hopkins University Press uses environmentally friendly book
materials, including recycled text paper that is composed of at least
30 percent post-consumer waste, whenever possible.

To my mom, Anne Marie Traflet

Contents

Acknowledgments

I extend my profound gratitude to my family, friends, colleagues, and mentors for helping me envision and finish this book. At Columbia University, Alan Brinkley, Elizabeth Blackmar, Kenneth Jackson, John Witt, and David Weiman were supportive in guiding me through the dissertation process. My sincere thanks also to M. K. Stack, retired member of the New York Stock Exchange, for his enthusiasm for this project and his keen insights, garnered from his more than three decades on Wall Street. Further enriching this book were my discussions as a graduate student with Rud Lawrence, former vice president of public relations at the NYSE during the Own Your Share years. In those talks, he awakened my understanding of the genuine passion that he and NYSE President G. Keith Funston exhibited toward their task of "democratizing" the stock market.

At key junctures in my work, I benefited from opportunities to do archival research supported by fellowships. An Alfred Chandler Fellowship at Harvard Business School allowed me access to a wonderful collection of material at Baker Library and the time to explore it. My thanks to Laura Linard and the rest of the dedicated staff at Baker Library for being so accommodating. A Rovensky Fellowship in American Business History also enabled me to deepen my research by exploring several archives, including the New York Stock Exchange Archive (NYSEA). I owe a significant debt to Steve Wheeler and Janet Linde at the NYSEA for their assistance and patience on my numerous lengthy visits there, with the most recent one being facilitated by an untenured leave grant from Bucknell University. I also thank the staff at the National Archives in College Park, Maryland, the Ad Council Archive at the University of Illinois (Urbana), and the Truman Archive in Independence, Missouri.

Many individuals provided much-needed encouragement along the way. My entire family, most especially my mom—Anne Traflet—as well as Dianne, Jeannie, Steve and Cathy, and Bob and Barbara, along with my nieces and nephews, deserve thanks, most particularly for having faith in this project and faith in me. Having successfully written her own book (albeit on sainthood, not Wall Street!), Dianne was an inspiration as well as a font of helpful advice. My twin sister, Jeannie, with her own career in public relations, helped shape this book on the NYSE's image transition in many key ways. Jeannie also provided great moral support, along with sustenance, on my research trips to New York City. To my mom, for her love and also for her contagious excitement about learning; I am much blessed. I grew up listening to her fascinating stories about her own childhood living on the Upper West Side in the 1940s and 1950s, and when I moved to New York City for graduate school, I found it every bit as stimulating as she had said. I thank my mom for encouraging me to go down the grad school path and also my dad, who had a deep interest in education and the stock market. With his wry sense of humor and his interest in Wall Street, he definitely would have gotten a kick that I had written this book.

I also had an amazing team of friends from Columbia who seemed to never tire of providing feedback. I thank especially Lisa Ramos, Nancy Kwak, and Betsy Herbin. At the Business History Conference (BHC) and the Economic Business History Society (EBHS), I took advantage of numerous opportunities to share my research on the stock market. Lynne Doti, Jeffrey Fear, Robert Wright, Neil Forbes, Stephanie Crofton, Luis Dopico, Erik Benson, Ranjit Dighe, and Jari Eloranta all helped sharpen my analysis. Ed Perkins, Matthew Fink, and Michael Adamson were very generous with their time and willingness to share their comments on various drafts. Ed Perkins also kindly shared with me material from his own collections to which I would never have had access otherwise. Friends and colleagues also were instrumental in helping bring this book to fruition, most especially William Gruver, Sue and Skip McGoun, Maria Fiori, Michael and Clare Coyne, Chris and Tammy Phillips, Tammy and Lee Masden, Mike and Sally Kobus, and last but not least, Karen, Joe, Dan, and Christian Gallagher. Friends provided food, sustenance, and even essential dog-sitting at critical points in the writing and research process. Not to be forgotten are my students who did their own part to help me better understand popular perceptions of equity investing, then and now. I thank Erin Mackin, Kaitlin Albright, Christie Longino, Alyssa DeLorenz, and Meghan Marks, as well as all the students in my Mass Investing capstone and my Bubbles and Panics courses.

At the Johns Hopkins University Press, Bob Brugger was unfailingly patient.

Pam Laird provided detailed and thoughtful commentary, and Helen Myers brought her careful eye to the manuscript.

While I did my best to incorporate the input of many talented individuals, any errors are my own. Thanks to everyone, named and unnamed, who helped make this book possible.

A Nation of Small Shareholders

Sowing an "Equity Culture"

> If we pursue our objectives with the strength of our convictions, we shall eventually approach our ideal, a nation of small share owners, a nation in whose material wealth every citizen has a vested interest through personal ownership, a nation which is truly a people's democracy.
>
> NYSE PRESIDENT KEITH FUNSTON, *NYSE 1951 ANNUAL REPORT*

For many people today, it is hard to remember a time when the gyrations of the U.S. and global stock markets did not command popular attention. During the second half of the twentieth century, the number of Americans owning common stock soared to unprecedented levels, stoked by a long bull market that lasted virtually uninterrupted from 1982 to early 2000. By the beginning of the twenty-first century, more than 80 million Americans—approximately half of U.S. households—owned equities, most through indirect holdings such as mutual funds and retirement accounts.[1] While millions of Americans are now "in" the stock market, though, the extent of most people's holdings is not all that high: according to 2007 figures, roughly two-thirds of investing households had stock holdings worth less than $6,000.[2] So not every American today even owns stock at all, much less owns a significant amount of it. Certainly, too, the wealthiest 5% of households still own the vast majority of common stock.[3] Yet the stock market undeniably has become ingrained in the national mass culture. Millions of citizens spanning the class spectrum pay attention to the Dow Jones Industrial Average (the DJIA, or "Dow"), the Standard and Poor's 500 Index (S&P 500), and other stock indi-

ces, believing that their material well-being, directly or indirectly, is con-
nected with the health of the stock market. Stock quotations are ubiquitous,
easily accessible online and in newspapers, and broadcast constantly on local
and national radio and television networks. Around water coolers as well as
dinner tables, people frequently discuss the merits of the market, individual
stocks, and other investments.

Indeed, an "equity culture,"[4] marked by widespread interest and participation in the stock market, has taken root in the United States and seems to
have endured even after the tumultuous 2008–2009 financial crisis. Admittedly, some individuals, in the wake of the recent turmoil, have questioned
the wisdom of investing in common stock.[5] Seeking purportedly safer terrain,
many have moved at least a portion of their money out of stocks and equity
funds and into bonds, bond funds, and other investments.[6] Nevertheless, the
common stock theory of investment—the idea that stocks are the best long-
term investment—still holds sway among legions of Americans. In 1901, the
journalist Charles Dow (who cofounded the financial publishing empire Dow
Jones & Company) advanced the common stock theory, which first gained
wide currency in the 1920s.[7] More than a century later, in an age when the
Occupy Wall Street movement has attracted attention to the growing problem of economic inequality, many Americans still perceive common stock
investing to be the most promising, albeit risky, route to amassing greater
personal wealth. In the United States, the so-called cult of equity remains
relatively strong.[8]

There was a time in this country, however, when Dow's common stock
theory of investment seemed defunct. During the Great Depression, Americans became disillusioned with common stocks. In the 1930s, officials at the
New York Stock Exchange (the NYSE, also known as the "Big Board," or simply "the Exchange")[9] feared that this popular disillusionment might be permanent, extending beyond the generation that had witnessed the Great Crash
of 1929. Would Wall Street—and Main Street—ever again witness the popular interest and participation in the stock market that had blossomed during
the golden bull market from 1923 to mid-1929?

While Exchange officials during the Depression and war years looked wist-
fully back upon the Roaring 1920s, that era had not truly been so golden, and
by no means had the market cast a spell on all Americans. Even before the
Great Crash, many doubted the morality of investing in the stock market.
Some citizens, farmers among them, maintained that buying stocks never

equated with "investing"; it always involved dangerous "speculation." They derided playing the stock market as gambling and called spoils gained "easy money," not "earned money."[10] Critics of the NYSE doubted that it cared about providing a fair and level playing field for all investors, big and small.[11]

At the same time, it was difficult for many Americans not to become transfixed watching stocks reach new highs almost daily. With numerous small investors being drawn into the 1920s market, journalist Frederick Lewis Allen described the bull market as having been "more than the climax of a business cycle; it had been the climax of a cycle in American mass thinking and mass emotion. There was hardly a man or woman in the country whose attitude toward life had not been affected by it in some degree." As Allen recalled, "The rich man's chauffeur drove with his ear laid back to catch the news of an impending move in Bethlehem Steel. . . . He held fifty shares himself on a twenty-point margin. The window-cleaner at the broker's office paused to watch the ticker, for he was thinking of converting his laboriously accumulated savings into a few shares of Simmons."[12] As Allen correctly intimated, in the 1920s a rising number of people from all walks of life had become shareowners. Exposed to the concept of investing through federal Liberty Bond advertising campaigns during the Great War and then lured by a bull market beginning in 1923, many Americans with disposable income, and even some without, grew willing to buy equities as well as bonds.[13] At the same time, it became easier to use margin (borrowed money) to purchase stock.[14] While it was hyperbole that "everyone," from the shoeshine boy to the elevator man, owned stock in the 1920s, approximately 15 to 20% of households did so—a significant number.[15] More might have been in the market if they had the money to invest or had they been willing to buy stock on margin.

The incipient equity culture collapsed along with the stock market, beginning on Black Thursday, October 24, 1929. Observing the DJIA fall almost 90% from its peak on September 3, 1929, to its low point on July 8, 1932, many Americans, even if they were not invested in equities, grew increasingly frightened of the stock market. By the summer of 1931, the "'liquidation of the common stock idea' [had become] one of the neatest and at the same time one of the most popular phrases generously utilized among financially-minded people," as statistician Lawrence Sloan bemoaned in his 1931 book, *Everyman and His Common Stocks*.[16] During the depths of the Great Depression, with a national unemployment rate of roughly 25% and rampant underemployment, few people had savings to invest in anything.[17] But even if they had money, many would not have placed it in the stock market. Public distrust of Wall Street only grew in the aftermath of a well-publicized government investigation into the stock market, headed by New York assistant district attorney Ferdinand Pecora.

This mistrust persisted, even after the passage of New Deal reform measures such as the Securities Act of 1933 and the creation of the Securities and Exchange Commission (SEC) in 1934. In a 1938 poll conducted by the American Institute of Public Opinion, 74% of those surveyed indicated that they believed Wall Street needed further government regulation to ensure fairness.[18] Writing in 1938, when the country was in the midst of a severe recession within the Great Depression, *Public Opinion Quarterly* contributor Howard Carswell emphatically noted, "the public is spectacularly *not* 'in the market.' "[19] A series of reforms in the 1930s had improved the substance of the Exchange, but its image remained weak, even after the Exchange underwent a major internal reorganization in 1938. Polls by Merrill Lynch in 1940 indicated that most Americans held Wall Street in low regard.[20] Keenly aware of these polls, Exchange personnel referred to themselves as laboring under the "Shadow of 1929."[21] They wanted Americans to see equity investing as an acceptable and desirable practice; they craved renewed legitimacy so that more of the public would invest.[22] Emerging from the Shadow of 1929 required actively building such legitimacy—the mere passage of time would not be enough to ameliorate the interrelated problems of low participation in the stock market, low faith in Wall Street, and a languid market.

More than two decades after the 1929 Crash, the Shadow of 1929 remained dark—despite rising disposable personal income levels and the related expansion of the middle class. Americans' collective disposable personal income grew from $92 billion in 1940 to $231.5 billion in mid-1952.[23] Given that the personal savings rate was relatively high at midcentury (approximately 7 to 8%),[24] many Americans possessed dollars that they could funnel into the stock market. Yet they overwhelmingly chose to place whatever savings they had into other vehicles, such as government and corporate bonds, life insurance, real estate, or simply savings accounts.

In 1952, according to a comprehensive study by the Brookings Institution, a think tank in Washington, DC, long known for its social science research, only 6.5 million Americans (4% of the U.S. population, or roughly 9.5% of households) owned any common stock—below the 1920s level of 15 to 20%

of households and far below the 2007 figure of 49.1%. In 1952, approximately half (46%) of equity investors owned only one issue. The few Americans who were in the market, often through an employee stock ownership plan (ESOP), were largely buy-and-hold investors, not active traders.[25]

So how and when did American investors rediscover the appeal of an equity culture that the Great Crash and ensuing Depression had crushed? What role did the world's largest stock exchange, the NYSE, play in that resurgence? To what extent did its leaders help rehabilitate the image of equities as a prudent long-term investment?

In the late twentieth century, a series of factors stimulated participation in the stock market. The list included a long bull market; retail brokerage innovations pioneered by industry leaders like Charles Merrill; heightened popular awareness of securities regulations implemented during the New Deal; the rise of mutual funds; the passage of the Employment Retirement Income Security Act (ERISA) in 1974; commission rate deregulation in 1975; the introduction of 401(k) private retirement plans in 1978; and the rise of equity derivative products.[26] All these factors being in play, the NYSE Board of Governors,[27] which made and enforced the rules for members (who held "seats"[28] on the Exchange) and listed companies, nonetheless, also played a crucial role in fueling popular interest in equity investing in the 1950s and 1960s. In so doing, they laid a foundation that others would build upon in later decades. The Board of Governors operated through a series of committees—law, admissions, business conduct, stock lists, finance, and, not unimportantly, public relations.

In scale, scope, and intent, the efforts of the NYSE to promote the stock market in the mid-twentieth century far surpassed a campaign it had undertaken in the early 1900s, when it had relied on a limited set of marketing tools, embracing public relations while largely rejecting traditional advertising.[29] Public relations aims to cultivate goodwill, often by currying favorable editorials or engaging in lobbying, ways that may be free for the sponsor.[30] Advertising, in contrast, generally involves paid promotion. For a long time, the NYSE actively discouraged member firms, never mind the Board itself, from advertising on any wide scale, even as advertising in other fields was rapidly growing.[31] The Board considered the financial profession akin to the medical and legal professions, which deemed advertising to be undignified and unethical. Allegedly, good commission house brokers, like good doctors and lawyers, need not advertise their services: word-of-mouth alone should suffice.[32]

Consequently, the NYSE in the early 1900s permitted member firms to use only a basic form of advertising, sometimes referred to as "tombstones," which gave information on a company's stock issuance that the underwriter (member firm) was bringing to market, and simply included the member firm's name and address.[33] The Exchange, with few exceptions, forbade members to use illustrations in their advertisements. The Board hoped that these restrictions would help disassociate member firms from fraudulent and unethical promoters of securities.[34] Operating on the fringes of Wall Street, less reputable brokerage firms unabashedly advertised and especially tried to attract small investors (sometimes called "dime" investors).[35] For a long time, the NYSE believed that the absence of advertising would only elevate their image.[36]

While slow to perceive the value of advertising, the NYSE rushed to embrace modern public relations practices. In 1913, as the government launched an investigation into the stock market, led by Louisiana Democrat Arsene Pujo,[37] the Big Board established its first public relations department (the Library Committee, renamed the Committee on Publicity in 1925, and then in 1935, the Committee on Public Relations). Concurrently, many of its listed companies, like AT&T, U.S. Steel, and Standard Oil, also instituted their own public relations departments, augmented sometimes by the retention of outside "publicity professionals" like Ivy Lee[38] or Edward Bernays.[39] Corporations wanted to burnish their images in part to refute Brandeisian criticisms that they were too big, not to mention "soulless," and lacking heart.[40] Though at the time the NYSE was an association, not technically a corporation,[41] Exchange leaders also wanted to demonstrate that their organization had a conscience that enabled it to act in the public's best interest. Seeking to disseminate the NYSE's "high standards" and "exemplary [self] regulation," Exchange publicists in the pre–World War II days employed a variety of tactics, such as press releases, films, speeches, books, and other promotional pieces. As part of their fight against Pujo's call for incorporation, which would have brought the NYSE under the authority and supervision of New York State, Exchange personnel pointed to the millions of small equity investors as evidence that economic power in the stock market was dispersed. Cultivating an image of popular shareownership, Exchange apologists hoped, would counter reformers' criticisms that the NYSE was a "private club" dominated by a wealthy elite.[42]

In an interview by *Collier's* magazine in 1923, Seymour Cromwell, NYSE president, 1921–1924, emphasized, "An analysis of the distribution of securities of any of our great corporations will demonstrate that the people, not the so-called interests, are their real owners."[43] Cromwell's successor, E. H. H. Simmons, NYSE president from 1924 to 1930, likewise tried to dispel the image of the Exchange as the province of rich, bloated stockholders. In a 1925 speech to the Credit Men's Association of Milwaukee, Simmons declared, "The small investor is the average investor." He and his colleagues frequently described the Exchange as the "people's market."[44] In an appearance before the Texas Bankers Association, Simmons insisted that "finance no less than business in this country has been vastly democratized, and . . . the ownership of our large business enterprises has been distributed through all classes and all sections of our population."[45] In truth, in the United States by this time, common stock voting rights constituted a plutocratic, rather than a democratic, arrangement, as one-vote-per-share had become standard, not one-vote-per-person.[46] Exchange executives, nevertheless, hailed wider share-ownership for achieving a "democratizing" effect on the American corporation. Richard Whitney, an Exchange governor who later became NYSE president, also repeatedly highlighted the presence of small investors in the market. The NYSE considered such speeches a critical component of their public relations.[47]

While the Board in the 1920s often, in their rhetoric, hailed small investors' presence in the market, hoping this would deter regulation, in their actions, they did not encourage the growth of retail investing. Exchange officials cannot take credit for inspiring the boom in stock ownership prior to the Great Crash; to the contrary, they discouraged members from using modern advertising methods that would have brought even more of Main Street to Wall Street. Many Board members feared that too many small investors would destabilize the market due to their allegedly irrational, panic-prone behavior. However, they did see some potential value in having more Americans as investors—presumably, investors would vote in alliance with the Exchange's interests. In short, Big Board leaders were conflicted: they wanted the image but not the reality of the "masses" being in the market. Broader participation in the stock market posed dangers, not just potential benefits for the Exchange and for the investors themselves.

Known as the "Old Guard," the group in power at the Exchange in the early 1900s was composed mostly of investment bankers and merchant bankers.[48] Factions within the Exchange membership that had a more vested interest in the business of small investors constituted a rival group known as the

"Reformers." Led by Paul Shields, W. Averell Harriman, E. A. Pierce, John Hanes, and John Coleman, the Reformers did not exert much influence until the late 1930s.[49]

As the Reformers' clash with the Old Guard illustrates, the Big Board has never been a monolithic entity with identical interests. All members ("seat-holders") are not the same. Three major groups comprise the membership base—specialists, private traders, and brokers. Each fulfills a unique function and caters to a different clientele. Specialists are in charge of "making a market" in their assigned stocks; they theoretically stand prepared at all times to buy and sell from and to other members. Their job is to ensure market liquidity (i.e., that a seller can quickly find a buyer). Besides trading on behalf of other members, specialists buy and sell for their own accounts, but never directly for nonmembers. Private and proprietary traders, as their name suggests, deal exclusively for their own accounts. Brokers include both independent brokers and commission house brokers. An independent broker (sometimes called a "two-dollar broker") is a business-to-business broker, executing orders on behalf of another member; he does not represent a specific firm or take direct public orders.[50] A commission broker (or "house broker"), also working on the floor of an exchange, is an employee of a member firm such as Merrill Lynch or E. F. Hutton, who executes orders for that firm and its customers. In return for that service, the broker receives a commission, or percentage, based on the transaction's value. In contrast to specialists, private traders, and two-dollar brokers, house brokers depend on outside customers ("individual investors" or "retail investors") for trading volume.[51]

In the early 1900s, house brokers and their firms had little presence on the Board of Governors, and this remained true, even as they accounted for approximately half of NYSE seats by the early 1930s. The Old Guard controlled the nominating committee that selected the Exchange governors who sat on the Board. According to the NYSE Constitution at the time, members had to be present to vote for candidates. This posed an impediment for many member firm commission houses that were headquartered out of town, such as Alex Brown (based in Baltimore, Maryland) and A. G. Edwards (based in St. Louis, Missouri). As a result, the majority of Exchange governors (roughly two-thirds) were specialists or private and proprietary traders. Possessing no direct interest in the business of small investors, they long dominated Exchange decision making, including policies on advertising and public relations.[52]

For some time, only a small minority of Exchange members dared to challenge the Old Guard's onerous advertising restrictions. Among them was a young Charles Merrill who, by the 1940s, would be leading the largest brokerage firm in the country, Merrill Lynch. As a broker on Wall Street prior to World War I, Merrill began to court small investors, realizing the enormous profit potential in this relatively untapped market. Rejecting the Exchange's dry tombstone advertising style, he experimented with effective newspaper advertisements geared toward a general audience. Not pleased with Merrill's aggressive salesmanship, the NYSE on several occasions reprimanded Merrill for running advertisements they deemed inappropriate, such as one that contained an illustration.[53]

Decades later, in the early 1950s, the Big Board decided for the first time to prioritize bringing more small investors into the stock market, and to use advertising to help accomplish this goal. Exchange governors agreed that promoting broader shareownership would be wise, as most member retail brokerage firms desperately needed more business. The Board also believed that shareowners would be more heavily invested in capitalism than nonshareowners, as they assumed that shareholding citizens would be more loyal to America and American companies.[54] As the Cold War deepened, keeping industry strong and cultivating economic citizenship seemed crucially important to the Exchange Board. Guided by these motives, the Board collaborated with advertising agencies, consultants, and retail member brokerage firms, especially Merrill Lynch, to forge a landmark marketing campaign for the NYSE.

The marketing campaign "Own Your Share of American Business" (OYS) ran from 1954 to 1969. The Exchange issued numerous advertisements that directly appealed to the public to come into the equities market. They helped spread shareownership by teaching retail member brokerage firms how to mass market effectively. Also, the Exchange worked with listed companies on initiatives that would make it easier for employees to become shareowners. The Cold War provided an ideological backdrop that made the NYSE's "buy stock" message resonate powerfully with the American public, even though that public still vividly remembered 1929.

With its emphasis on advertisements, the Own Your Share (OYS) marketing program in the 1950s and 1960s marked a radical departure from the Board's narrow conceptualization of marketing, and it signified the Board's newfound appreciation of Merrill's mass marketing approach. The shift in Board policy occurred in part due to the end of the Old Guard's reign, triggered by events stemming from the 1929 Crash. A new era opened at the NYSE in which retail-friendly Exchange governors could finally work with member firms in forging a marketing program to encourage more citizens to become shareholders in American enterprise. While the Big Board tapped into many public relations and marketing strategies that the Library Committee had utilized in earlier years (such as promotional films, books, and educational seminars), the Own Your Share campaign was first and foremost an advertising program.

The main goal was the expansion of shareownership. The Board hoped that the achievement of this goal would improve the Exchange's reputation, rebuff communism, and restore profitability to member retail brokerage houses. Unlike their predecessors in the 1920s, the NYSE Board of Governors in the 1950s and 1960s would not just talk about small investors who were already in the market; they would actively encourage more Americans to become "shareholders" in American enterprises. They began to substitute the word "shareholder" for "stockholder," believing that "share" had a more positive connotation.[55] Resuscitating the 1920's theme of "democratizing" the stock market, the NYSE in the mid-twentieth century became newly committed to "broadening the shareholder ranks." Own Your Share marketers encouraged Americans to open brokerage accounts with member retail brokerage firms, so as to boost business and strengthen the NYSE as a citadel of capitalism.

An analysis of OYS advertisements illuminates the values of those crafting them, and reveals how the creators perceived their intended audiences.[56] Rather than providing an exact mirror into a particular moment in time, advertisers selected and enhanced certain images.[57] In its OYS advertisements (echoing earlier rhetoric propounded by the Library Committee), the NYSE frequently depicted the United States as an egalitarian country where families were growing ever more prosperous.[58] Wide shareownership, the Exchange contended, was helping the country progress toward reducing class differences and ameliorating tensions between management and labor. Capitalism, not communism, Exchange leaders emphasized, was the better economic system, and "American capitalism" was particularly benign and egalitarian.

While NYSE Board members were far from ideologically homogeneous, the idea of "American capitalism" dominant at the Exchange at this time differed from that articulated by economist John Kenneth Galbraith in his 1952 book, *American Capitalism: The Concept of Countervailing Power.*[59] Both the NYSE Board and Galbraith agreed that capitalism in the United States had been transformed in the early postwar years. Galbraith emphasized how the rise of giant corporations had stifled pure competition and necessitated the "countervailing" power of strong unions and government regulation. Exchange leaders, however, focused on broad shareownership in the United States as a key feature of American capitalism and noted how shareownership was growing more widespread and diffuse, especially compared with other countries with stock markets. Big Board officers frequently pointed to the rising numbers of small shareholders in large companies like American Telephone and Telegraph (AT&T) as evidence of dispersed economic power and a sharing of profits in American enterprise. As the NYSE emphasized, in the United States, workers increasingly owned the means of production, but, unlike the Soviet Union, they did so through the vehicle of shareownership.

That the NYSE Board was even advertising the virtues of shareownership is significant. The revised marketing strategy sheds light on the NYSE's evolving perceptions of small investors and its new thoughts on the potential and ideal size of the nation's shareowner base. Besides wanting to help struggling member retail brokerage firms, during the Cold War years, the Board found the image of a marketplace with many little investors appealing. Anxious to be operating in the public interest and to be known as doing so, the NYSE Board welcomed the opportunity to show equity investing as a way to fight communism and keep America and American industry strong. In his letter prefacing the NYSE's 1951 Annual Report, Keith Funston, NYSE president from 1951 to 1967, passionately emphasized that expanding individual shareownership was in everyone's best interests. He reiterated to audiences beyond the Wall Street community the lofty goal of a "nation of small share owners."[60] Funston was not the first NYSE president to articulate that vision of mass equity investing. Yet he and his colleagues were atypically intent on transforming their ideal into a reality. In their eyes, the Own Your Share public relations and advertising program was the prime mechanism to facilitate the spread of individual retail investing,[61] thereby keeping communism at bay.

In the viewpoint of many Exchange officials, the NYSE's raison d'être—raising capital as well as providing a fair and orderly marketplace—meant the organization was the beating heart of capitalism and hence a natural defender of that system. In selling Americans on the benefits of shareownership, Big Board executives gave added momentum to the efforts being made by big business to sway public opinion toward the private enterprise system.[62] As Funston proclaimed, "I believe with all my heart that a nation of capitalists—

and certainly anyone who owns one share of stock or one thousand is a capitalist—is an effective answer to communism's false doctrines."[63]

The NYSE was at a critical nexus for helping defend free enterprise, given the organization's contact with more than 1,300 individuals or firms owning seats on the Exchange and more than 1,000 listed companies. The NYSE was in a unique situation in the early 1950s as it began the quest to enlarge share-ownership; although the lingering Shadow of 1929 hampered efforts to promote equities, tapping into escalating anticommunist sentiment during the Cold War provided a way to relegitimize the stock market, weaving it into the American way of life.[64]

In an age when civilian defense and air raid drills in schools were as common as fire drills, Exchange officials hoped that advertising equity investing to children as well as adults might strengthen capitalism. It also would build business for retail-oriented members. Like many of their predecessors, they theorized that a shareownership campaign might be an effective way to build a nation of investors and also de facto lobbyists for the nation's securities markets; presumably, shareholders would be more likely to favor policies that the exchanges endorsed, such as lower capital gains taxes. The Exchange Board had faith that the OYS campaign would enhance the NYSE's reputation as a publicly minded private institution. The expansion in marketing activities also reflected the Board's reconceptualization of the NYSE's duties and responsibilities to investors and the nation.[65]

How the Big Board sought to engineer a comeback after the Great Crash of 1929 and why the NYSE was more successful in doing so in the 1950s and 1960s than in earlier decades are the animating questions of this study. To no small extent, orchestrating a comeback involved the NYSE making a determined Cold War effort to rebuild its status and credibility and, in the process, inspire public trust and popular participation in the nation's securities markets.

CHAPTER ONE

Reeling from the Great Crash

Like 1066, 1776, and 1914, it [1929] was a year that no one would forget.
JOHN KENNETH GALBRAITH, *THE GREAT CRASH* (1951)

In 1950, the "Shadow of 1929" still cast its pall on the New York Stock Exchange, impeding a resurrection of an equity culture as well as inhibiting a return to profitability for many member retail brokerage firms.[1] What happened during the Great Crash of 1929 to cast such a long shadow? Why did the NYSE's reputation, not just the image of equity investing, deteriorate so badly? Later in the 1950s and into the 1960s, the Big Board finally began to step out from the Shadow of 1929 with the development of their Own Your Share of American Business (OYS) marketing campaign. To appreciate how the OYS campaign helped overhaul the Exchange's tarnished image requires understanding what transpired during the Great Crash and the ensuing Depression years.

What became known as the "Great Crash of 1929" quickly became seared in the collective American memory. Commanding the front pages of the nation's newspapers that late October, the market's plunge frightened investors and noninvestors alike. Worried that the media attention accorded the Crash might further undermine faith in the stock market and also damage confidence in the broader economy, Paul T. Cherington, a senior executive at the

J. Walter Thompson advertising agency, conferred with his staff on Black Tuesday, October 29th. He told them, "I think we have to realize the fact that this is a thoroughly well-advertised flurry. This is a real feature of the situation and a rather unfortunate one." Cherington hypothesized that the heavy media coverage occurred because "The panic (if you want to call it a panic) or the 'securities flutter' comes at a time when there is nothing else to occupy the public attention." He added that if the Crash occurred during the World Series, it would be a different story. Cherington concluded, "As a result this is probably the best advertised of the market flurries that has occurred in recent years."[2]

Of course, it was not just a temporary "market flurry," nor did the Crash just extend from October 23rd through October 31st, 1929.[3] The Dow Jones Industrial Average (DJIA, also known as the "Dow") did not reach a post-Crash low until July 8, 1932, by which time it had fallen 89% from its all-time high. Likewise, the NYSE's image did not decline all at once. After actually enjoying a brief upward surge in the first few days after the Crash, the Big Board's status suffered in the 1930s from widely publicized congressional hearings into stock market practices. It did not help the Exchange's image that from 1929 to 1938, the Old Guard, comprised mostly of bankers and traders, still controlled the NYSE Board, despite the rising number of commission brokers purchasing seats and becoming members. The organization's reputation finally reached its nadir in 1938, a year after another collapse in equity prices, coinciding with a sharp recession. The public's tendency to conflate the NYSE with Wall Street worked to the Big Board's disadvantage during the Great Depression years. The Exchange also caused some of its own public relations problems, such as the scandal in 1938 that engulfed its once revered president, Old Guard leader Richard Whitney.

Blaming the "Little Fellow" after the Great Crash

Immediately after the October 1929 Crash, it was the small investor, not the NYSE, who was on the defensive. Many bankers blamed little investors, with their allegedly panicky behavior, for exacerbating a market decline into a full-fledged crash. To some in the financial community, the Crash proved that most people did not belong in the market; "public investors" had engaged in volatile and heavily emotional trading. Guaranty Trust, conducting a survey on the causes of the Crash that autumn, attributed the disaster to "thousands of the public, who had become 'investment-minded' and the victims of their own lively imaginations . . . [selling] out in a rush." The quotation marks around "investment-minded" suggested disbelief that most working-class and middle-class Americans were capable of savvy participation in the market, as opposed to wealthier and better-educated investors, who presumably were more competent traders. Guaranty Trust insisted that "thousands of inexperienced persons [entered] into the ranks of stock market speculators where neither their financial knowledge nor their financial strength entitled them to be." In the bank's view, small investors typically were "uninformed as to intelligent procedure in buying and selling securities . . . [and] easily subjected to psychological reactions of an exaggerated sort, buying and selling en masse without any clear understanding of the reasons for doing so." Noting the herd mentality in the market, Guaranty Trust observed, "Although there has always been an element of mob psychology in the actions of the investing public, this element has been increased manifold by the changes of recent years." The bank concluded, "the small investor is, then, to a large extent, the victim of his own imagination."[4] Media reports also highlighted mass panic among investors, although a few reporters disagreed and suggested that most investors reacted to the calamity with eerie calm, akin to shell shock. When *Saturday Evening Post* writer Edwin Lefevre visited multiple brokerage offices on Black Tuesday, he noted, "nowhere did I see the hysterical melodrama that people always expect in Wall Street at such times."[5] But the dominant early version of the Crash, perpetuated both by Wall Street and the media, was that investors—particularly small investors—had panicked and thus accelerated the decline with their crowd mentality.

Indeed, Guaranty Trust's reference to an "element of mob psychology in the actions of the investing public" reflected a common worry on Wall Street that the investing public constituted an unthinking "crowd" or a "mob." A favorite book of many financiers was Gustave LeBon's *The Crowd: A Study of the Popular Mind*, originally published in 1895. LeBon wrote, "Under certain given circumstances, an agglomeration of men [a 'crowd'] presents new characteristics very different from those of the individuals composing it. The sentiments and ideas of all the persons in the gathering take one and the same direction, and their conscious personality vanishes. A collective mind is formed." LeBon called the gathering a "psychological crowd" and contended that it "forms a single being and is subjected to the *law of the mental unity of crowds*." LeBon argued that the psychological crowd often acted irrationally, as it was prone to suggestibility and the "contagion" of thoughts.[6]

The rise in the number of shareowners after World War I had lowered the quality, some feared, of the investing "crowd." As at Guaranty Trust, some executives at J. P. Morgan & Company disparaged small investors after the Crash, though Morgan partners were more inclined to voice their criticisms privately. Senior partner Thomas Lamont blamed the Crash in part on too many Americans of modest means buying stock on margin. As he told a colleague, "If and when we ever get back to normal," stock market authorities should "make it much more difficult for every Tom, Dick and Harry, [for] every hairdresser and manicurist all over the country to speculate in stocks." Acknowledging that "almost every man has a speculative streak in him and it is bound to expose itself in some way," Lamont wished that such dangerous speculation "be confined to the ponies or football games or," he said, with a touch of sarcasm, "to political results." When the gambling instinct leads to stock speculation, not only does it "ruin the small speculator himself" but it "brings distress to the community." To Lamont, one lesson from the Crash was clear: the NYSE should "devise some method of discouraging people of small means from attempting to speculate or ever to buy securities—even the best—on a margin."[7] Lamont's criticisms were not entirely fair. According to later estimates, fewer than 600,000 shareholders, of every economic class, were operating on margin in 1929.[8] Of those few small investors who had borrowed money to buy stock, many met the first, and often, the second and third rounds of margin calls. This was, of course, unfortunate, as the market continued to decline. As a result, many investors, caught without the additional cash to meet later margin calls, eventually found themselves "sold out."[9]

Bankers like Lamont were not the only ones who focused blame on little speculators. Even some former advocates of popular shareownership, like Yale professor Irving Fisher, now joined the scapegoating. Professor Fisher derided small shareholders as the "lunatic fringe" in the market. The Crash, Fisher contended, ultimately was a "healthy development" because it would "shake out" this undesirable element, returning the shareownership base to wealthier, allegedly more responsible investors. Distressed investors responded to Fisher's comment with a mixture of anger and betrayal. As one writer complained to the *New York Times*, "[the] dismissal of the late unpleasantness as a 'healthy reaction' brings up the time-honored puzzle when reaction ceases to be healthy and why its salubrious character is not recognized while it is going on." The writer added, "The description never under any circumstances appealed greatly to amateur speculators who on such occasions are left on the market's door-step, nursing their financial wounds. But the further and equally familiar moralizing on 'reaction' by those whom the sufferers had once regarded as friends and guides does not even spare sensitive feelings."[10]

While small investors initially surfaced from the Crash with a wounded image as well as a diminished net worth, the NYSE's Old Guard conversely emerged with an enhanced reputation, though the popularity surge would be brief. Engineering the post-Crash image spike was not the Big Board's public relations department, but one key individual. It was not the famous banker J. P. Morgan Sr. (he had died in 1913). Neither was it his son, Jack, although the House of Morgan, as usual, played a pivotal behind-the-scenes role. Neither was it the Exchange's president, as E. H. H. Simmons was vacationing in Hawaii at the time of the Crash. In October 1929, the NYSE's man of the hour was its acting president, Richard Whitney.[11]

Richard Whitney: The Hero of 1929

Head of his own firm, Richard Whitney & Co., Richard Whitney had long been part of Wall Street's exclusive inner circle, often representing J. P. Morgan & Co.'s orders on the floor. At the time of the Crash, he had been a Governor of the Exchange for almost a decade and a seat-holder since 1914. He maintained close connections to many J. P. Morgan partners, in part because he knew the Morgans from his childhood days. Richard's older brother, George, was himself a partner at J. P. Morgan & Co., as was Richard's former classmate, Thomas Lamont. Despite his prominence on Wall Street, Richard Whitney was not well known in the rest of the country—that is, until the Great Crash made the stock market front page news. With Simmons away in Hawaii, the burden of managing the crisis fell to Whitney, the next in command. Due to an adroit publicity stunt on the Exchange floor, Whitney emerged as the nation's hero on Black Thursday, October 24th, and the most nationally recognized executive in the Exchange's history to that point.

In the heat of the panic, Whitney calmly strolled over to Post No. 2, where U.S. Steel traded, and placed an order that soon became famous. He announced a $205 bid for 10,000 shares of Steel, bidding through the market above the current market price. By volunteering to pay more than the stock's current sales price, Whitney indicated his belief that the stock eventually would rise well above $205, and that he, therefore, would profit from the transaction. The bid was a symbolic gesture designed to elicit confidence in the faltering market. For a brief time, the tactic worked to lift the price of that stock as well as several others. Traders correctly interpreted Whitney's order as a sign not just that Whitney personally believed in the market, but that banker support had materialized—that in this Crash, as in other panics, the nation's most powerful bankers would provide a floor beneath which equity prices would not fall. Ultimately, however, not even the banker's syndicate would be able to stem the market collapse. Thomas Lamont was the Morgan partner who organized the syndicate, which included among others, Albert Wiggins of Chase National, William Potter of Guaranty Trust, George Benson Jr. of First National, and Seward Prosser of Bankers Trust.[12]

Richard Whitney, therefore, was essentially a front man for this bankers' pool. That Whitney had placed his order for U.S. Steel was significant; Steel was a Morgan client as well as a Morgan creation, and the House of Morgan led the bankers' rescue operation.[13] Whitney used the syndicate's money, not his own, to prop up the stock. Glossing over this detail, colleagues hailed Whitney's action, passing resolutions praising him for his "courage, resourcefulness, and . . . rare qualities of leadership." Issuing admiring reports, the press made Whitney into a bona fide celebrity.[14]

The acting President of the NYSE seemed to fit (and enjoy) the part. An imposing figure at six foot two and a muscular two hundred and twenty pounds, Whitney had "Hollywood looks" and exuded a debonair sophistication, according to reporter Matthew Josephson. Educated at Groton and Harvard and trained in the Wall Street school of manners, Whitney seemed to epitomize the gentleman banker. Basking in the media attention that autumn of 1929, Whitney strove to appear upbeat and self-assured, convinced that his confidence would be contagious. He encouraged his fellow bankers to project optimism as well. As they were about to emerge from one of their emergency closed-door meetings conducted in rooms beneath the trading floor, Whitney instructed his colleagues to prepare for the waiting reporters: "Now get on your smiles, boys." Rewarding him for his job in managing the Crash, the Board of Governors elected Whitney president of the New York Stock Exchange in 1930. It would be the first of four consecutive terms.[15]

Immediately upon his election, Whitney embarked upon an extensive lecture circuit to revive faith in the stock market. He was not alone in believing that the very act of encouraging optimism was a way to end the financial crisis. As Josephson recalled, "When the world's greatest financial bubble burst in the autumn of 1929 . . . [our leaders in business] . . . could agree really only on one thing: 'Above all, that precious, elusive thing Confidence must be restored.'"[16] Among the many businessmen who tried to stem the panic with reassuring words that October, John D. Rockefeller Sr. of Standard Oil issued a rare public statement, which newspapers across the country printed. He said, "Believing that fundamental conditions of the country are sound . . . my son and I have for some days been purchasing sound common stocks."[17] Perhaps the most famous (or infamous) of the morale-boosting efforts was President Herbert Hoover's statement: "The fundamental business of the country, that is production and distribution of commodities, is on a sound and prosperous basis."[18]

Unlike Hoover, Whitney did not offer what would prove to be false words of cheer. He did, however, repeatedly try to restore confidence by emphasizing the high character of the NYSE and its listed companies in his speeches to chambers of commerce, colleges, business groups, and other gatherings. In one popular speech, "Business Honesty," he encouraged companies to earn the public faith, for he saw widespread confidence in an ethical corporate environment as key to recovery.[19] In many speeches, Whitney dwelt on what caused the Crash—and also, what did not cause it. Perhaps his most emphatic contention was that the NYSE was not to blame. Like the House of Morgan and Guaranty Trust, he sometimes pilloried small investors for upsetting the market. However, in other speeches, Whitney, anxious to build public support for a continued "free," unregulated NYSE, alternatively praised small investors for "democratizing" the market. In a speech to the Boston Chamber of Commerce in 1931, Whitney, echoing his predecessor E. H. H. Simmons, declared, "From every point of view, this great distribution of securities among our people seems to be a source of strength." He added, "If a substantial part of the people can participate in American industry not only our economy but also our political stability is made more certain."[20] Later, in a radio address over the National Broadcasting Company (NBC), Whitney averred, "the interest in securities and securities exchanges is not limited to a small or privileged class." With some exaggeration, he continued, "It is truly national and embraces every family in the land."[21]

In acting as the Big Board's spokesman, Richard Whitney was not setting a precedent. Since the creation of a public relations department in 1913, "whoever happened to be president of the Exchange made speeches from time to time before various organizations," as one Exchange member recalled in 1931.[22] Yet much smaller audiences, mainly inside the tightly knit Wall Street community, heard those earlier speeches. After the 1929 Crash, comments about the stock market attracted heightened popular interest. Exchange President Whitney obliged by not only addressing the usual groups, such as accountants and investment bankers, but also wider, national audiences. Much like President Franklin D. Roosevelt who, beginning in 1933, famously employed "fireside chats," Whitney used the radio to inspire public confidence. Whitney instructed his staff to transcribe many of those speeches into book form, so they could be widely disseminated.[23]

Such speech making posed risks for the NYSE. Potentially, anything that the Exchange president said reflected on the organization, but if listeners misinterpreted the intended meaning that reflection could be negative. Furthermore, audiences were prone to assume that Whitney as president articulated the Exchange's official point of view. Yet, due to the diverse membership base, the NYSE represented many points of view, and the president did not reflect all of them. In fact, on the controversial topics, it was likely that Whitney, part of the Old Guard minority, would not represent the majority view. On other topics, Whitney might articulate his own thoughts, expressing neither the Old Guard nor the majority viewpoint. Neither the Board of Governors nor the Exchange's public relations department was afforded the opportunity to approve the speeches prior to their delivery: a wild card factor existed.

After the Crash, some Exchange members urged a halt to this growing habit of executive pontification. In a long letter to Thomas Lamont, one critic, banker L. Criscuolo,[24] complained that speeches were not even within the Exchange's purview. He explained that the Big Board's function was simply to bring buyers and sellers together in a central location where they could trade securities listed on the Exchange. "It is not," Criscuolo said, "the function of the Exchange to explain economic conditions or to make alibis for panics, declines in the price of commodities, or other factors which are beyond the control of the Exchange and its individual members."[25] Considering that "even the best minds in the country have been at a loss to explain the reasons for the trends in prices of securities and commodities," he warned that the NYSE president was venturing into dangerous territory by tackling these subjects. Any misstep threatened to "exacerbate the already widespread distrust of the securities market." Taking aim at Whitney, though not specifying him by name,

Criscuolo noted, "people who are assumed to be [Exchange] leaders are often prone to make statements which are devoid of ordinary business sense." Even assuming satisfactory content, the mere fact that a president of the NYSE presumed to speak on certain matters might send an incorrect message. "The moment the Stock Exchange attempts to explain the reasons for the violent advances or declines in the market the investing public immediately assumes that the exchange is responsible for all these conditions." If the Exchange simply refrained from making "alibis for conditions which are beyond its control," Cricuolo contended, "there would be less and less talk in this country of people being ruined by Wall Street."[26] Richard Whitney reacted angrily, accusing Cricuolo of "butting into a situation which is . . . none of *his* business." He continued his speech-making unabated.[27]

Surviving the Great Bear Hunt (1931–1932)

Much to Whitney's and the Exchange's chagrin, by 1931, popular theories about the causes of the continued bear market had changed, with the small investor being transformed from culprit to victim. Blame shifted to an unidentified group of malicious "bear raiders" who allegedly had "sold America short."[28] Many, especially those in agrarian areas, had never approved of "short selling," the process of selling stock one does not currently own in the hopes that the stock price will go down by the time the short seller buys it back. Critics of short selling questioned the morality of earning money as a stock went down, and they impugned the patriotism of those betting against stocks of American companies. In contrast, the NYSE always upheld short selling; the public relations department for decades had tried to explain that it was legitimate and useful, as short selling added to the market's liquidity.

While defending short selling, the Big Board, however, did not condone bear raiding. As Whitney explained in a speech to the Boston Chamber of Commerce, whereas short sellers "genuinely believe the price of a particular security is too high," bear raiders offer "securities in volume and in a manner calculated to depress prices with the hope of profiting by the depreciation in value which his own transactions have created." Whitney defended the short sale as "an essential part of the machinery of any great open market for securities," and clarified, "I wish to emphasize that bear raiding and short selling are not synonymous." Despite the Exchange's efforts to educate the public about the differences between the two, many Americans tended to lump them together. In early 1931, Whitney delivered a speech about bear raiding to local chambers of commerce and other groups across the country, trying to reassure his listeners that the NYSE's Business Conduct Committee carefully watched for any trading activity "that looked like bear raiding." He contended that the Business Conduct Committee warned members, "such activities were a violation of the Constitution of the Exchange and that participation by them directly or indirectly in such transactions would subject them to drastic discipline." Whitney emphasized that the Exchange had absolutely no evidence suggesting "any concerted action to depress the market."[29]

Whitney's speech on bear raiding had gone through multiple drafts, and the original version illustrates Whitney's frustration with the public's misperceptions of the Exchange. He circulated this draft to his brother, George Whitney, and Thomas Lamont for input. George read it first, marking several passages that he felt needed to be rewritten. Lamont read it next. Lamont observed that Richard Whitney sounded as if he were "ill-natured and altogether out of patience with the community which attacks the Stock Exchange." Noting the "questionable phrases" that George had highlighted, Lamont commented, "I have not only marked more of these, but have indicated how *dreadful* I thought some of them were." Lamont warned that if the speech remained unmodified, the Big Board "will lose completely whatever sympathy the general public has [for it]." For the sake of the Exchange, Whitney needed to stop "indulg[ing] in so many diatribes against the people who are disturbed over the question of short-selling." From a public relations standpoint, it was unwise to aggravate and insult critics. Lamont recommended that Whitney adopt an approach "far more sympathetic for the people who have suffered heavy stock losses and who honestly think that these losses are largely due to short-raiding." Whitney should pay tribute to their "honesty" rather than attack them as "blankety-blank fools or worse." The speech needed "a complete recasting . . . as it stands now, the text contains many exceedingly offensive phrases."[30]

Whitney heeded the advice. In its final version, Whitney attributed the bear raiding myth to a misperception that the NYSE was "an influencer of markets." Trying to correct this misperception, he employed the metaphor of a mill's water wheel: "While the useful power and pressure seem to come from the axle, it is, nevertheless, generated at the circumference. Anyone who believes that the Exchange is an influence which controls the price of securities is as much mistaken as a man who thinks the axle of a mill-wheel originates the power which runs the mill." There had been a time when bears could influence the market, Whitney admitted, but Wall Street was different then: "only a comparatively small group of wealthy men were interested in securities. . . . The system of distributing quotations was extremely crude and . . . the number of stocks listed on the exchange was small enough to cause the fluctuations of one or two to influence the whole market." Those conditions no longer existed on the modern NYSE, where millions of share-holders engaged in trades and where more than 1,200 stocks were listed. "Today bull and bear markets cannot be made to order." Stock prices were produced, not by a few lone wolves, but by "the mass psychology of the hundreds of thousands and millions of persons who are interested in securities either as investors or speculators."[31] In that last sentence, Whitney implied— yet wisely did not state—that small investors were responsible for the low level of the stock market.

Despite the Exchange's efforts to deny bear raiding, the idea persisted, even fueled by Republican President Herbert Hoover, who suspected that prominent Wall Street Democrats, such as John J. Raskob and Bernard Baruch, had plotted the market collapse to discredit him in the upcoming U.S. presidential election. Prominent Republicans Whitney and Lamont urged Hoover in vain not to make the charge. When Hoover did, the bear raiding accusation unfortunately struck a chord of plausibility among Americans predisposed to condemn short selling and inclined to view the NYSE as a rigged marketplace.

Upon Hoover's request, in early 1932, a Senate Banking and Currency Committee began to investigate allegations of nefarious short selling: it became known as the "Great Bear Hunt." As Whitney had predicted, the committee found absolutely no evidence of a conspiracy to topple the stock market. Despite that conclusion, and despite Whitney's speeches, popular suspicions about organized bear selling persisted.[32] In May, reporter Matthew Josephson wrote in the *New Yorker* that bear raiding was "a topic without which no good dinner party is complete nowadays."[33] However, the media assiduously disassociated the NYSE president from the black sheep in the Exchange fold (or, more aptly, the black bears). Reporter John Flynn hailed Whitney as a Wall Street broker of the highest caliber.[34] Whitney was still the hero of 1929.

Although the Senate Banking and Currency Committee had detected no signs of organized short selling, the Great Bear Hunt had unearthed, incidentally, other market abuses which provoked the committee, chaired by Senator Peter Norbeck of New Jersey, to expand the scope of its hearings. In April

1932, a subcommittee convened to investigate the extent to which unfair market manipulations like pools and corners had pervaded the 1920s market. The proceedings gained momentum in early 1933 when Senator Norbeck appointed Ferdinand Pecora, a well-known New York assistant district attorney, as the chief counsel. In February, the proceedings commenced. A month later, President-elect Franklin D. Roosevelt assumed office. With these two events—Roosevelt's inauguration and the Pecora investigation—the NYSE's post-Crash public relations disaster began to unfold in earnest.

The NYSE's Public Relations Disaster Accelerates (1933–1934)

By the time President Roosevelt assumed office on March 4, 1933, the nation was mired in the depths of the Great Depression, with approximately 25% of the country unemployed and more than 11,000 banks having failed.[35] New Dealer and eventual Supreme Court Justice William O. Douglas recalled that Roosevelt faced a "desperate situation" because "a nation of investors had suffered untold losses as a result of secretive, excessive and fraudulent practices of promoters, bankers and issuers."[36] Some of those scandalous market practices already had come to light in the early phases of the Senate subcommittee hearings; others would soon surface as the Pecora investigation gained steam. In his inaugural address, President Roosevelt sought to reassure the nation, famously insisting, "the only thing we have to fear is fear itself—nameless, unreasoning, unjustified terror which paralyzes needed efforts to convert retreat into advance."[37] Two days later, to revive confidence in the teetering banking system, Roosevelt declared a "bank holiday." All financial institutions would be temporarily closed, and only the ones deemed solvent would reopen. During the bank holiday, from March 6th to March 15th, even trading on the NYSE was halted. Had he been alive at the time, J. P. Morgan Sr., who had struggled to keep the Exchange open during other crises, would have recoiled in horror. The NYSE had not shut its doors, even in the frenetic days of October 1929. Not since the outbreak of World War I in 1914 had Big Board operations been suspended.[38]

To the Old Guard, the closure of the NYSE during the bank holiday was an ominous sign of the Roosevelt administration's hostility toward the stock market. The President's inaugural address was another portent, as Roosevelt essentially blamed the NYSE for the nation's woes: "Plenty is at our doorstep, but a generous use of it languishes in the very sight of the supply. Primarily this is because rulers of the exchange of mankind's goods have failed through their own stubbornness and their own incompetence. . . . Practices of the unscrupulous money changers stand indicted in the court of public opinion, rejected by the hearts and minds of men." Roosevelt conceded, "True they have tried" to inspire confidence, yet "their efforts have been cast in the pattern of an outworn tradition." Roosevelt continued, "Stripped of the lure of profit by which to induce our people to follow their false leadership, they have resorted to exhortations, pleading tearfully for restored confidence. They know only the rules of a generation of self-seekers. They have no vision, and when there is no vision the people perish." Roosevelt contended, "The money changers have fled from their high seats in the temple of our civilization."[39]

As Roosevelt began his administration, Ferdinand Pecora energetically sought to speed the exodus of the moneychangers from the temple. He called prominent men in the financial district, like Jack Morgan Jr. and Richard Whitney, to testify. Pecora aimed not only to expose specific misdeeds but also to illuminate what he saw as Wall Streeters' elitism and their lack of commitment to providing a fair marketplace. Pecora's investigation revealed numerous unscrupulous securities marketing tactics, insider trading and stock manipulations, as well as general corporate misdeeds such as Chase President Albert Wiggins' selling short his own company's stock and National City Bank President Charles Mitchell's alleged income tax evasion.[40] In the public eye, the NYSE seemed to have failed to ensure a level playing field.

The Pecora hearings and subsequent investigations also uncovered abuses committed by several investment trusts (also called investment companies). At the time, closed-end funds, which had a fixed number of shares outstanding, dominated the investment trust business. In contrast, open-end funds (mutual funds) were just beginning to become popular. An open-end mutual fund continually sold shares to anyone who wanted to purchase them, so anyone who wanted to sell would receive the net asset value (NAV) per share on the day he or she sold. During the Crash, both closed-end and open-end trusts plummeted in value, but losses in closed-end funds were more severe, in part because they had been much more leveraged. Closed-end trusts also suffered from several scandals, such as embezzlement accusations.[41] In contrast, the open-end funds were relatively devoid of such stains, yet they, too, suffered a loss of business and prestige, as a confused and disillusioned public in the 1930s tended to blur together all investment companies (closed- and open-end).[42] After the Pecora hearings concluded, the government undertook further investigations of the investment company industry, and passed legislation to tighten its regulation: the Investment Company Act of 1940 and the Investment Advisors Act of 1940.

But, by the spring of 1933, the Pecora hearings had already exposed sufficient evidence on other fronts to propel the passage of two critical pieces of banking legislation: the Federal Securities Act (enacted May 27, 1933) and the Banking Act of 1933 (enacted June 16, 1933), also known as the Glass-Steagall Act. The Banking Act contained a series of measures, such as the creation of deposit insurance by the Federal Deposit Insurance Corporation (FDIC). Glass-Steagall's provision separating commercial banking from investment banking was the item that most concerned the NYSE. Big Board officials referred to the Banking Act in terms of a "blow," and the big banks bore the brunt of it especially the most prominent house on Wall Street, J. P. Morgan & Co. Partners at the House of Morgan, though aggrieved, quietly accepted the legislation, viewing any efforts to overturn it as likely futile.[43]

Less onerous to the NYSE was the Securities Act of 1933, which had two primary purposes: providing full disclosure to all investors (which would end the information disparity that had existed between "the public" and insiders) and eliminating fraud in the selling of securities. Requesting Congress to enact it, President Roosevelt explained, "This proposal adds to the ancient rule of *caveat emptor* the further doctrine, 'Let the Seller Beware.'"[44] The Old Guard did not strongly object to the Securities Act, realizing that the Roosevelt administration was under enormous public pressure to address the disturbing Pecora findings by implementing some market reforms. Moreover, the Old Guard understood that the Securities Act, as New Dealer William O. Douglas later explained, was "restricted in purpose and effect. . . . Once the truth is disclosed (and absent fraud) . . . industry then can sell what it pleases."[45]

The NYSE's Business Conduct Committee already had strict advertising policies. Nevertheless, they ostentatiously cooperated with the new act. During a brief stock market rally, when a member firm wanted to run an advertisement entitled "Reconstruction *Is* Under Way," the Committee insisted that the copy be changed to read "Reconstruction *May Be* Under Way." It warned the firm to "consider the new Federal Securities Act," the new truth-in-securities law, when composing future advertisements. In "truth," recovery from the Depression was not underway, though at the time, no one, including the Business Conduct Committee, could have known this. In another example of zealous monitoring, the Committee objected to four advertisements submitted by banking house Brown Brothers Harriman & Company because they included pictures of one of the firm's founders. The NYSE maintained that such illustrations violated the approved tombstone style of "direct and simple" advertising.[46]

In addition to scrupulously observing the new Securities Act, the Old Guard tried other ways to boost the organization's image with both the Roosevelt administration and the public. A Special Committee on Customers' Men implemented a few reforms such as higher educational standards, hoping to improve the character of those selling securities—a group known as "customers' men." The Special Committee also now officially discarded that name for the new moniker, [retail] "broker." The old term had become the subject of too many jokes. As one committee member explained, "they say he is paid to go out and exploit the public to get their money in here." "I haven't been able to go to a rough show when there wasn't some crack about a customer's man." Another member concurred: "The average person's idea of a customer's man is awful bad for us and the customer's man, and for the Exchange." They also objected to "customer's man" because it sounded too friendly, too eager to serve small clients, more befitting "a type of servant or menial rather than a high class business man." Conversely, "broker" presumably would "elevate and dignify" their job.[47] As these examples illustrate, the NYSE after the Crash initially engaged primarily in symbolic reforms. In retrospect, the period between the Crash and the end of Roosevelt's First Hundred Days was a grace period for the Exchange to improve its form and substance that its leaders did not properly utilize. Consequently, when New Dealers shifted focus from regulating the initial issuance of securities to regulating the market as a whole, the Exchange lay exposed to the charges that it had poorly patrolled the marketplace before 1929, and also had inadequately engaged in reforms afterward.

The Old Guard viewed Pecora's "inquisitorial" hearings as an insult to their dignity as well as a violation of their privileged relationship with their clients. Citing privacy concerns, Whitney refused Pecora's "request" that he send all Exchange members a detailed questionnaire about their clients and client trading activity. But Pecora persisted and sent two emissaries to Whitney's office for the purpose of securing his cooperation. One was reporter John Flynn, the man who had hailed Whitney's character in 1931. Whitney again refused, and he dismissed Flynn and his colleague allegedly with the words, "You gentlemen are making a great mistake" in trying to reform the marketplace; the Exchange was already "a perfect institution."[48] Reported by Flynn, Whitney's comment seemed to capture the institution's stubborn refusal to admit mistakes and its callous disregard for investors' welfare. In light of the scandals unearthed by the Pecora Committee, the contention that the Exchange was a "perfect institution" seemed laughable. Whitney later contended that he had been misunderstood: he did not mean to deny that scandals had occurred, just that the NYSE possessed within its own structure the capacity to prevent their reoccurrence. The flaw resided in the administration of the Exchange's rules, not the actual rules. The Exchange, Whitney argued, was fully capable of cleaning its own house and improving rule enforcement: it needed no "cop on the corner."[49]

Disagreeing with Whitney, the Pecora Committee in June 1934 concluded that federal regulation was "necessary and desirable" considering the "evils and abuses which flourished on the exchange and their disastrous effects on the entire Nation." Likewise, a House committee report endorsed federal regulation, declaring that exchanges should no longer be allowed to operate as "private clubs" that promote only their members' interests; instead, they needed to be treated as "public institutions . . . affected with a public interest in the same degree as any other great utility."[50] In February, Senator Fletcher drafted a bill to empower the Federal Trade Commission (FTC) to oversee the Exchange, even before the Pecora Committee issued its final report in June. The Old Guard objected, but the minority Reformers declared their willingness to work with the federal government to modify the bill. Four months later, shortly after the Pecora Committee ended its investigation, the Securities Exchange Act became law.

The Creation of the SEC (1934)

To craft the legislation that became the Securities Exchange Act of 1934, Felix Frankfurter, one of Roosevelt's trusted advisors, recruited a team that included Benjamin Cohen, Thomas Corcoran, and James Landis. Cohen and Corcoran, both lawyers who worked at Wall Street law firms, possessed an unusually strong understanding of the complex securities industry. Landis, who had studied at Harvard Law under Frankfurter and who had once clerked for Supreme Court Justice Louis Brandeis, also proved influential, particularly in his advocacy for keeping the NYSE as primarily a self-regulatory organization.[51] As Landis explained, "Self-government is, of course, the desirable thing. Everyone will admit that the less regulation there is, the better it will be, provided the objectives are always kept clear; and the better the self-government, the less need there is for regulation." While committed to preserving self-regulation as much as possible, Landis also endeavored to design the legislation so as to improve the Exchange's character and its sense of responsibility to the public. As Landis later explained, the key was to make the NYSE's "loyalty . . . to the broad objectives of government a condition of its continued existence, thus building from within as well as imposing from without."[52]

The Securities Exchange Act of 1934 contained several key provisions, such as the stipulation that companies with stocks listed on the NYSE or other exchanges publicly disclose their financial information. Per the Securities Act of 1933, new companies going public already had to disclose their financials, but now, existing publicly traded companies had to do so as well. The Act also created the Securities and Exchange Commission (SEC), a five-man panel that essentially would coregulate the Exchange. The president of the United States would appoint the commissioners, who had to be confirmed by Congress. The SEC officials, while theoretically empowered to alter the rules of the Exchange, would act only if the Exchange proved incompetent in making needed changes. Reflecting Landis' influence, the SEC was supposed to intervene only when self-regulation failed. As William O. Douglas, the third chairman of the SEC and future Supreme Court justice, later noted, the idea was to "keep the shotgun, so to speak, behind the door, loaded, well-oiled, cleaned, ready for use, but with the hope that it would never have to be used."[53]

At the NYSE, the creation of the SEC provoked mixed reactions. The Board was relieved that the new legislation left the Exchange as primarily a self-regulatory organization. Also, the Board appreciated that at least it was not the FTC coregulating the NYSE, as the Fletcher-Rayburn bill had originally proposed. But the Old Guard resented any organization overseeing the Exchange. The group was not mollified when Roosevelt selected as the first SEC chairman not Ferdinand Pecora, as the NYSE had feared, but Joseph Kennedy—a man thought by some to be friendly to business and thus likely to be a lax SEC administrator, given his well-known stock market exploits in the 1920s. Kennedy, however, was not well-liked by the Old Guard; as President Roosevelt was well aware, there had been a showdown between Kennedy and J. P. ("Jack") Morgan Jr. in the 1920s when the upstart Kennedy had tried to buy his way into the Old Guard by engineering control of Columbia Trust Company. In considering Kennedy for the position, Roosevelt liked that Kennedy was not enmeshed with the Old Guard. Also, Roosevelt wanted to repay Kennedy for his support during the 1932 presidential campaign. Finally, Roosevelt believed that someone inside Wall Street, familiar with the tricks of the trade, would be best qualified to patrol the marketplace.[54]

Beginning his tenure as SEC chairman, Kennedy proclaimed on nationwide radio the agency's "two major objectives": "One is the advancement of protection of decent business; and the other—even more important—is spiritual, and I do not hesitate to employ that word in connection with finance. We are seeking to re-create, rebuild, restore confidence."[55] Evidently, Kennedy, too, was on the confidence bandwagon. Surprising many, Kennedy sought to achieve that confidence by advocating serious reforms. Most controversial were proposed changes in the Exchange's management structure that would increase the power of the commission brokers. Since these members relied upon retail investors for business, presumably they would better champion the investing public's interests.

Not wishing to surrender any power to the commission brokers, the Old Guard refused to consider changing the NYSE's management structure. However, they began to enact some meaningful reforms. They finally banned market manipulations that unfairly influenced a stock's price. Also, becoming more serious about curbing the front running of orders, the Old Guard forbid specialists from disclosing information regarding any orders they were filling or from acting on the information to benefit themselves. The Business Conduct Committee began to strictly enforce these new rules, and also tightened its enforcement of older rules.[56] While applauding these changes, the SEC, however, still desired substantial changes in the Exchange's management structure. The reforms also seem to have been ineffective in validating the institution in the public eye; the NYSE was caught in a catch-22 situation: the more the organization proclaimed its legitimacy, the more people seemed to question it.[57]

In October 1934, Big Board President Richard Whitney distributed an opinion questionnaire to the Exchange community. Circulating it to "Members, Partners, Branch Office Managers and Correspondents," Whitney solicited advice on how to restore public confidence and eradicate popular misunderstandings. In the cover letter, Whitney wrote, "You are familiar with conditions in your city and district. You have knowledge of the attitude of your customers, your business friends, the editorial position of your newspapers. You know the general and basic criticisms in their minds." Whitney asked: "Will you write frankly and tell me, in as much detail as possible, the conditions in your locality and the things which beget criticism and antagonism to our business? Will you give me these items of criticism and misinformation; also the attitude of your newspapers and what they find fault with? Give me, please, the facts concerning the situation, no matter how critical." Carefully emphasizing, "The Exchange does not intend to indulge in propaganda or mere business boosting publicity," Whitney promised, "We shall represent facts only."[58] No records exist of responses to the questionnaire, perhaps because few answered it, at least in writing. The House of Morgan, for example, issued no formal reply, as Morgan's in-house publicist Martin Egan had advised Lamont, "I don't believe that you should send any response to this circular letter. . . . I am sure if you have any views about the NYSE there are other means of communicating them instead of taking part in this questionnaire."[59]

Whatever the results of the questionnaire, Whitney did not lessen his criticism of New Deal measures. In his radio addresses and personal appearances in the late autumn of 1934, Whitney sharpened his criticism of the SEC, vilifying the agency for worsening the Depression as well as threatening the country's "economic freedom." He vainly portrayed himself as a martyr on behalf of both capitalism and the Exchange, the symbol of capitalism. He lamented that when equity prices fell, "the president of the New York Stock Exchange inevitably became a mark for the hunters," even though the market was merely a "recording instrument," a "barometer" of business conditions, not the maker of prices. Because "the intangible character of value made it difficult to trace this shrinkage to its sources . . . the popular sense of frustration and the demand for a feeling victim turned the general wrath against the Stock Exchange" and against Whitney.[60]

Speaking before the Chicago Association of Stock Exchange firms in December 1934, Whitney avoided his earlier gaffe of hailing the Exchange as a "perfect institution." This time, he admitted that mistakes had been made and some reforms were necessary. He did not condemn criticism: "it is well for established institutions to be exposed to the discipline of public study. The spirit of penance and self-reform is aided by the occasional exasperation of a hair-shirt." Whitney carefully emphasized "self-reform." He implored his audience "to weigh judiciously the clamor for penalties and reform, raise his eyes from the distress of the hour, and looking down the perspective of time, judge these institutions by their over-all performance." Distinguishing "honest criticism" from the current assault on the Exchange, Whitney warned that "when [an attack] serves no other purpose than the glorification of a self anointed critic, it bears the seed of great mischief." He concluded, "It is the duty of every intelligent citizen to maintain these markets inviolable against the mischievous proposals of misguided visionaries. In so doing it is the conservative and not the radical who best assures a higher standard of material welfare for all our people."[61]

Internal and External Power Struggles at the NYSE (1935–1938)

Reformers at the NYSE argued that Whitney's thinly disguised attacks on Roosevelt as well as his rigid adherence to the status quo hurt more than helped the Exchange. At a divisive Board of Governors meeting, floor broker John Hanes accused Whitney of maintaining outmoded policies and refusing to acquiesce to public demands for serious changes in Exchange protocol. Even some Old Guardsmen began to agree that Whitney's arrogance, if not his actual policies, was becoming a liability. In March 1935, during a nominating meeting preceding the Exchange's annual election, several members questioned Whitney's continued fitness for the job of president. "The criticism hing[ed] loosely on the question of public relations," the *New York Times* reported. Two weeks later, the NYSE Board appointed Charles Gay to the top post, a long-time Exchange governor who was a partner at Whitehouse & Co. Viewing Gay as a moderate, many members along with the SEC preferred him to Whitney. Even a contingent of the Old Guard saw value in having Gay as president; they believed that having a moderate nominally in charge of the Exchange would be a good public relations move to mollify the SEC.[62] Along with Gay's ascension to the presidency, the Board made other concessions to the Exchange's moderate wing, such as appointing Maurice Farrell, a prominent Reformer, to chair the Committee on Public Relations. Yet the Old Guard retained control over other critical Exchange committees, such as Business Conduct, Law, and Admissions. Despite no longer being president, Whitney remained a powerful Exchange governor.[63] The organization began to operate in effect two divergent public relations programs—the official one in which the commission brokers, under Farrell, exercised influence, and an unofficial one, led by the Old Guard.

That March, the Old Guard proposed appointing a "czar" to oversee the Exchange and assure its integrity. Providing oversight, of course, was the SEC's function. The Old Guard secretly hoped that a czar eventually might replace the SEC. On the surface, it might appear as if the NYSE would object to a czar just as strongly as it did to the SEC, as a czar would still subject the Exchange to external regulation. Yet there was a key difference: the president of the United States appointed the SEC commissioners, who also had to be confirmed by Congress, whereas the NYSE Board of Governors would appoint, and probably control, a czar. While technically overseeing the NYSE, an outside czar, the Old Guard presumed, would not threaten the Exchange's independence.[64] Recognizing the Old Guard's ulterior motives, the media lambasted the czar idea as yet another token effort by the recalcitrant Exchange to give the appearance, not the substance, of reform. Even the normally conservative, probusiness *New York Sun* satirized the proposal in a poem:

We [the NYSE] need a czar, a pleasant one,
Like Landis or like Hays,
To step into the Stock Exchange
And bring it better days . . .
A czar who knows the public mind,
And who can skillfully
Present us in the public eye
The way we like to be.[65]

"Kensaw Mountain" Landis and Will Hays, the czars of movies and baseball, respectively, had helped those once scandal-stained institutions regain credibility.[66] However, the Big Board was not yet fully committed to genuine reform, whether imposed internally or externally. The Old Guard wanted to preserve the status quo, and yet somehow cultivate a better image. Capturing the NYSE's concern with its public face, the *Sun* remarked:

We need some glorifying done,
And we need it badly now;
Oh, won't some volunteer step forth
And kindly show us how?
We want that chilly mask removed—
That manner cold as ice;
The public should be made to feel
We're really very nice.[67]

For more than a century, the Exchange had cultivated a formidable aura, epitomized by the polished marble of its headquarters at 11 Wall Street on the corner of Broad Street, across from the offices of J. P. Morgan & Co. at No. 23 Wall. Now, however, the institution wanted to be perceived as friendly and perhaps above all, as moral and respectable:

> Judge Landis bless'd the game of ball,
> Will Hays made Hollywood;
> Oh, why can't we be sanctified
> And made correct and good?
> The Stock Exchange is just a place
> Where stocks are traded in.
> Why should it be regarded as
> Some dark abode of sin? . . .
> Oh, educate the public well—
> This moral tale unfold;
> No matter what the ticker does,
> It has a heart of gold![68]

The czar proposal captured the Old Guard's determination to fight external regulation. The SEC, now headed by James Landis, who succeeded Kennedy in 1935, had hoped that Gay's appointment to the NYSE presidency would diminish the grip held by the Old Guard and unleash a new era of cooperation between Wall Street and Washington. To the SEC's disappointment, the change in power from Whitney to Gay was only superficial; the Board, more than the presidency, was the epicenter of Exchange policy-making, and Old Guard leaders like Whitney still served on key committees, such as Business Conduct and Law.

Besides underestimating the strength of the NYSE Board, the SEC had misjudged Gay's ideological leanings.[69] Gay shared Whitney's tendency to champion the specialists and floor traders, not the retail commission house floor members. Like Whitney, Gay began to openly disparage the small investor. In one speech, Gay dismissed the public as "a Gargantuan entity, often maladroit, given to extremes of gloom and of optimism."[70] As his term progressed, Gay increasingly criticized the SEC, as he did in his preface to the NYSE's *1936 Annual Report*. For many years, the NYSE's annual report format had included just a basic income statement and a balance sheet. However, in 1935, as part of its public relations endeavors, the Big Board began including a letter from the president to the Exchange community. (At this time, some listed companies were also beginning to use their annual reports as a public relations tool.[71]) However, in the NYSE's case, that public relations initiative backfired, as Gay, in his letter, blamed the SEC for creating an "illiquid market," a comment that incensed the SEC. Less than two months after the NYSE published its *1936 Annual Report* with Gay's criticism, the stock market collapsed again.[72]

The ensuing Recession of 1937 perplexed and frustrated government, business, and Exchange leaders, who frantically endeavored to deflect hostile public opinion. President Roosevelt blamed the lingering Depression on a "capital strike" by Republican business leaders, while the NYSE blamed the SEC, and the SEC, in turn, blamed the Exchange.[73] These groups were all battling for legitimacy, believing that if one group achieved legitimacy, another would lose it. The SEC wanted the Stock Exchange to "take the rap" for the 1937 market collapse, as the *New York Sun* noted. However, according to the newspaper, "the Stock Exchange has no intention of being a lamb on the sacrificial altar."[74] Boding badly for the Old Guard, William O. Douglas, with the help of New Dealers Thomas Corcoran and Benjamin Cohen, became the new chairman of the SEC, succeeding the more moderate and patient Landis on September 21, 1937. Gay's remarks in the *NYSE 1936 Annual Report* infuriated Douglas, who feared that his SEC might be scapegoated for the October market crash. Deriding the NYSE as an antiquated "private club," Douglas threatened to nationalize the Exchange unless it cooperated with the SEC and reorganized its management structure to ensure the organization operated more in the public interest. President Roosevelt supported Douglas' ultimatum, and Reformers on Wall Street, led by Pierce and Shields, urged Gay to take the threat seriously.[75] The NYSE's self-regulatory structure, basically intact even after the creation of the SEC, seemed in imminent jeopardy unless the NYSE engaged in a substantial internal reorganization.

The strengths and the weaknesses of the Exchange's structure became an area of academic interest in 1937. At the Harvard Business School, the NYSE's self-regulatory status was the subject of an examination question in a Business History class taught by professors Norman Gras and Ralph Hower. Professor Hower saved the exam of one exemplary student, Harry Hanson. Hanson responded that self-regulation afforded the Exchange a "clearer understanding of its problems and how to meet them than any outside regulatory governmental organ." After citing other advantages of self-regulation, he pointed out three major disadvantages of the associative structure. First, "Unethical action of one member tends to cast unsavory publicity on the other members. In other words the association is, in a sense no stronger than its members." Second, "In times of distress and shaken confidence the association becomes the butt of criticism . . . in many cases undeservedly." Finally, "Long-standing traditions foster a resistance to change to meet new conditions. It is only recently that the NYSE has taken aggressive and overt action toward getting favorable publicity." He elaborated: "An early policy of the organization was extreme privacy. Later, and especially in the last dozen years or so, we have seen an exact reversal of this policy—an attempt to acquaint the public with the nature of the organization, functions, manner of doing business, etc."[76] However, the Exchange's efforts to "acquaint the public" with its virtues did not prevent a showdown with the SEC in the autumn of 1937.

Fearing that the new SEC chairman was not bluffing in his threat to nationalize the Exchange, Gay appointed a committee to propose an internal reorganization, and in late 1937, the committee began its work, led by Carle Conway, chairman of the board of Continental Can Company. Conway viewed Exchange reorganization as imperative in order to facilitate more cordial relations between Wall Street and Washington, which he saw as necessary to fuel recovery. Conway was close friends with Hanes, the Reformer who, in 1932, had attacked Whitney for being unresponsive to public opinion. Other members of the Conway Committee included Maurice Farrell, chairman of the Public Relations Committee and associated with F. S. Smithers & Co.; Kenneth C. Hogate, president of the *Wall Street Journal*; Adolph A. Berle Jr., lawyer and member of President Roosevelt's inner circle; William McChesney Martin Jr., a partner in the St. Louis brokerage house, A. G. Edwards & Co.; Thomas H. McInnerney, president of National Dairy Products; and three well-respected Exchange members, John Prentiss, Trowbridge Callaway, and John A. Coleman.[77] The completed Conway study, published on January 27, 1938, recommended a reorganization replete with a paid independent presidency and a heightened role for commission house floor brokers. Buckling under the pressure of Douglas' threat to nationalize the Exchange, the Board of Governors unanimously approved these recommendations. (Whitney conspicuously abstained.) The SEC initially thought it had won a clear victory. However, to die-hard Old Guardsmen, the approval only meant that they theoretically would reorganize the Exchange at some undesignated future time. In the meantime, they would continue to resist reform. Once again, progress was at a standstill, with the Old Guard and the SEC mired in deadlock.[78]

The Whitney Scandal and the NYSE Reorganization of 1938

Only a scandal emanating from the Exchange community's highest ranks in 1938 finally broke the hold of the Old Guard. The year before, Harvard Business School student Harry Hanson had listed as a major disadvantage of the Exchange's association structure that "unethical action of one member tends to cast unsavory publicity on the other members. . . . The association is, in a sense, no stronger than its members."[79] Hanson had been reflecting upon the member firm scandals that Ferdinand Pecora had brought to the public eye in 1933 and 1934. However, in retrospect, his comment foreshadowed what would bring the NYSE to its lowest point yet—unethical action by one of its most prominent members. In 1938, this member was caught stealing funds from the Stock Market's Gratuity Fund; he was the leader of the Old Guard, five-time president of the NYSE, Richard Whitney. He did not steal directly from public investors. (The Gratuity Fund was a retirement account for Exchange employees.) However, the crime symbolized everything popularly deemed wrong with the NYSE: the arrogance of its leaders, the way the club protected its own, and the perceived immorality of Wall Street.[80]

The "Whitney affair" stigmatized the NYSE not just due to the actual crime, but also the way the financial community first ignored the problem and then tried to conceal it. Whitney's financial problems had been evident to many colleagues since at least 1930, when he began borrowing heavily from them to cover losses in highly speculative real estate and stock investments. He then borrowed more funds to repay these loans as they matured. He did so in part by illegally pledging customers' securities as collateral and by using the Gratuity Fund as his personal bank. Whitney's distress selling should have triggered an Exchange investigation into his firm's affairs, but his position on the Board and the Business Conduct Committee enabled him to escape detection for eight years.[81] Even after an Exchange employee, George Lute, alerted the Board to the disturbing irregularities in the Gratuity Fund account, the scandal did not immediately become public knowledge. Richard's brother, George, at J. P. Morgan, tried to rescue him by offering to pay the exposed deficit. Meanwhile, Richard Whitney attempted to strike a deal with his friend, President Gay: he would sell his Exchange membership if the charges against him were dropped. This, Whitney argued, would not just be in his own best interests, but also those of the NYSE, because "I'm Richard Whitney, and I mean the Stock Exchange to millions of people." A scandal tainting him tainted the entire Stock Exchange. Gay refused, and on March 1, 1938, he solemnly ascended the rostrum on the trading floor and announced that "an examination of the affairs of Richard Whitney & Company [uncovered] evidence of conduct apparently contrary to just and equitable principles of trade."[82] After being expelled from the Exchange, Whitney was convicted of embezzlement and sentenced to a term at Ossining State Penitentiary ("Sing Sing") in Westchester County, New York. The "Whitney Affair" also prompted an SEC investigation. In the final report, the SEC castigated the Exchange for attempting to cover up Whitney's crime. The NYSE was not a private social club, where the misconduct of a key member could be treated as a private matter of no public import.[83] With Whitney's conviction and the SEC report, the NYSE's reputation plummeted. However, the Whitney affair ironically served a useful purpose; by hastening the collapse of the Old Guard, it opened the path to meaningful internal Exchange reform. Indeed, the crisis led to a new NYSE—new first in substance and then, eventually, new in image.

The Exchange's quest to eradicate the Whitney stain began immediately. Two weeks after the NYSE expelled Whitney, the Board sought the assistance of expert image-maker Edward Bernays, one of the founders of modern public relations. When news of the private meeting was leaked to the press, the Committee on Public Relations clarified that the Exchange had not employed Bernays, but had merely consulted with him.[84] Seizing the opportunity presented by the Whitney power vacuum, the Reformers lost no time in restructuring the NYSE according to the already approved Conway plan. By June, only a few months after Whitney's indictment, they completed the Reorganization of 1938. The presidency became a paid post to which William McChesney Martin, a leading Reformer and a member of the Conway Committee, ascended. Possessing an impeccable reputation, Martin was the anti-Whitney. The former Old Guardsman was arrogant; Martin was humble. Whitney enjoyed gambling and drinking; Martin preferred reading and hot chocolate. Martin, who had once seriously considered the Presbyterian ministry, presented the right image for an institution desperate to repair its public standing.[85] In addition, the Exchange expanded the number of Governors, and mandated that it include three representatives of "the public." The posts of "public governors" came to be typically occupied by industry leaders and sometimes educators. The first three public governors were Carle Conway, Robert M. Hutchins, and Robert E. Woods. The SEC was pleased with the Exchange's new structure. Finally satisfied, William O. Douglas declared an end to the "crackdown on Wall Street," proclaiming, "The prosperity of the Stock Exchange is not incompatible with the national welfare."[86]

The Whitney affair was the last of a series of scandals to engulf the Exchange in the turbulent decade after the Great Crash. Yet the Shadow of 1929 did not immediately dissipate after the 1938 Reorganization. Despite internal and external reforms of the organization, and a new president who was beyond reproach, public confidence in the stock market's integrity did not follow, as opinion polls taken between 1938 and 1940 confirmed.[87] Factors impairing the Exchange's ability to convey its reforms included the institution's bias against advertising as well as its history of misdirected public relations during the Great Depression years. Consequently, a confidence gap existed between the Big Board's improved substance and public perception.[88]

CHAPTER TWO

Experimenting with Advertising

> Advertising is a mode of education by which the knowledge of consumable
> goods is increased. . . . Its success is measured by the amount of buying
> which it stimulates.
>
> EMILY FOGG-MEADE, "THE PLACE OF ADVERTISING IN MODERN
> BUSINESS," *JOURNAL OF POLITICAL ECONOMY* (1901)

By 1939, a year after the NYSE Reorganization, the stock market still languished, and many member firms, suffering from a dearth of business, struggled to survive. The Dow, only reaching 158.41 that year, was nowhere near its pre-Crash high of 381.17. Annual stock volume was 262 million shares, as opposed to more than 1.1 billion shares in 1929, and the meager stock turnover level of 18% in 1939 paled in comparison to 119% a decade earlier. Reflecting Wall Street's woes, a seat on the Exchange in 1939 sold for a low of $51,000, as opposed to a high of $625,000 in 1929.[1] The Big Board's problems stemmed not just from a Depression-era reduction in personal savings that could be channeled into investments but also from shattered public trust in their institution and widespread disenchantment with equities as a prudent investment. Exchange leaders wrestled with how to overcome these challenges.

James W. Young, an advertising executive at J. Walter Thompson agency, once insisted that advertising could be "the greatest single force for informing and inspiring public opinion which the world has ever seen."[2] But the Big Board was slower than "Big Business" to appreciate the power of advertising.

Historically, the Old Guard had severely restricted member firm advertising, believing that this would enhance the association's image as a lofty professional organization. They also had resisting advertising the Exchange itself or the merits of investing.

In the NYSE Reorganization of 1938, however, the Reformers who gained power were amenable to change.[3] Due to competing interests, the Reformers soon fractured into two groups: a neo–Old Guard, dominated mostly by specialists, and the commission house brokers. Despite this division, the NYSE Board of Governors was able to agree on some initiatives, including liberalizing member firm advertising. The Board understood that many commission houses desperately needed a larger, more active client base. The Board was still unwilling to directly help struggling member firms market their services, yet they grew open to letting member firms help themselves. On April 13, 1939, the Board informed member brokerage firms that they could advertise more freely, as long as advertisements were truthful and in good taste. The NYSE's revised advertising policy "caused a considerable stir in Wall Street," the *New York Times* reported, as commission houses debated how advertising might help and which of their competitors would be the first to take advantage of the loosened rules.[4]

A Trickle of Member Firms Enlarge Their Advertising (1939–1940)

Fenner & Beane, one of the largest commission houses in the country, second only to E. A. Pierce, moved quickly.[5] Only two weeks after the new policy went into effect, Fenner & Beane launched a three-week series of advertisements in newspapers and magazines across the country. The advertisements are notable for what they did not attempt to do: they did not specifically mention the firm's competitive strengths; rather, they promoted the NYSE and sought to correct misperceptions about the marketplace. The first advertisement, "Mass Opinion Makes Fair Prices," challenged the notion that a handful of insiders manipulated stock prices. As the advertisement stressed, stock prices were the product of the opinions of the masses, not of a privileged few who allegedly operated the Exchange at the expense of the rest. In another advertisement, "Why a Stock Exchange?," Fenner & Beane explained why the public should place their faith in the NYSE: "When an investor purchases securities through a firm that holds membership in the NYSE or the New York

Curb Exchange [later renamed the American Stock Exchange], he is dealing with organizations that are financially responsible, for those [running the] Exchange regularly review the financial status of all members, and their financial requirements are high and rigid."

Cognizant that many Americans were unaware of the SEC's purpose or even its existence, Fenner & Beane also conveyed the new investor safeguards that were now in place on established exchanges like the NYSE, attempting to dissuade investors from doing business with bogus brokers or those on less reputable exchanges. The copy emphasized, "These safeguards for the investing public explain why most of the country's leading corporations list their securities on a recognized exchange, and why so many institutional and individual investors prefer to purchase listed stocks and bonds through member firms." The only mention of Fenner & Beane was at the very end, where the firm listed its name, offices, and NYSE affiliation. The *New York Times* remarked that Fenner & Beane was "advertising not itself but the organized exchanges of the country on the theory that public understanding of their functions is not all that it should be."[6]

Philip W. Russell, senior partner at Fenner & Beane, supported his firm's campaign and enthusiastically approved the NYSE's more permissive attitude toward advertising. He explained, "We believe that the new rules promulgated recently by the Stock Exchange with regard to member firm publicity and advertising will open a new era in the relations between the Stock Exchange and the investing public. It is our hope that our series of announcements will contribute to the new understanding between the public and organized securities exchanges, which will result from the relaxation of the rigid restrictions formerly imposed by the New York Stock Exchange on member firm advertising."[7]

In his comment, Russell, like many Exchange members at the time, used the rather ambiguous term of "investing public." Who was the "investing public," and to what extent, if any, did they differ from the regular "public"? Fenner & Beane's advertisements did not encourage existing investors to trade more frequently or encourage new investors to come to Wall Street. The promotions, although designed to increase the firm's business, focused on improving the image of Wall Street among the American public, the vast majority of which were noninvestors.[8]

Fenner & Beane hired Doremus & Co., founded in 1903 by *Wall Street Journal* owner Clarence W. Barron and one of only a few advertising agencies that specialized in the small field of financial advertising. During World War I, Doremus had initiated the first major advertising campaign promoting Liberty Bonds for the U.S. Government.[9] Now, a quarter century later, Doremus helped Fenner & Beane create a series of newspaper and magazine advertisements. These advertisements emphasized that contrary to the "prophets of doom," actually, "no country in the world has a greater future than America." Philip Russell explained to the *New York Times* the need for the campaign: "We owe it to ourselves and to the public to call attention to the solid background for individual success and general recovery that exists in the heroic heritage of this country and in its resources." Denying that his firm's advertisements were predicting a boom in securities prices and an immediate return to prosperity, Russell declared, "We are simply trying to restate an American philosophy that was an accepted commonplace to earlier generations of Americans."[10]

In wanting to use advertising to attract small investors, Charles Merrill was a kindred spirit with Philip Russell. Merrill had left Wall Street in 1930 to pursue opportunities in the chain store business, and E. A. Pierce & Co. had acquired the brokerage business of Merrill, Lynch & Co.[11] A decade later, Merrill returned to Wall Street after Winthrop Smith, a partner at E. A. Pierce, had invited Merrill to join his firm, which needed an infusion of capital. In considering the offer, Merrill consulted polls by Elmo Roper and the NYSE, and conducted his own survey.[12] The results uniformly confirmed that Americans still distrusted securities salesmen and the NYSE, but Merrill, nevertheless, accepted the challenge. Emboldening Merrill was his observation that the burgeoning middle class constituted a great market, his success in the 1920s cultivating small customers, and his ideological commitment to capitalism, perhaps heightened by the deepening world war.[13] Merrill enjoyed a strong reputation with investors, who remembered his advice before the Great Crash to take their money out of the market. In a letter to his customers on April 1, 1928, Merrill had urged them to reduce their margin accounts "or, better still, to pay them off entirely." While not encouraging his clients to "sell securities indiscriminately," he did advise them "in no uncertain terms [to] take advantage of present high prices and put [their] own financial house in order." Reporting on Merrill's advice to "sell enough securities to lighten . . . obligations," the *New York Times* had commented, "This is the most outspoken advice of the kind that has been given by any firm to its customers in the present phase of the market. Mr. Merrill does not say that he expects prices to fall;

he simply emphasizes that it is a good time to realize profits."[14] For his timely warning, Merrill earned a reputation for being a friend of the "little guy"—the small investor on Wall Street.

In April 1940, Charles Merrill and his colleagues outlined a business strategy that used advertising to reach small investors. At a conference of the branch office managers, Merrill emphasized that public relations was no substitute for advertising, explaining, "Unfortunately, most of us have, oh, a vague, general idea that it is very nice to get your name in the paper and have a write-up, and they call that publicity. Well, I call it applesauce. It has no more to do with publicity, or not as much, as the honest, forthright advertisement bought and paid for with your own money and published in the paper." He insisted, "All that sort of publicity in the world won't bring you one new customer, and, besides that these newspaper fellows are pretty smart. They represent the public and they can pick out a stuffed shirt. . . . They just go to them like a bird dog goes to a quail. We will hand out no more boilerplate publicity." Merrill realized, "Publicity is a very dangerous weapon. It is a two-edged sword, and it is sharp on both sides." He was not saying that the firm would cease all public relations efforts, but he wanted to embrace advertising, convinced of advertising's power to tell the firm's story persuasively and directly.[15]

In 1941 Merrill's house merged with Fenner & Beane, becoming Merrill Lynch Pierce Fenner & Beane (hereafter abbreviated "Merrill Lynch").[16] The firm continued to grow its customer base, and Charles Merrill credited the expansion to "aggressive advertising and merchandising."[17]

As Merrill Lynch increased its advertising, other commission brokerage firms were struggling to stay afloat. Due to strained finances, few advertised after the liberalization in NYSE policy. Needing business, they were, however, hesitant to spend on advertising, which they saw as a discretionary item. They worried that the payoff from advertising, if any, would be long in coming. Companies in other industries also questioned whether advertising was worth it, finding it difficult to measure the return on their investment. Advertising apologists insisted that advertising was indeed worth it, helping companies differentiate their products from those of competitors and serving to educate consumers.[18]

Despite these advantages, many companies in a variety of industries slashed their advertising budgets during the Great Depression. P. T Cherington, the J. Walter Thompson executive who had warned that the Crash was a "well-advertised flurry," remarked in 1931, "When the treasurer says there is no money for advertising unless the sales payroll is to yield it, or when there is a serious shrinkage in the value of securities which might be used as collateral for a loan to finance any aggressive selling, there is not much to be done about it." He continued, "The short and terrible period of descent from prosperity to depression is one in which any urging of advertising is impractical. This stage in the business cycle, for most business concerns, is so full of defensive action, and so encumbered with previous commitments that the main job is to sustain life." Cherington and his colleagues, nevertheless, tried to convince their corporate clients that it was wise to advertise, even if the public did not have money to buy their products. The idea was to keep a company's brand names memorable with consumers so that they would return once the economy recovered. Cherington argued that actually advertising was most needed during a depression: "manifestly, those who aggressively push sales during such times can count on increasing their proportionate share of the shrink[ing] market at the expense of those who are less alert. During such times, also, competition is of the sharpest and most determined sort, and advertising takes a logical place in such competition as one of the most economical and effective of competitive devices."[19]

Unlike companies in the automobile industry and other consumer-goods oriented fields, NYSE member brokerage firms had not yet embraced advertising, and to begin this in the midst of the Depression would have been a major leap of faith. Nevertheless, a few large commission houses such as Fenner & Beane and J. S. Bache did make that bold move into advertising in the late 1930s and early 1940s. Smaller commission houses hoped that the pro–stock market messages promoted by the larger firms would help all member firms. This multiplier effect, however, was not immediately materializing.

The NYSE Flirts with Institutional Advertisements (1939)

Concerned about many member firms' dwindling business, the Board of Governors contemplated an action that previously would have been unthinkable: collaborating with member firms in an advertising campaign geared toward the mass market. The Old Guard had not seen advertising as part of their role providing a "just and orderly marketplace." However, leaders of the reorganized NYSE interpreted their mandate more broadly. According to the new rationale, an "orderly" market had to be liquid, and liquidity depended on a market with many shareowners.[20] Advertising that brought more investors to Wall Street could be justified, and in October 1939, the Board planned for an institutional advertising campaign to be conducted jointly with member firms.

Unlike product advertisements that aim to sell products and services, institutional advertisements make more expansive claims, often emphasizing the advertiser's broad contributions to society and perhaps a way of life.[21] Some companies such as AT&T and U.S. Steel had advertised since the early twentieth century, but in the 1930s, more firms began appreciating its value, including some who sought to undo public relations damage inflicted by the Nye Committee. In 1934, the Nye Committee, chaired by North Dakota Senator Gerald Nye, had investigated the country's leading armament manufacturers to assess whether they had dragged the United States into World War I so they could profit from increased sales. The investigation found no proof of war profiteering, but the targeted companies, nevertheless, suffered from Senator Nye's charge that they had been "merchants of death."[22] Some turned to institutional advertising as an image recovery strategy. Determined to recover its once stellar reputation, from 1935 to 1953 DuPont sponsored a radio show entitled "Cavalcade of America" which, in a series of half-hour segments, dramatized episodes in American history. Interspersed were repeated promotions of DuPont's new tag-line: "Better things for better living . . . through chemistry." Rather than directly refuting Senator Nye's allegations, DuPont's advertising emphasized the company's positive contributions to society, and "Cavalcade of America" helped DuPont improve its reputation.[23]

While DuPont and other companies tapped the power of institutional advertising, the securities industry hesitated. With its 1939 promotions, however, Fenner & Beane pointed the way for the NYSE. Their advertisements did not try to sell the firm's products or services; they emphasized the benefits the NYSE brought to the nation, such as providing a free and open marketplace. In the late 1930s, therefore, the NYSE Board was relying on a handful of member firms to tell the Exchange story. Resisting a direct engagement in institutional advertising, Exchange officials had explained and extolled the NYSE's work in other formats, such as books and films, lecture tours, and radio programs. Yet all the preaching of the stock market's virtues seems to have had little effect, judging by the Exchange's ongoing image problems. However, the NYSE had not yet tried to advertise in mass circulation newspapers and magazines. In late 1939, this apparently was about to change.

On October 18, 1939, a headline in the *New York Times* proclaimed, "Exchange Pushes Its Ad Campaign." As the *Times* noted, "For years the Exchange has been considering institutional advertising, designed chiefly for education of the public as to the services offered by the market place." Now the Exchange seemed ready for a campaign that would include "a schedule of thirteen full pages in leading newspapers." Contending that the NYSE's public relations department was nearing the completion of its plan, the *Times* explained, "the main burden of expense [would be] borne by member firms, with the Exchange itself possibly carrying a small portion in addition to sponsoring and supervising the advertising."[24] The *Times* emphasized this would constitute a NYSE precedent: "The Stock Exchange has never advertised, even on a small scale. Members, of course, have done so from time to time, but mainly in the direct line of business."[25] While the majority of the *Times* report was optimistic about the proposed advertising plan being implemented, the conclusion raised doubts: "In Exchange circles emphasis is placed upon the statement that plans so far are nebulous, that the scheme is by no means assured of passage and that two important questions remain unanswered. First, can enough money be secured from Stock Exchange houses [member firms] to carry through the program on anything like the scale originally envisaged? Second, will the governors of the Exchange vote the funds necessary to pay the Exchange's share, whatever that may be?"[26] Shortly following the *Times* report, upon canvassing members, the Board of Governors determined that too few brokerage firms were willing to contribute significant funds to the campaign. In addition to their strained finances, many brokerage firms were concerned about how the stock market might react if another world war erupted, and the Exchange closed as it had done temporarily after the start of World War I. Once the NYSE Board realized that member firms were not going to pay for a master advertising campaign, the governors balked at the NYSE shouldering the burden, and in late 1939, they shelved the idea, at least temporarily.

Exchange Soldiers and Sellers in World War II

The eruption of World War II profoundly affected the NYSE. President William McChesney Martin surprised the Exchange community and government officials by enlisting as a private in the U.S. Army rather than seeking an exemption. President Roosevelt and former SEC chair William O. Douglas, having had a role in selecting Martin for the presidency during the 1938 Reorganization, were disappointed in Martin's decision and urged him to reconsider, arguing that he could better serve the Allied cause by staying at home and ensuring the capital markets continued to function smoothly. Operating from the sense of morality that had made him an attractive president for a scandal-stained Big Board, Martin refused to be dissuaded from what he perceived was his ethical duty to serve his country in battle.[27]

Martin's successor, a New Dealer chosen by the commission broker faction led by Reformer Paul Shields, was quite different from prior Exchange presidents. Emil Schram had never been a member of the NYSE nor was he even particularly knowledgeable about the securities markets. Prior to being selected for the presidency position, Schram never had even been inside the NYSE, and he joked about not knowing where to find the entrance to the building. Schram also did not have the family pedigree of the typical NYSE executive: he was born and raised in Indiana to a poor farming family and had not attended college. After finishing high school, he worked on construction projects, which led to a job with the Reconstruction Finance Corps (RFC), where he eventually became agency head. Despite his unusual background, both the commission broker and neo–Old Guard factions saw potential in Schram. The Board wanted an individual that the Roosevelt administration would find acceptable; this was the Exchange's first opportunity after the Reorganization to choose its president without the government overseeing the appointment, and the NYSE was anxious not to lose this independence. The neo–Old Guard also wanted a president who would be pliable to their agenda. Schram seemed to fit the bill: a suitable token gesture toward the New Deal. To make sure that Schram did not threaten their power, the neo–Old Guard also had thought to amend the NYSE Constitution, confining the president's role mostly to public relations. At the same time, they enhanced the scope of the chairmanship position, and a prominent neo–Old Guardsman, specialist Robert Stott, now occupied that key role.[28]

President Schram, thus, was supposed to be the spokesman, not the architect, for Exchange policy. In June 1940, celebrating Schram's installation at a dinner at the Hotel Commodore in New York City, Stott told Exchange members and guests that Schram was going to be the NYSE's "spokesman—before the public, with the press, and in Washington."[29] In truth, contrary to the neo–Old Guard's plans, Schram, and especially his successor, Keith Funston, came to exert significant influence on the substance of the NYSE, as the public relations role became more important than anyone ever envisioned. In his inaugural speech, the unassuming Schram said he thought his role would be limited. Possessing no grandiose visions about transforming the Depression-ridden Exchange, he warned, "I am no Aladdin with a magic lamp, no Moses promising to lead you out of the wilderness."[30] As Schram implied, there were no easy answers to the Exchange's problems, no solutions that he, as president, was ready to propose or empowered to deliver.

After the entrance of the United States into World War II, Schram and the Board came to see the war as a chance for the NYSE to rehabilitate its image. In his letter prefacing the 1942 *Annual Report*, Schram told the Exchange community, "we are [afforded] an opportunity not only to render a patriotic service of incalculable value, but to demonstrate anew the indispensable usefulness of this industry." Schram vowed that the Exchange, guided by "stewardship" and a "deep sense of responsibility," would zealously assist the nation during the crisis. Schram's words capture a new language of "service," "usefulness," "stewardship," and "mission" that permeated the NYSE during World War II. In the Schram era, the Exchange, which had once taken pride in its "private club" status, was beginning to envision itself as a "quasi-public" institution. The NYSE's annual reports, beginning in 1942, described the Big Board as "essentially a service organization providing market facilities to the public through its members and member firms."[31]

In the 1940s, Exchange "service" also connoted military service. In the Exchange community at large (members, clerks, Exchange employees, and member firm employees), approximately six thousand individuals (or roughly 15%) served in the armed forces, a number that would have been even higher had it not been for the relatively old age of many working on Wall Street.[32] Schram emphasized that all those fighting for the Allied cause had a "right to expect that those of us who remain at home will preserve this and other free institutions in health and usefulness." Therefore, on the home front, all Exchange personnel needed to put forth "the utmost exertion and sacrifice to the end that the war may be brought to a victorious conclusion as speedily as possible." In this way, "we can best protect our civilian economy and insure a stable order after the war has been won."[33]

The Exchange boasted that its members had put their financial expertise at the government's disposal immediately after war was declared, selling government war bonds for no commission as their predecessors had done during World War I. In the *Exchange Magazine* as well as the organization's annual reports, the NYSE in a self-congratulatory manner hailed their own contributions to the war finance program. As Schram noted, "We are carrying a share of responsibility proportioned to our position in the nation but that is our privilege. It is not a task that has been laid upon us, but a service we are cheerfully performing." Schram added, "Our organization has supplied not only the executive direction of War Bond campaigns in various localities, but also a corps of experienced salesmen numbering many thousands. Their knowledge of securities, and of the personal advantages of War Bond ownership to the buyer, as well as their understanding of the problem of financing the war, specially qualifies them for these activities."[34] The NYSE carefully tracked the dollar amount of member bond sales, citing these statistics as evidence of the Street's "vital" contribution to the government's war finance program. From 1941 to 1945, in each of the six war loan drives mounted by the U.S. Treasury, NYSE members sold an average of approximately one billion dollars worth of bonds.[35]

While war bond sales were brisk, equity trading volume remained abysmal, falling in 1942 to its lowest level since 1914.[36] Schram, nonetheless, claimed he was "confident" that this would "prove to have been the lowest ebb of the prolonged depression through which this industry has been passing."[37] In retrospect, he was right. In public, Schram and his colleagues blamed the low trading volume on war-induced disruptions and uncertainties. Privately, they worried that popular distrust in the Exchange's integrity, lingering from the Depression years, might also be stifling a market recovery. Yet Schram in official pronouncements expressed his confidence that the NYSE now enjoyed widespread public faith. As he said in the *1943 Annual Report*, "the Exchange today deserves the public confidence which it more and more enjoys."[38] From Schram's point of view, the Exchange's image should have been improving, considering Wall Street's patriotic wartime service and the reforms that had corrected "various mistakes of the past."[39] Some outside experts concurred that the NYSE had improved from its earlier freewheeling days. In 1938, even SEC chairman William O. Douglas had said that the Stock Exchange was now "not incompatible with the national welfare"—a powerful statement considering its source. Others praised the Exchange's progress in "cleansing the financial stables." Benjamin Graham and David Dodd, professors at Columbia Graduate School of Business and coauthors of *Security Analysis*, lauded the Depression-era market reforms as "sweeping and efficacious." As they noted, "the great majority of the abuses [such as pools and corners]. . . have now all but disappeared." Professors Graham and Dodd credited the

NYSE (as well as the SEC) with "indeed a striking accomplishment"—the "virtual ending of stock-market manipulation."[40]

While the NYSE arguably now deserved trust, by the end of the war the public still lacked confidence in the Exchange's integrity.[41] The stock market's performance also was weak. Although common stocks yielded decent dividends (typically in the 4–6% range), stock prices overall remained depressed.[42] The NYSE's selling of war bonds did not work out exactly as Big Board officials had hoped. While beneficial to the nation, the bond drives had not significantly improved Wall Street's image, nor did they seem to engender interest in stocks, contrary to what had transpired after World War I. Yet in ways that they did not fully realize, NYSE members had learned a great deal about mass marketing methods during World War II. To enable millions of Americans of all backgrounds and ages to respond to patriotic calls to buy war bonds and war savings stamps, the purchase had to be made easy and convenient. Available in a variety of denominations, war bonds could be purchased in multiple venues, including through installment payment plans with employers.[43] In the 1950s, NYSE members would begin to adopt similar strategies to make stock ownership more attractive to average-income Americans.

In sponsoring war bond messages, the NYSE community also had honed its skills in institutional advertising. Individual member firms paid for war bond advertisements, but so too did the Association of Stock Exchange Firms. The headline of one such war bond advertisement sponsored by the Association, featured in the *New York Times* in March 1942, was, "The New York Stock Exchange Recommends a Security for Only the Second Time in 150 Years," the first time being during World War I. Of course, the security that the NYSE was recommending was government bonds, not stocks. The NYSE Board, as the advertisement pointed out, never recommended specific common stocks to the public. The association, however, had recommended Liberty Bonds to support the fighting effort during World War I, and now the Exchange intended to do so again. Notably, the 1942 advertisement glorified the NYSE as "the World's Greatest Free Marketplace."[44] At the time, the institutional character of the NYSE's war bond advertisements garnered no media attention, as reporters did not see it as an important turning point in advertising policy. It seemed to be simply an emergency war measure. However, after victory in 1945, something new happened at the NYSE: unlike in 1918, the Board of Governors retained the newspaper space, substituting the war bond advertisements with promotions that hailed the institution as operating "in the national interest."

The NYSE had finally begun to advertise itself. In the NYSE's own annals, the precedent was not well remembered. In the 1960s, compiling a brief historical overview of Exchange advertising, executive Gene Miller dismissed the rollover of wartime ad space as a "non-decision" that just happened.[45] But advertising had not surreptitiously entered the Big Board by the back door; it had been a conscious decision, a decision that the Board had not taken lightly.

NYSE president Schram addressed the change in the Exchange's advertising in the *1946 Annual Report*. Speaking on behalf of the Board interests he represented, Schram recommended that the new print promotions "be a regular, consistent part of the Exchange's duties." Schram did not expect the advertisements to immediately transform the NYSE's image, nor did he expect them to suddenly unleash mass stock sales. As Schram contended, "the strength of advertising is in its cumulative nature." Adopting a long-term perspective, he believed that if the NYSE repeatedly propounded its integrity and concern for the national welfare, eventually citizens would be enlightened and would flock to patronize member firms.[46] Schram's emphasis on "regular, consistent" promotions reflected a prevalent idea in the advertising profession. As N. W. Ayer, the country's first advertising agency, had said in the early 1900s, success depended on "keeping everlasting at it: You can't cut a giant oak down with one stroke of the ax—you must keep on chopping if you ever expect to accomplish anything. If it takes 50 strokes to fell a tree and you deliver 49 and quit, you have wasted your time and effort with no result. It is the last stroke on top of the other 49 preparatory strokes that does the business."[47] The NYSE, as Schram implicitly recognized, was just beginning to deliver the first few strokes of chopping away at the popular misconceptions of the market. To make advertising pay, the NYSE had to commit to the effort. As the Ayer agency once commented, "The business man who tries advertising and then says that advertising does not pay, quite as frequently fails because he has not tried *long enough* and *hard enough*, as he does because he has *not tried right*."[48] The NYSE had to persevere long and hard.

The NYSE's new appreciation for advertising reflected a general upsurge in legitimacy accorded to the advertising profession during World War II. Advertisers had rather successfully countered criticisms that they fomented economic waste, encouraged profligate spending and crass materialism, and contributed to moral degeneration.[49] Many of the charges leveled at advertisers in the 1930s were similar to those being levied at securities salesmen. Analyzing these charges and how the advertising industry overcame them during

World War II illuminates how the NYSE in the 1950s began to craft its own recovery strategy.

In the 1930s, criticisms of advertising, like criticisms of Wall Street, gained in venom. Allegedly, advertisers irresponsibly sold products to gullible Americans who could ill-afford them, while securities salesmen unethically prodded naïve people to purchase securities inappropriate for their income levels or investment objectives. Purportedly, advertisers also incited Americans to buy recklessly on credit, while stock salesmen supposedly promoted excessive use of margin. Permeating these criticisms was a disbelief in most Americans' capacity to manage sophisticated financial transactions or withstand sales pitches. In more laissez faire times, ignorant citizens who were duped received little popular sympathy. However, during the Great Depression, popular sentiment grew that industry or the federal government needed to protect those unable to take care of themselves. In the 1930s, a consumer protection movement gained strength, pressuring selling industries to increase self-regulation or face government controls.

The advertising industry, like the securities industry, confronted regulatory proposals. In 1933, the same year that the Securities Act prohibited the fraudulent sale of stocks and bonds, New Dealer Rexford G. Tugwell drafted legislation that prohibited deceptive advertising of food, drugs, and cosmetics. Like the NYSE's attitude towards the truth-in-securities bill, many advertisers viewed federal truth-in-advertising legislation as inevitable, considering public outcry for industry reform. Therefore they pragmatically lobbied for modifications to the bill. Advertisers especially wanted the burden of proof to rest with the government (not the company) for proving false advertisements, and they wanted "falsehood" to be defined explicitly as advertisements that were materially misleading. The 1938 Wheeler-Lea Amendment, which empowered the Federal Trade Commission (FTC) to issue "cease and desist" orders and fine promoters of false advertisements, contained these points.[50]

Relieved that Wheeler-Lea was diluted in potency, advertisers, though, soon faced another pressing concern: how the eruption of World War II would affect their industry. Businesses, mobilizing to retool their production to meet the government's heightened needs, would presumably slash their advertising budgets, perceiving little purpose in stimulating consumer demand for products that the government was rationing. The curtailment in advertising expenditures might be more severe if advertising were disallowed as a tax-deductible business expense. The American Association of Advertising

Agencies (A.A.A.A.) and the Association of National Advertisers (A.N.A.) met in November 1941 in Hot Springs, Georgia, to craft a "survival" strategy, hoping that a coordinated defense would help them weather the hostile regulatory environment. Notably, one attendee was Carle Conway, the public governor of the NYSE who had spearheaded the Reorganization of 1938.[51]

In arguably the most important speech of the conference, James W. Young at the J. Walter Thompson agency attributed animosity to his profession primarily to the public's tendency to associate advertising with capitalism, at a time of pervasive dissatisfaction with capitalism. In a thinly veiled attack on Roosevelt and the New Deal, Young commented that even in "certain influential quarters, notably government circles," there were individuals who would "modify the economic system of which advertising is an integral part." Young offered a solution: as "masters of the techniques of using [persuasive] channels," they, as advertisers, were uniquely well positioned to defend themselves and the "American system." He stated, "We have power. Why do we not use it?"[52] Proposing essentially to "advertise advertising," Young revived an idea conceived by the country's oldest advertising agency, A. W. Ayer. Shortly after World War I, Ayer spearheaded a cooperative agency campaign to highlight the merits of advertising. Those promotions touted no products and featured no agency names; they just promoted the idea of advertising.[53] Roughly two decades after Ayer's endeavor to justify advertising, Young suggested, in similar vein, "we ought to prepare the Case for Advertising—an open and frank case." Embracing Young's suggestion, the participants pledged to publicize the benefits that advertising provided to the nation.[54]

The United States' entry into the war a month later influenced the campaign. Like NYSE leaders, advertisers put aside their disagreements with the Roosevelt Administration, hoping that doing so—and helping the country win the war—might improve their image and their profitability. But while the NYSE during World War II primarily placed its faith in actions, not words, to reap an image transformation, the advertising industry rested its hopes in both actions and "fighting words" that would "speed victory" and, along with it, the recovery of the advertising profession's stature.[55]

The Rise of the Advertising Council

Formed in the aftermath of the Hot Springs meeting, the War Advertising Council (WAC) was a voluntary, nonprofit organization established by a wide array of advertising constituencies—"owners and principals of magazines, newspapers, radio, outdoor, printing and direct mail, the country's advertising agencies, and the great industrialists who use advertising," as its first chairman, Chet LaRoche, boasted. According to LaRoche, these executives had gathered for an "entirely unselfish" and "nonpolitical" purpose—to help sell Americans on the war by using the vehicle of "war advertising." He defined this as *"advertising which induces people, through information, understanding or persuasion, to take certain actions necessary to the speedy winning of the war."*[56] Adopting the sword and quill as its logo, WAC encouraged citizens to buy bonds, plant victory gardens, donate rubber and other needed supplies, and conserve essential resources. Industry executives designed and promoted, free of charge to the government, more than one hundred public service campaigns valued at more than a billion dollars. Big Business readily cooperated with the Council's call to put a "War Message in Every Ad."[57] WAC also collaborated with the federal government, especially the Office of War Information (OWI), directed by Elmer Davis.[58] To inspire Americans to voluntarily take actions necessary to achieve victory, both OWI and WAC relied on institutional advertising, which WAC defined as promotions that advanced "the public interest." In their promotions, WAC played upon wartime patriotism and citizens' willingness to sacrifice.[59] Grateful for WAC's assistance in mobilizing the nation, the government never tampered with the tax deductibility of advertising expenses and never, despite wartime paper shortages, restricted advertisers from continuing to promote their products and services in newspapers and magazines.[60]

At the war's end in 1945, the image of the advertising industry was healthier and more robust than it had been in 1941. WAC had helped illustrate that, as Council member Paul West explained, "all advertising can and does by its very nature have an important effect on our public relations. . . . Every advertisement can do a constructive public relations job for its sponsor." West was using "the term public relations here in the most modern sense—not our prewar concept of it." A new conception of public relations was emerging, rooted in the idea "that we should make no fallacious distinction between product advertising and public relations advertising." As West observed, the chasm that existed between public relations and advertising was fading, and along with it, the ad industry's problems.[61] WAC highlighted advertising's rising stature, citing its national opinion polls that showed the public applauded "the advertiser who enlisted in the public service." A 1944 article in *Collier's* magazine, exploring the advertising industry's wartime transformation, noted that the quality of advertising had improved, as the WAC had performed "tasks essential to the U.S. and to a free world." The industry, rising to the challenge of the war emergency, had infused itself with "a new importance and a new dignity."[62] Both President Roosevelt and President Truman praised the role played by advertising during the war.[63] Anxious to preserve their enhanced legitimacy, advertising executives in 1945, nevertheless, worried whether the American free enterprise system—and, by implication, their own profession—were secure from potential attacks at home or abroad.

Many corporate leaders were similarly uneasy. Crediting wartime deficit spending with propelling the nation out of the Great Depression, they, like many Americans, worried that the economy would regress upon the removal of the wartime stimulus, as it had after demobilization following World War I.[64] Conservative industry titans also feared that peace might bring a return to what they perceived to be the antibusiness climate of the New Deal, like the imposition of onerous regulations, the convocation of "inquisitorial" hearings, and threats of nationalization.[65] As *Collier's* remarked, "Business got a black eye during the depression and during the succeeding years never quite regained its self-confidence."[66] A dire WAC report in 1945 captured businesses' fears, warning of the threats posed by communism and socialism, as well as the revival of "group clashes" and "old hatreds" on the "home front." In light of these dangers, advertising executive Theodore Repplier declared, "Everyone agrees that the American enterprise system [still] needs 'reselling.'" Repplier vowed his industry would continue to work closely with government and business, and he proposed reconfiguring the WAC for peacetime needs.[67] Supporting the continuation of WAC, Big Business and Madison Avenue renewed their commitment to selling free enterprise and also to the practice of "idea" or institutional advertising, hoping in the process to protect their corporate images.

President Roosevelt and his successor President Truman both perceived value in extending the Council's life beyond the wartime emergency. Roosevelt had emphasized that, once the war was won, there would still be "many critical national problems requiring the understanding and cooperation of every American." Likewise, Truman emphasized that the government would need the "cooperation of American business on questions which will be vitally in the interest of all the people." The Council could be a way to achieve that cooperation.[68] Therefore, WAC morphed into a postwar "Ad Council." The executive leadership remained basically unchanged, with Theodore Repplier and James Young continuing as president and chairman of the Board of Directors, respectively. However, the Ad Council no longer automatically supported campaigns "suggested" by government agencies. Instead, a Public Policy Committee (PPC) voted on proposals, rejecting ones that seemed not to be in the organization's spirit, which, in theory at least, was strictly nonpartisan. In addition, a new Business Advisory Committee (BAC), chaired by Charles Wilson of General Electric, hoped to facilitate closer cooperation between Big Business and Madison Avenue. Several active members of the BAC, such as Charles Wilson, Carle Conway, and Clarence Francis, also served as public governors for the NYSE and had a role in the NYSE's eventual decision to expand its concept of public relations to include more institutional advertising.

In the early postwar years, BAC and PPC implemented public service campaigns, some themes of which were "Confidence in a Growing America," "Democratic Capitalism," and "Miracle of America." Beginning in the 1950s, the Ad Council impacted NYSE public relations initiatives, as the two organizations began to collaborate on some campaigns. However, in the earlier postwar period, the NYSE remained undecided about its long-term marketing direction. The Exchange had not grasped that it, like the advertising community, could bridge the gap between public relations and advertising, and in so doing, help resolve pressing image and profitability problems lingering on Wall Street from the Great Depression years.

The NYSE's Use of Advertising Agencies in the Early Postwar Era (1945–1947)

Seeking to reinvigorate public faith in equity investing and in their own institution, after World War II, the NYSE resumed its search for outside image assistance, and this time, the Board decided to hire not a public relations professional, but an advertising agency. Bringing "outsiders" into the traditionally private Exchange served a function that management did not at the time fully appreciate: these advertising experts brought fresh perspectives. Wall Street had been suffering from myopia, accentuated by the dearth of new brokers entering the securities industry in the Depression years. Most of those on Wall Street in 1945 had been there since the 1920s, and these veterans seemed unable to establish the critical distance necessary to understand the problems confronting their ever-evolving industry.[69] Although Exchange officials vaguely sensed that the securities industry's lackluster image was impeding a market recovery, they needed external assistance to pinpoint their core problems. At first, the NYSE retained the services of Gardner Advertising Company. Best known for its outdoor promotions, that agency, however, was not the best match for the Exchange, which preferred the print media (in part, because the NYSE felt that newspapers deserved their advertising business since they published the stock tables). In the spring of 1947, the NYSE replaced Gardner with a larger, more prestigious firm: Batten, Barton, Durstine & Osborne (BBDO).[70]

At the time of BBDO's appointment, fears of a postwar recession had not completely dissipated. In a 1947 article entitled "Must We Have Another Depression?," economist Leon Keyserling warned, "While all economists do not agree as to the causes of the last depression, a listing of the causal factors generally agreed upon indicate that many of these factors are again present now or will be present within a few years." He listed numerous warning signs, such as "the tendency of our productive capacity to outrun our mass buying power; the chronic weakness of such bellwether industries as residential construction, the seemingly reluctance of capital investment to expand as dynamically as once it did . . . the enormous disparities in the price and wage structure, and huge differentials in the price of the enjoyment of national income by regions and individuals."[71] The NYSE Board found the projections of economic decline frustrating and ironic. As Schram noted, "relative inertia" characterized the securities markets at the same time that "high employment, increased earnings and record production prevailed in the nation's industries." Wall Street, said Schram, was enduring a "trying" period.[72]

While Wall Street lay in the doldrums after the war, tensions were escalating between the Soviet Union and the United States and its allies, as Joseph Stalin moved to consolidate control in Eastern Europe and expand communist influence elsewhere. Visiting Westminster College in Fulton, Missouri, on March 5, 1946, British Prime Minister Winston Churchill told the audience that "a shadow" had fallen upon the Allied victory: "Nobody knows what Soviet Russia and its Communist international organization intends to do in the immediate future, or what are the limits, if any, to their expansive and proselytizing tendencies." Churchill said, "From Stettin in the Baltic to Trieste in the Adriatic an iron curtain has descended across the Continent." To counter the communist influence and prevent another world war, Churchill believed in the importance of fostering "the establishment of conditions of freedom and democracy as rapidly as possible in all countries." Recognizing that "the United States stands at this time at the pinnacle of world power," Churchill implored the United States to recognize its sense of duty and not "reject it" or "fritter it away." He said, "It is a solemn moment for the American democracy. For with primacy in power is also joined an awe-inspiring accountability to the future."[73]

To stop the spread of communism and to acknowledge the obligations of the United States as a world power, in 1947, President Harry Truman outlined the policy of containment in his Truman Doctrine. At the time, Greece was embroiled in a civil war between the old monarchical military regime and communist-led revolutionaries. While noting, "the Government of Greece is not perfect," Truman emphasized that Greece was a democratic country and must remain so. Truman requested that the United States extend financial assistance to Greece as well as Turkey. Truman stated, "I believe that it must be the policy of the United States to support free peoples who are resisting attempted subjugation by armed minorities or by outside pressures. . . . I believe that our help should be primarily through economic and financial aid which is essential to economic stability and orderly political processes."[74]

Shortly thereafter, in June 1947, the United States enacted the Marshall Plan (also known as the European Recovery Program), named after U.S. Secretary of State George Marshall. The Marshall Plan pledged economic assistance to Europe to help countries rebuild and recover from the war. By stimulating a return to prosperity and helping make European countries strong again, the United States hoped to thwart the spread of Soviet communism. During the life of the Marshall Plan, from 1948 to 1952, the United States provided $13 billion in economic assistance to European countries participating in the Organization for European Economic Co-operation.[75]

The onset of the Cold War influenced the NYSE, as its leaders increasingly saw their organization as a bastion against communism, and sought to communicate that image to the public through its advertising and public relations efforts. Just as there was bipartisan support in Washington for the Truman Doctrine and the Marshall Plan, at the NYSE, a consensus developed that the NYSE had a duty to contain the spread of communism, and that a strong, vibrant stock market with many small investors would serve as an excellent deterrent. The Big Board by the 1950s and 1960s would not just be advertising the Exchange's importance to the nation, but would be actively trying to make the NYSE more of the "people's market" that it had invoked since the early 1900s.

In the late 1940s, the NYSE began to ramp up its advertising in this direction. With the aid of BBDO, the NYSE launched a series of advertisements in mass circulation magazines like *Time, Look,* the *Saturday Evening Post,* and *Collier's,* highlighting the stock market's democratic composition. The NYSE wanted to bring more business to Wall Street by emphasizing that shareownership was already diffuse. In truth, at the time, the NYSE had very little knowledge about the composition of the nation's shareownership base, as the organization had never conducted shareowner censuses. (It only would start to do so in 1952.) In the late 1940s, the NYSE only knew the number of shareholders in individual listed companies, but it had no way of knowing the extent of duplication in the shareowner lists and hence could not establish the total number of shareowners in the country. Even without a formal census the NYSE understood in 1947 that most Americans did not own stock. The NYSE's advertising campaign did not claim this to be the case; advertisements conveyed the idea that the average shareowner was an average, middle-class American, not that the average American was necessarily a shareowner. It was a critical difference.

One such NYSE advertisement featured a table filled with many different styles of hats, including a ten-gallon cowboy hat, a denim cap, a crushed fedora, a derby, a wide-brimmed straw hat, and a ladies' fur neckpiece. The copy beneath the lead caption of "Stockholders' Meeting" announced, "They come from everywhere . . . from every income group, from every community. . . . They are women as well as men, employees as well as executives, farmers as well as businessmen. They are typical stockholders, the owners of business."[76] Another NYSE advertisement featured people from different professions all "Working 9 to 5" while keeping their "surplus dollars on the job 24 hours a day."[77] These advertisements showcasing the democratic nature of the marketplace were innovative for the NYSE, yet some listed companies had employed similar institutional advertisements for decades. Perhaps most prominently, AT&T for years had run advertisements heralding the diversity inherent in their company's shareownership lists. AT&T advertisements, beginning in 1911, tended not to focus on the product they offered (telephone service) but that the company was an "investment democracy" owned by many ordinary, average citizens. As AT&T executives had hoped, the campaign indeed was effective in defusing criticisms that the organization was a dangerous monopoly.[78] In their tone and content, the NYSE's advertisements in 1947 bore a striking resemblance to AT&T's early institutional advertisements.

In the aftermath of the 1947 campaign, several magazine stories and newspaper editorials picked up on the theme undergirding the Exchange's advertisements and conveyed similar points about the stock market's democratic character. The *Saturday Evening Post,* for instance, raved, "The Investor Is Almost Everybody." It contended, "The investor may be a millionaire, although millionaires represent but an infinitesimal fraction of investors. Far more likely, the investor is You. . . . In a society based on investment, it would be pretty hard to pick out anybody outside the almshouse and guarantee that he isn't in some respect an investor. . . . When you come down to earth, we are all investors."[79] The NYSE carefully tracked these positive stories and tried to cultivate reporters by sending them press releases and other material that favorably portrayed Wall Street. The NYSE had long tried to build a network of supporters, to help them thwart opponents in the U.S. government who saw Wall Street as inimical to the national welfare. Now, with the onset of the Cold War, the NYSE recognized the importance of cultivating popular understanding of the Exchange as a barrier against communism.

Reporters began helping the NYSE promote itself,[80] although a few critics objected to the elevated claims about the stock market's composition. J. A. Livingston, author of *The American Stockholder* (1958), derided the NYSE for suggesting in its advertisements that "Corporations are owned by everyone" and that "Wall Street is not a rich man's preserve." He poked fun at the egalitarian picture painted of Wall Street as a place "where Main Street as well as Park Avenue puts its savings, where the millions of the millionaire and the tens and twenties of the widow and the schoolteacher commingle." Livingston argued that this image was erroneous, yet it was what Wall Street wanted the American public to believe, and what Exchange members themselves "wanted to believe."[81]

The NYSE's initial postwar advertising approach deserves note for what it did not do: advertisements did not explicitly invite Americans to buy stock. The Board seemed to have agreed to cultivate the public as lobbyists, but not (at least not yet) to court them as customers. In the 1947 campaign, advertisements depicted existing, not new, customers and issued no call for the uninvested to go "own a share of American business," as later Exchange advertisements would convey. The Exchange's long-standing resistance to inviting the public into the market did not dissolve all at once.

Merrill Lynch: A Leader in Mass
Marketing with Few Followers

In the late 1940s, most member firms were still not advertising widely, with some notable exceptions, the biggest being Merrill Lynch. After the merger with Fenner & Beane in 1941, Merrill Lynch Pierce Fenner & Beane ("Merrill Lynch"), now the largest brokerage firm on Wall Street, courted the small investor, and was the dominant player in the financial advertising field. Charles Merrill's commitment to bringing mass merchandising principles to Wall Street was a key factor in the firm's success. He understood that the burgeoning middle class held great potential for the securities industry, and that small investor accounts might eventually mature into larger accounts. In the 1930s, while away from Wall Street, Merrill had honed his mass merchandising skills as an executive with the Safeway Stores, a large grocery chain. He brought the lessons he had learned in the chain store business to Merrill Lynch. Explaining the firm's philosophy, Merrill stated, "Our business is people and their money. We must draw the new capital required for industrial might and growth not from among a few large investors but from the savings of thousands of people of moderate incomes. We must bring Wall Street to Main Street—and we must use the efficient, mass-merchandising methods of the chain store to do it."[82]

Merrill focused on making his staff trustworthy and competent. His employees underwent more specialized financial training than the NYSE required. To enhance the profession's demeanor, Charles Merrill renamed his brokers "account executives." Underlying such changes was Merrill's commitment to providing customers with superior service. As he told his colleagues, "Now, I contend that, win, lose, or draw, we must treat all customers exactly the same. It is not their fault that we accept business from small people. That is our responsibility. When we open our doors to all classes of customers, we have simply got to nail the policy to the mast that anybody that comes in this shop is going to receive the squarest and best treatment on the lowest competitive terms."[83]

Merrill Lynch's advertisements, in contrast to Wall Street's typical cold tombstone advertisements, were friendly and conversational in tone, emphasizing that the firm was just as concerned with the business of small clients as it was with the big ones. In one representative Merrill advertisement, entitled

"What Keeps a Customer Happy," a fictional customer cited several factors that kept him a loyal and content Merrill Lynch client: a long relationship with the same account executive, "consistently high caliber service," and complimentary investor reports. The customer concluded, "Over the years . . . I've found that Merrill Lynch is just as concerned with an order for 10 shares as it is for 100, and handles it just as efficiently. But looking back over 20 years, the thing that stands out most in my mind is *that you never tried to sell me a thing*—never pushed for that extra commission."[84]

Far from "push[ing] for that extra commission," Merrill Lynch eliminated the commission structure, instead paying its account executives fixed salaries, a policy that remained for decades. The underlying idea was that account executives should give clients advice motivated not by a desire to boost their commissions, but by a sincere concern for the welfare of their clients, big and small. Removing commissions engendered customer trust, and willingness on the part of Merrill Lynch employees to develop smaller accounts. As Merrill explained to his office managers at a company conference in 1940, "Now, having established a basic principle that everybody is working on a definite compensation, a definite salary, then we removed instantly the desire on the part of the manager or partner to hog the so-called good accounts [the big accounts]." Wanting to more sensibly assign and distribute clients to employees, Merrill explained, "Accounts are to be analyzed, put in groups, by account, by size of it, by the requirements of the investor or speculator, [and] geographically as to districts in a town." He recommended that the firm study its sales representatives, to better understand the type of client with which they worked best. Those who had the ability to handle particular types of customers (like small or large, or more investment or speculation-oriented) would be matched with them. As Merrill said, his firm needed to "put the round pegs in round holes."[85]

Most importantly, Merrill Lynch welcomed all customers—a fact that Merrill Lynch advertisements consistently emphasized. "How Big Is a Customer?" asked one Merrill Lynch promotion. As the text explained, "That's a hard one for us to answer. Because here at Merrill Lynch they come in all sizes. The important point in that *your* account is big business to us—regardless of size!" The copy continued: "We help lots of people whose portfolios run to hundreds of thousands of dollars, and lots of people with only hundreds to invest. We thought most investors knew that, but lately we've had a number of letters from people who seemed to think we wouldn't bother with accounts as small as theirs. So let's make this plain. *No* account is too small! Regardless of size, we'll give it the best service we can."[86]

Merrill Lynch cultivated the small shareholder in other ways, such as in the late 1940s sponsoring radio broadcasts about the market, and conducting investment seminars, including ones geared to women. In 1949, for instance, Merrill Lynch placed a small advertisement in a local newspaper for an upcoming women's investment seminar. The firm was deluged with so many applications that it had to schedule additional seminars to handle the overload. "We never thought the ladies would be so interested in stocks," one of Merrill's brokers reportedly said, although for years, the firm had stressed the vast market potential inherent in small investors, women as well as men.[87]

A handful of other brokerage firms engaged in similar tactics to attract more customers. In the summer of 1949, a Cleveland firm, Prescott & Company, began mass marketing stocks at a local flower show. Lloyd Birchard, a partner at that firm, had suggested to his colleagues, "If the grass-roots people of this area won't come to a brokerage firm, let's take our office to the grass roots." The firm decided to open a booth at the festival in order to, in Birchard's words, "sell securities, just as weed-killers, saws, and garden appliances are merchandised—with simple words, pretty pictures, and gadgets." When thousands of Flower Show attendees flocked to the Prescott booth, the firm was reportedly "astounded."[88]

That summer, a few other firms, including Merrill Lynch and E. F. Hutton, set up information booths at state and county fairs. They preached to potential clients a similar message: "it's just as easy to buy a security as a loaf of bread." A few months later, J. S. Bache defied the conventional norms of the securities industry by placing advertisements in subways—a strategy that provoked a combination of "sneers" and "jealousy" among more risk-averse competitors.[89] At midcentury, in their efforts to woo the masses, Merrill Lynch, E. F. Hutton, and J. S. Bache were atypical among even retail-oriented brokerage firms.

"Small Investors: Wall Street Dynamite?"

In an analysis of the marketing situation on Wall Street, *Forbes* reported that most brokerage houses, though coveting the success of Merrill Lynch and other Wall Street renegades, were "not jumping on the promotion bandwagon."

Many brokerage firms, particularly small ones, still feared that small accounts would not be profitable; the only way it might work is if they built a sufficient volume of small accounts to gain economies of scale. Merrill Lynch, like J. S. Bache, was taking a risk going after this market. The *Forbes* article downplayed the profitability question, and instead ascribed the reluctance to advertise to another factor: "Deep in the minds of the skeptics lurks the conviction [that] promising and profitable as the small-investor market might be, there is dynamite in the Main Street trade. Nobody is certain it will ever go off. But neither is it felt safe to tamper with the detonator." The stick of dynamite wielded by the "Main Street trade" was the vote. As *Forbes* reported, "conservatives shudderingly remember that burned investors are also voters. Increasing numbers of new investors only make the prospect more appalling."[90]

The *Forbes* article raises an interesting point. While the NYSE had long recognized the importance of cultivating the public as lobbyists, it was not necessarily true that shareownership made the public more favorably inclined toward Wall Street. A lot depended on individuals' experiences in the market; negative investing results could make people antagonistic toward the Exchange, particularly if they felt they had been improperly treated. If they felt wronged, they might turn to Washington to impose sanctions on Wall Street.

There was another negative scenario associated with bringing more Americans into the market: the masses in the market might renew government attention to Wall Street. In the early 1900s, the NYSE had proudly pointed to the millions of investors as evidence of the Exchange's good public character, but critics had cited this as proof of the need for external market regulation. Purportedly, if the public were involved in the market, they needed protection—protection that the NYSE at the time seemed inadequately prepared to provide.

Some at the NYSE, particularly from the investment banking sector, feared that if stocks collapsed as they had in 1929, this might incite another spate of federal legislation that could sap the vitality of the market. Many brokers also feared that average income investors might destabilize the market, if not by their alleged psychological shortcomings, then by their lack of robust incomes. As *Forbes* noted, the middle-class investor seemed particularly vulnerable to "bad economic weather" because his "working investments are also reserves. If he is hit hard enough, he has to recall his invested capital. If it's because of a general recession, he has to pull out his capital just at the worst time."[91] Thus, for many reasons, the brokerage fraternity's consensus at midcentury, with the exception of outliers like Merrill Lynch, was to avoid appealing to small investors, lest Wall Street, in *Forbes'* words, risk incurring "another disastrous black-eye."[92]

The NYSE's Special Advisory Committee on Public Relations (1949)

To help the securities industry recover, the NYSE executive organization needed to assume more leadership. In 1949, the NYSE convened a Special Advisory Committee on Public Relations, a temporary committee charged with exploring how Exchange public relations, including advertising, might be used to increase trading volume. Chaired by Harold Scott, who a few years later would rise to Chairman of the NYSE Board, the Advisory Committee declared four major policy objectives: "to increase public confidence in the integrity and usefulness of the Exchange; to foster a realistic understanding by the public of stock ownership; to create a more favorable atmosphere for wider use of member firms' services; and to increase public understanding of the role of equity capital in finance, industry, jobs, and production."[93] None of the objectives mentioned broadening the shareowner base, but the phrase "wider use of member firms' services" was promising. "Wider use" could mean wider use by existing brokerage customers, or it could mean tapping into a wider array of customers, or it could mean both. By the mid-1950s, the NYSE would decide to focus more on cultivating new business than on encouraging heavier trading by existing customers. The Advisory Committee initiated a dialogue along these lines. But obstacles to broadening the market remained, including the question whether the NYSE itself (not just member firms) should advertise.

The Advisory Committee accepted advertising as a viable way to accomplish its stated objectives. Yet several other Board executives, along with many rank-and-file members, insisted that the NYSE already spent too much on promotional campaigns: "the lavish expenditure for advertising the stock exchange has served its purpose and [should] be curtailed," said one member.[94] At the time, the "lavish" expenditure was only $500,000, and the contention that advertising had "served its purpose" was questionable, considering the poor financial condition of many member retail brokerage firms, who suffered from a dearth of business. At this juncture in 1949, with the NYSE still quite divided upon the legitimacy of resorting to Exchange advertising to help members, President Emil Schram announced his decision to retire. The charged ideological atmosphere accompanying the intensifying Cold War influenced the choice of his successor—as well as the course of NYSE advertising and hence the path toward mass equity investing.

CHAPTER THREE

Marketing the "Own Your Share" Program

> We should leave no stone unturned in making the most of this opportunity.
> We should take any and all practical steps to assist our Member Firms in
> merchandising to the mass of the American public. Since the Exchange
> itself must never attempt to sell securities to anyone, the only way that it
> can get at the problem is by helping our Member Firms.
>
> NYSE PRESIDENT KEITH FUNSTON, JUNE 1953

When NYSE President Emil Schram announced his decision to retire in 1949, China had just "fallen" to communism, and Stalin had already instituted the Berlin Blockade, cordoning off West Berlin to prevent food and other supplies from reaching the city.[1] After the United States and other countries conducted the Berlin Airlift, Stalin finally lifted the blockade in May 1949. Other crises ensued. In June 1950, while the NYSE searched for a successor to Schram, North Korea invaded South Korea. At home, in the context of these foreign policy crises, concern mounted over the loyalty of government officials, actors, directors, and other Americans, fueled by the accusations of the junior senator from Wisconsin, Joseph McCarthy. Before a Wheeling, West Virginia, audience, Senator McCarthy dramatically brandished a list that purportedly contained the names of 205 communists in the U.S. State Department.

Wall Street never succumbed to McCarthyism. Nevertheless, in a subtle, "soft" way, anticommunism permeated its sphere, elevating the ideological as well as practical value that Exchange officials and others attached to common stock ownership.[2] Perceiving widespread shareownership as a weapon to fight communism and also keep American companies strong, the NYSE Board grew amenable to the Exchange mass marketing the concept of equity investing. And because the stock market seemed an embattled symbol of capitalism, the financial community accorded the Big Board presidency higher importance. The NYSE chose as its new president Keith Funston, a business executive with considerable marketing experience who emphasized the importance of market research. Early in Funston's tenure, the NYSE commissioned two important studies of the stock market. The first was the nation's first ever shareowner census, administered by the Brookings Institution and summarized in the Brookings Report. The second was a merchandising analysis conducted by Stewart, Dougall & Associates, which explored ways in which the NYSE could stimulate business for its member retail brokerage firms. After examining the conclusions of the Brookings Report as well as the numerous options outlined by Stewart, Dougall, the Big Board settled on a recovery strategy that aimed to broaden shareownership. They created a Market Development Department that, by 1953, was hammering out the program that became known as "Own Your Share of American Business" (OYS).

A Pivotal Interlude: The Search for a New Exchange President

In the 1950s and 1960s, Keith Funston served as the NYSE's chief spokesman for broad shareownership, the ideal of "democratic capitalism," as well as the Own Your Share program. In 1949, however, it was far from clear who would succeed the retiring Emil Schram. The NYSE assembled a special executive search committee, consisting of Winthrop Smith (from Merrill Lynch), Hugh Baker, John Coleman, Richard Crooks, Joseph Klingenstein, Robert Stott, Jay Whippe, and Robert Boylan. Exchange members, corporate executives, and concerned citizens recommended candidates to replace Schram, and offered advice. Dominating their correspondence to the search committee was a common theme: the Exchange needed an effective communicator who could project a positive image not just for member firms, but also for American business, stock markets, and the free enterprise system. The ideal president should be "an authoritative spokesman, if not the chief exponent, of corporate enterprise in terms of securities ownership and its role in our economic life," said one writer. Since "the American system of private enterprise and private investment" lacked a "real spokesman," "the head of the Stock Exchange could fill that assignment," commented another. There was a "new need . . . for a figure who can dramatize . . . the fact that the machinery of the Stock Exchange offers a channel for achieving economic security."[3] As one corporate executive observed, "During the next five years or so, when we are apt to be engaged in either a hot or cold war with the communist world, the position of President of the Exchange will assume even far greater importance." The Big Board leader needed to counter Soviet propagandists' portrait of the Exchange as an elite, undemocratic club. Inspiring faith in the market system's fairness also would encourage people to trade more. An active stock market would help ensure that American businesses possessed sufficient equity investments to grow and hence provide products and services that would help the country fight the Cold War while maintaining a high standard of living at home.[4]

In 1950, new issues of common stocks contributed only a small share to the financing of industrial growth. Reviewing the five-year trend in corporate financing, Exchange officials highlighted an "equity gap": from 1945 to 1950, American industry raised $148 billion in capital for expansion, but only $18 billion (less than 13%) came from new issues of common stock. To finance expansion, American industry primarily relied upon retained earnings ($75 billion), followed by bonds and other debt instruments ($55 billion). Big Board leaders insisted that firms needed to "tap a lot of new springs of capital," which meant getting more Americans currently not in the market to buy stock.[5] They expected that the new NYSE president should help close the equity gap by selling noninvestors on the value of becoming investors and by selling corporations on the value of issuing common stock. The long-suffering investment banking and retail brokerage sectors hoped that the incoming president would help address their respective problems. Investment banks had suffered from corporations' decreased use of the equity market. Until the 1930s, many corporations had relied upon stock issuances to finance expansion. Even though the Great Depression had ended, corporations remained hesitant to tap the equity market for various reasons, including the continued depressed market in the 1940s and early 1950s; the availability of other financing options; and, at least according to the NYSE, the SEC's onerous and expensive new disclosure requirements. Nonetheless, Schram's successor would need to rekindle corporate management's interest in the stock market.

The new president also would need to be adept at improving government relations. As the search committee noted, he should "know his way around Washington," not just Wall Street. Having finally decided to accept the division of banking and the other requirements of the Securities Exchange Act, the Big Board desired a leader who would be able to smooth relations with the SEC and who would be adroit at dealing with the Federal Reserve, which now had the responsibility for setting margin rates. A president with preexisting ties to influential business and government leaders might succeed in lobbying for lower capital gains taxes and other measures favorable to the market.[6] Summarizing the president's duties, Exchange member Charles Ros concluded, "As executive head of the world's principal securities market, he is expected to exercise such leadership among its members and member firms as will assure the soundness, integrity and efficiency of its operations and practices; inspire the confidence of the investing public and of the corporations that the Exchange serves; enlist the understanding cooperation of governmental authorities and increase the public's recognition of the essential function that the Exchange performs."[7]

Having heavily advertised the position—something the Exchange had not done in prior executive searches—the committee received many applicants. In handwritten letters, some small businessmen, such as an attorney in Virginia, a broker in Massachusetts, and a manager in Texas, nominated themselves. The committee seriously considered more than one hundred candidates. The lead contenders were William McChesney Martin (former Exchange president), General Douglas MacArthur (recently relieved of his duties by Truman), and several Board members like Robert Boylan, the current Chairman, and Robert Hardenbrook, who was endorsed by the conservative National Association of Manufacturers (NAM). None of these men, however, got the job. MacArthur did not want it; Martin had been nominated by Truman to serve as Federal Reserve Chairman; and selecting an Exchange Governor for the post was too internally divisive, as specialists, floor traders, and commission brokers all wanted a governor who represented their specific interest group.[8]

G. Keith Funston Joins the Exchange: "Salesman and Educator"

After a prolonged search lasting more than a year, the Committee appointed to the $100,000-a-year post 40-year-old G. Keith Funston. *Forbes* described him as a "handsome and boyish" character who "seems at first like an all-American fullback blessed by distinguished birth and enjoying membership in the right fraternity." Funston was "engaging in speech, convincing in manner, [and] courteous in approach."[9] A coworker described him as possessing "all the Boy-Scout qualities, and I mean that sincerely."[10] Yet, personality aside, Funston possessed few obvious qualifications for his new post. Like Emil Schram, he was neither a former Exchange executive nor had he ever worked on Wall Street. Funston's major qualification was his skill in selling. As a student at the Harvard Business School, Funston had come to appreciate marketing and advertising principles. He was particularly wedded to the importance of using "scientific" measurements—like polling—to understand one's target audience. After obtaining his MBA in 1935, Funston first applied the lessons he learned to his job as assistant sales director at the American Radiator Company. In 1940 he moved to Sylvania Electric, where he analyzed market and distribution patterns. With the entry of the U.S. into World War II, Sylvania's president, B. G. Erskine, introduced the young Funston to Goldman Sachs partner Sidney Weinberg. Weinberg, who was helping Donald Nelson organize the War Production Board (WPB), convinced Funston to apply his skills to the new organization. In both his work for the WPB and his later position as a lieutenant commander in the U.S. Navy, Funston developed a strong network of contacts in both business and government. When the war ended, Funston assumed the presidency of his alma mater, Trinity College in Hartford, Connecticut, which at the time was in financial straits. Determined to put the college back on a firm financial footing, Funston embarked upon an ambitious fundraising campaign, targeting not only alumni, but also local businesses, particularly Hartford's large insurance companies. To sell Trinity, Funston focused on improving the college's image, including its physical appearance. Refusing to bow to budgetary pressures, he insisted that the campus be renovated and buildings painted. As he told his colleagues, "Gentlemen . . . in order to be successful you must look successful." The strategy worked. By 1950, Trinity was not only on more solid financial ground, but its academic reputation was also rising. In the business world, Funston's reputation likewise ascended, attracting the attention of his mentor from the WPB, Sidney Weinberg, who had been elected to the Exchange's Board of Governors during the 1938 Reorganization but had since retired from the Board. Nevertheless, Weinberg was well aware that the Big Board, like Trinity College, was in need of a revamping as well as a new president. Weinberg recommended Funston, and after a series of interviews with the college president, the Exchange's executive search committee ended its long search.[11]

From 1951 to 1967, to the American public and the world, G. Keith Funston represented the NYSE, which in turn represented capitalism. He became the "symbol of the symbol," and the leading voice for an expanded Exchange public relations program that sought, through mass advertising, to encourage Americans to buy stock.[12] With the Exchange's hiring of a "salesman-educator" as its new president, the tentative early postwar years of only flirting with experimental promotions ended. The Exchange's historic resistance to advertising the stock market finally had been decisively broken.

Shortly before Funston assumed his position, a new Public Reception and Exhibition Room opened at the Exchange, in the 20 Broad Street building, adjacent to the visitors' gallery. In retrospect, the facility symbolized a new era of Exchange public relations in which Big Board officials would strive in new ways to convey to a doubting public that their institution operated "in the national interest" and that their "friendly" member firms really welcomed the small investor.[13] The president's office got a face-lift and a change in locale, a brighter room that Funston decorated with a few meaningful personal items. Most prominently, he hung a picture of Independence Hall behind his desk, a reminder, he said, "that freedom is the basis of everything in this country," and that the New York Stock Exchange was the "epitome of free enterprise. Once that's lost, we're gone."[14] Funston was a salesman who believed in what he was about to sell.

Who Owns Industry? The Brookings Report

As *Forbes* noted, Funston's job demanded "internal as well as external salesmanship"; he needed to develop an advertising attack plan to reach the masses, and then he had to sell Exchange members on its merits.[15] In devising a marketing strategy, Funston had the help of his staff and also an external advertising agency. By the time Funston assumed office, BBDO had been retained by the NYSE for more than two years. With his Harvard MBA background and his marketing experience, Funston had his own ideas about crafting a successful sales strategy. He upheld the relatively new notion that a company needed a solid, scientific understanding of its customer base. Such knowledge provided a yardstick to measure sales growth, facilitated the development of initiatives to keep customers happy, and often led to the development of effective ways to attract new customers.[16]

Funston was surprised and upset when he discovered that the Exchange lacked even a broad understanding of its shareowner base. No one—not Gardner Advertising Company, not BBDO, not Exchange managers, and not member retail brokerage firms—had ever precisely ascertained shareowners' aggregate numbers. (To its credit, though, Merrill Lynch was beginning to conduct shareowner samplings to better understand clients' investment objectives, their economic backgrounds, and other characteristics.) Estimates of the nation's total shareowner base ranged from 15 to 20 million individuals, but these amounted to little more than educated guesses. The extent to which one company's shareholder lists overlapped with those of other companies was an unknown. For example, AT&T and GE boasted at midcentury more than one million and 400,000 shareholders, respectively, but no one knew how many shareowners held stock in both companies.[17] A national shareowner census would have aided marketing efforts, but member firms had never been prepared to spend the money. It was a classic catch-22 situation. Brokerage firms struggling for profitability did not want to allocate scarce funds to marketing research, yet they lacked business in part because they did not understand their client base.[18]

Funston prodded the NYSE to commission the country's first formal survey of shareowners. Conducted by the Brookings Institution, Lewis Kimmel and the other architects of the study devoted enormous thought to developing comprehensive survey methods that would yield reliable data on the extent of shareownership. Their first step involved contacting 5,002 corporations and requesting them to submit data on ownership of their outstanding stock issues. The study sought to accumulate ownership information of not only the 1,074 NYSE-listed corporations, but also the 577 companies listed on the New York Curb Exchange (later renamed the American Stock Exchange), the 18 other major exchanges in the United States (with 673 listed corporations), as well as 373 unlisted banks, 149 unlisted investment companies (including open-end mutual funds), and 2,147 other unlisted companies of all types (including companies whose stock was traded over-the-counter). The National Association of Securities Dealers (NASD) and the National Association of Investment Companies (NAIC) joined the major exchanges in helping the Brookings Institution canvass and obtain raw ownership data. Ultimately, the Brookings Institution received usable data from almost 3,000 corporations. NYSE-listed corporations were particularly compliant, with 993 of the 1,074 corporations (92.5%) responding with the requested information. With the help of International Business Systems (IBM), the Brookings consultants began the laborious task of sifting through the lists to eliminate duplicate names. The study also probed into the true owners of shares registered in the names of broker-dealers ("street names") as custodians for their clients. Statisticians, the media, and NYSE officials uniformly applauded the Brookings Institution's rigor in conducting the study.[19]

In the 140-page report released by Brookings in the summer of 1952, one statistic particularly captured Funston and the Board's attention: only about 6,490,000 Americans were shareowners. This was less than half the number they had projected. Funston and his colleagues were unpleasantly surprised. Although they were aware that brokerage firms had been losing business and that trading volume had declined, the problem was worse than they had thought. 6,490,000 investors represented just 4.2% of the population, or 4,750,000 household units, or 9.5% of American families (see table 3.1). Of the nation's shareowners, moreover, 72% owned stock in only three or fewer companies.[20] In contrast, 104 million Americans owned life insurance; 53 million, savings accounts; 43 million, Series "E" U.S. savings bonds; and 14.5 million, annuities and pensions. Illustrating just how uncommon common stock ownership was in 1950, nearly twice as many citizens (more than 12 million) owned interests in consumer cooperatives (see table 3.1).[21] *Forbes* referred to the NYSE as a temple "long neglected while its former devotees sought other idols."[22] Only a few months before the release of the Brookings Report, Funston had declared in his annual letter to the Exchange community that the Board's goal was "a nation of small share owners, a nation in whose material wealth every citizen has a vested interest through personal ownership, a nation which is truly a people's democracy."[23] With only 6.4 million investors, the country was not yet on the path to universal shareownership.

Funston and his peers heralded in public the Brookings Report's positive findings to the end of projecting an image of shareowner diversity. They noted that three out of four investors had annual incomes of less than $10,000 a year ($81,218 in 2010 dollars). Women were slightly more likely than men to own shares. Thousands of salespeople, foremen, clerical workers, and housewives, in addition to business executives and other professionals, owned stock. The market, in this rosy scenario, was a melting pot. Although the wealthy still owned the majority of shares in the market, and were also much more active traders than smaller investors, the NYSE extolled the class and gender diversity of the shareownership ranks. As one NYSE employee proudly announced, "We found American investors in overalls, as well as pinstripe busi-

Table 3.1   Americans' investing patterns in the early 1950s

Type of investment	% of total family units with one or more owners	Estimated no. of family units with one or more owners
Life insurance (including G.I.)	82.30	41,160,000
Savings accounts	52.80	26,390,000
U.S. Series "E" bonds	41.90	20,940,000
Annuities and pensions (exc. Social Security)	20.90	10,470,000
Publicly owned stock	9.50	4,750,000
Other government bonds	5.50	2,760,000
Privately held stock	4.60	2,300,000
Real-estate mortgages and bonds	2.70	1,370,000
Corporate bonds	1.30	640,000

Source: Brookings Report, chart reprinted in *Fortune,* "Who Owns Business?" September 1952, 87.

ness suits. We found them in sunbonnets, as well as chic chapeaus. We found that the American of average means dominates the investing population."[24]

The NYSE's investor relations department sent press releases, along with a ten-page compressed summary of the Brookings Report, to prominent reporters, many of whom responded accordingly with stories with headlines such as "Who Owns American Industry?"[25] It was a question the answer to which Wall Street historically did not like. In the 1930s, journalist Ferdinand Lundberg contended that America was "owned" by sixty families. President Franklin D. Roosevelt and other New Deal government officials took their cue from Lundberg and criticized the increase in economic concentration. Criticisms within the United States about "Who Owns America," however, faded after World War II, in part because prosperity had resumed, and also because attacking the system increasingly seemed un-American.[26]

Thus, when reporters in 1952 used the headline, "Who Owns America?," to discuss the Brookings results, they did so to highlight capitalism's democratic nature, to emphasize that ownership of the means of production was indeed widespread in the United States. Reporters overwhelmingly celebrated the shareownership survey, using it as ammunition to counter the "Soviet hate campaign" then directed at Wall Street. As a *New York Daily News* editor proclaimed, the census "kicks the props out from under the Red-Pink Ballyhoo about how great, soulless corporations owned by a handful of rascally millionaires rule this country."[27] In a more restrained tone, the *New York Times* commented, "One of *Pravda's* most cherished propaganda notions is the idea that the American economy is essentially owned and operated by a small group of 'Wall Street Capitalists.' The fallacy of that idea has long been obvious to anyone familiar with this country, but precise and concrete data for demonstrating that fallacy have been lacking for the most part. That lack has now been remedied by the Brookings Institution's survey."[28]

Even newspaper political cartoons, a form that gravitates toward satire, celebrated the report. In one cartoon, a casually dressed man and woman, representing Mr. and Mrs. John Q. Public, stood in front of a billboard on which was emblazoned "6,500,000 Americans Own Stock." With no sarcasm intended, the man happily remarks to the woman, "Looks Like <u>WE</u> Are the 'American Capitalists!'"[29] Contrary to the cartoon's message, considering that only 4% of citizens (or less than 10% of households) owned stock, it was more likely that "we" were not a shareowner. While the average American investor might have been "middle class,"[30] the average middle-class American was not an investor. And, depending on the presentation of Brookings' statistics, the shareowner base could seem quite unequal. For instance, Funston often boasted that Brookings found that families with annual incomes of less than $5,000 owned one-third of individually held shares. Conversely phrased, the fact that one-quarter of all families with incomes of more than $5,000 owned nearly two-thirds of individually held shares was considerably less impressive. Moreover, in 1952, people earning less than $5,000 a year—a third of stockholders—comprised 57% of the adult population. The Exchange's definition of the "middle class" or the "average American" was not constant.[31]

Furthermore, 98% of shareholders were adults, and more than half of them were over 50 years old. The majority of all common shareholders lived in either New York, California, Pennsylvania, Illinois, or Massachusetts; almost 20% of the nation's shareowners resided in New York alone.[32] Also, the statistic that women owned slightly more shareholdings than men was misleading, considering that many husbands put stock in their wives' names for tax purposes. Only a few writers pointed out these distinctions and criticized the Exchange's interpretation of the study. Joseph Livingston, author of the *American Stockholder* (1958), vehemently objected to the portrayals of widespread stockownership, deriding the assertion as a "pathetic fallacy" and a "vicious lie." Though less biting in its remarks, *Fortune* was also critical, calling the broad stockholder base "a beguiling illusion," and Brookings' results, "little cause for rejoicing." "Figures may superficially suggest that Main Street and Wall Street have already merged, but that is hardly the case." *Fortune* concluded, "some of the capitalist cheering is a bit premature. What the report actually portrays is not so much a capitalist achievement as a capitalist opportunity."[33] This mirrors the Exchange's private reactions. A 4% rate of share ownership neither appeared to be a strong barrier against the spread of communism, nor did it augur well for brokerage firm profitability. Livingston captured the Exchange's evolving reaction to the Brookings findings: "At first, Wall Street was shocked and shrunken. But then a new thought struck: Only 6,500,000 shareholders! In a country as big as America! My, we haven't begun to tap the market! The 6,500,000 estimate became a new credo, a goad to expansion, a promise to salesmen."[34]

While the Brookings Report prodded the Exchange to market shareownership more aggressively, so, too, did another report which also appeared in the summer of 1952. Trading volume in the first half of 1952 was only 196 million shares, a significant decline from 275 million shares in the same period the prior year. Ironically, the decrease occurred at the same time that the Dow rose. The brokerage fraternity, according to the *Magazine of Wall Street*,[35] viewed the coexistence of a "persistent strong price pattern" with "limited" public participation as "disconcerting."[36] The magazine's editor, C. G. Wyckoff, attributed the poor trading volume to many factors, including inflation worries, concern about the Korean conflict, and uncertainty about the upcoming presidential election (General Dwight D. Eisenhower was running against Adlai Stevenson, the Democratic Senator from Illinois).[37] Yet in the eyes of many in the securities industry, the primary problem was one of public relations: too few Americans understood the stock market's importance to the national welfare, and too few citizens trusted securities salesmen. "Somewhat belatedly," reported the *Magazine of Wall Street*, Stock Exchange officials were beginning to recognize that a "new approach must be made to the investing public."[38]

Who should primarily direct that approach—member firms or the Exchange itself—was not yet clear. The Board of Governors expected President Funston to educate the country on the Exchange's general role, and to urge more member firms to follow Merrill Lynch's example and mass market securities. But, in 1952, the Board had not yet explicitly directed Funston to encourage "the public" to become actual shareowners. The president's job was limited then to soliciting general popular support of, not necessarily participation in, the stock market. Cold War exigencies and the securities industry's continued depressed state compelled the NYSE Board to reevaluate Funston's responsibilities and to enlarge their perceptions of who should be classified as desirable members of the "investing public." The NYSE, with Funston as its main spokesman, eventually would guide member firms in marketing share-ownership to the country. This was not immediately obvious, however. The Board still needed to do more homework before it would make that decision.

The Stewart Dougall Merchandising Study (June 1953)

In late 1952, the Board commissioned the consulting firm Stewart, Dougall & Associates to conduct a "merchandising study" to "suggest the proper balance of responsibility and effort required from the exchange itself and the individual membership in advertising and merchandising the securities and services they have to offer the public." Another purpose was to examine options for reinvigorating trading volume.[39] In their analysis, the consultants treated stocks as a product that was bought and sold, as any other. "It is axiomatic in merchandising manufactured goods, especially consumer package items, that sales gains can be achieved in three basic ways: creating new users; increasing the number of users; and, increasing the amount of use." The Stewart Dougall consultants reasoned that the NYSE could raise trading volume by cultivating new market participants, enticing existing shareowners to increase their holdings, or encouraging current shareholders to trade their shares more frequently. Stewart Dougall did not seem to fully appreciate the fact, however, that the key to solving trading volume issues was cultivating more active traders (either existing or new shareholders), not simply attracting more buy-and-hold investors.

The Stewart Dougall researchers favored getting existing stockholders to buy more shares (but made no mention of actively trading them). In making their recommendation, they were guided by a core tenet of marketing, namely, that it is easier to get existing customers to buy more of a product than it is to attract new customers. A shampoo manufacturer, for instance, can generate higher sales by convincing preexisting consumers simply to use more each time they wash their hair, or to wash more frequently. In focusing on preexisting shareowners, the researchers carefully considered the Brookings results. Of the 6.5 million equity owners, 4.5 million (nearly two-thirds) possessed less than four stock issues, though they could afford more. Importantly, Brookings found that most of the 6.5 million shareowners held their stocks on a permanent or semipermanent basis.[40]

In June 1953, Stewart Dougall suggested a modest goal: getting 10% of these 4.5 million "low users" to increase their holdings.[41] They also suggested that the NYSE strive for a 10% gain in shareowners over a three-year period, increasing shareowners to 8.5 million. The Stewart Dougall "10 percent solution" recommendations were not as focused on raising trading volume as they might have been. But the "10 percent" idea suggests that radical solutions were not necessary for the retail brokerage industry (small at the time) to recover profitability. Not every American needed to buy stock. If existing customers simply traded more frequently, brokerage firms could have increased their profitability without adding one more American to the shareholder lists. The NYSE weighed the Stewart Dougall recommendations and eventually adopted an ambitious solution (mass shareownership) to a problem that could have been solved in less drastic ways.

In searching for a viable solution to restore vitality to Wall Street, Stewart Dougall researchers emphasized that responsibility resided not just with the Exchange's Board of Governors, but also with listed companies and member brokerage firms. Invoking the "need for unity and cooperation" in spreading the shareownership message, the Stewart Dougall Report stressed: "Foremost, in our judgment, it is imperative to the success of the merchandising program . . . that there be understanding, wholehearted belief and interest in the goals, and full cooperation from the entire New York Stock Exchange community in working to achieve them." Commenting that the Exchange "maintains a clean house" and "has the public trust and welfare in mind," the report concluded, "In merchandising language, those who deal on the Exchange have quality products to offer to the public: products which represent a major portion of America's industrial might and recorded business successes." Nevertheless, the study added, "the burden of contacting and communicating with the currently non-investing public cannot be dependent upon the necessarily broad-scale contributions of the Exchange proper. It is a function of the 'merchants' and 'salesmen' to participate in communicating facts about the merits of the product and the services they offer to the buying public."[42] Member firms in the early 1950s needed this reminder. As the Stewart Dougall Report noted, most of them marketed inadequately if at all. The NYSE had to change that pattern, and eventually they would do so by making it easy and inexpensive for members to participate in a campaign masterminded by the Exchange.

Institutional Equity Investing: An Alternate Route to Improved Broker Profitability and "Democratic Capitalism"

The Stewart Dougall Report focused on stimulating retail individual investing, because retail investors at midcentury accounted for approximately 80% of trading volume on all the stock exchanges in the United States and held 94% of the total outstanding equities.[43] Cultivating more institutional equity investing was another way for the NYSE to enhance profitability for member brokerage firms. Institutional investing also could help the NYSE achieve broader shareownership, by providing the public with another, albeit less direct, route into the stock market.

Yet, in the early 1950s, most institutions, such as pension funds, commercial banks, and life insurance companies, did not include equities to any great extent in their portfolios. Commercial banks, the biggest group of financial institutions by size of assets, held only a negligible amount of corporate stock due to regulations. Life insurance companies and mutual savings banks held a mere 1.3% and less than 1%, respectively, of their assets in common stock.[44] Private pension funds, too, historically had purchased little stock; at the end of World War II, pension funds held less than $300 million of either common or preferred stock, which translated to a mere one-tenth of their total assets and only one-fifth of 1% of all corporate stock outstanding.[45]

Law and custom sharply restricted most institutions from buying significant equity shares for the portfolios under their control.[46] The philosophy was that institutions had a profound responsibility to be careful in their investing choices because preserving capital was critically important when dealing with "other people's money."[47] Equities seemed too risky to be a substantial part of institutions' holdings. In many states, institutional managers had to abide by "prudent man" laws, which limited their investing choices. These laws were the outgrowth of the "prudent man rule," first articulated by Justice Samuel Putnam of the Supreme Judicial Court of Massachusetts in 1830. This ruling concerned the behavior expected of managers overseeing personal funds held in their trust, although the standard eventually spread to encompass other institutional money managers. In his opinion, Justice Putnam declared, "All that can be required of a Trustee to invest is that he conduct himself faithfully and exercise a sound discretion. He is to observe how men of prudence, discretion, and intelligence manage their own affairs, not in regard to speculation, but in regard to permanent disposition of their funds, considering the probable income, as well as the probable safety of the capital to be invested."[48] In the Depression years, with a renewed, post-Crash sensitivity to the need for "sound discretion" and "probable safety" of funds under their control, institutional managers typically chose investments with perceived minimal risk, such as high-grade corporate bonds and government securities.[49]

The NYSE, though, had reason to anticipate that institutions might come to exert a larger presence in the market. Some institutional money managers were rethinking their aversion to stocks: postwar inflationary fears were a catalyst inspiring their changed outlook. Searching for hedges against inflation, an increasing number of professional money managers were attracted to stocks of well-established companies such as AT&T and GE. At a time when rising prices were eroding purchasing power, fixed income investments seemed almost too conservative. As Funston noted, there was a "growing realization that at times great risks can frequently be avoided, instead of assumed, through the institutional ownership of sound common stocks."[50] The resurgence of the common stock theory of investment, which posited that common stocks, not bonds, were the best long-term investment, strengthened institutional managers' receptivity to buying stocks.[51] Also influential was the rise of modern portfolio theory. In a 1952 article on "Portfolio Selection" in the *Journal of Finance*, the young economist Harry Markowitz emphasized that while it was impossible to eliminate all risk, it could be minimized by maintaining a well-diversified portfolio. The key was not to focus on the risk of one investment in isolation, but rather, to focus on the risk relative to other assets in the portfolio. The idea of diversification long preceded Markowitz, but his quantification of the process made it seem scientific.[52] In subsequent years, economists such as William F. Sharpe further advanced financial theories regarding risk and securities pricing.

Prudent man laws needed to be liberalized for institutional managers to embark on their new direction. New York was one of the first states to pass the enabling legislation.[53] On July 1, 1949, a new law permitted fiduciaries to invest up to 35% of their funds in common stocks. As the NYSE announced in its *1950 Annual Report*, the revised law "represented a looser, more common-sense approach to the long-standing 'prudent man rule' as it afforded trusteed funds more freedom to decide their portfolio content." The Big Board predicted that this would have "deep significance for future operations of the Exchange, particularly as new reservoirs of capital are built up in the corporate pension funds."[54] The NYSE was right to see these pension plans as a huge market for stocks. Charles Wilson, chief executive of General Motors, had recently pioneered new possibilities for the portfolio content of corporate pension funds; in 1950, in contract negotiations with Walter Reuther, president of the United Auto Workers (UAW), Wilson had proposed giving employees a fully funded pension plan that would be permitted to invest some assets in common stocks. Wilson's proposal was revolutionary, allowing a private pension plan to invest in many stocks rather than only the employer's stock. Emphasizing diversification, the plan stipulated that no more than 5% of the fund's assets be invested in any one stock. Reuther agreed.[55]

In the early 1950s, life insurance companies and other institutional players also were reevaluating their aversion to buying stocks. In 1951, several New York–based life insurance companies requested that state regulators permit them to invest a maximum of 2% of their assets in equities. Their success encouraged life insurance companies in other states to follow suit. Although 2% of a life insurance company's assets in stocks may seem inconsequential, the size of these companies' portfolios (in the billions of dollars) meant that having even a small percentage in stock would significantly bolster stock market volume.[56]

Noting the rising level of common stock purchases by pensions, life insurance companies, and savings banks, the NYSE forecast, "The spread of the 'prudent man' rule among fiduciary investors is potentially of far-reaching importance."[57] Yet the Exchange was ambivalent about the revolution that was unfolding. The rising tide of institutional equity investing posed significant challenges for their organization, not just potential benefits. One worry was that institutional fund managers, owing to the size of their shareholdings, might wield excessive power over corporations, and hence over the NYSE.[58] Another concern involved institutions' enormous block trades—orders of a large amount of a stock all at one time, usually more than a few thousand shares.[59] These block transactions might hurt the market's liquidity—the ability to bring "buyers and sellers together quickly and hold price changes to a minimum."[60]

Despite such fears, the Big Board embraced the incipient institutional buying trend. Institutions had begun increasing their equity buying in the early postwar period, while Wall Street remained mired in the Depression and hungry for business. At a time when total trading volume, institutional and individual combined, had not recovered to pre-Crash levels, a modest growth in institutional trading was a lifeline for the floundering securities industry. Institutional equity purchases only constituted 20% of trading volume at mid-century, but this was more than in the prewar period, so institutional sales were rising as retail continued to stagnate. As the *Magazine of Wall Street* reported in 1952, "It is obvious that whatever demand has existed [for stocks that year] has come from large institutional buyers such as investment trusts, pension funds and the like. Buyers of this type are extremely sophisticated and presumably believe investment opportunities are still available." In contrast to institutional interest, individuals still seemed apathetic toward the market. As Wyckoff commented, "The public, on the other hand, seems more preoccupied with the political outlook [Eisenhower versus Stevenson], the Korea situation and personal problems relating to the high cost of living and taxes. Undoubtedly this has played a part in their relative inactivity in the market." Wyckoff also noted, "It takes enthusiasm and, frankly speaking, a pronounced tendency towards speculation to bring the public into the market on a large scale. Obviously, such an atmosphere has been lacking for a considerable period."[61]

Institutional investing helped revitalize Wall Street. As later Exchange president Robert Needham recalled, "During the worst years, the institutions were in the market when nobody else was. . . . They saved the market from disintegration."[62] Institutional trading eventually proved to be a boon for many of the Exchange's members, particularly specialists and brokers dealing with the public. Since NYSE rules at the time prohibited institutions from holding seats on the Exchange,[63] institutions needed to route their trades through NYSE members and pay them commission fees. With fixed rates (the rule at the Exchange since its founding in 1792 up until 1975), brokers earned the same percentage on transactions regardless of their size.[64] In the early postwar period, the Big Board could charge these relatively high fees because it had little competition for institutions' business. Over-the-counter (OTC) dealers, who belonged to the National Association of Securities Dealers (NASD), conducted little business in large blocks; they dealt mostly in securities of small companies unable to meet an exchange's listing requirements.[65]

OTC securities, then and now, are traded through a dealer network, versus a formal exchange such as the NYSE. Exchange-listed stocks also can be traded over-the-counter between brokers who do not belong to the NYSE and institutional investors.[66]

The NYSE's increased efforts in the early 1950s to cultivate little retail investors does not mean that the Big Board was oblivious to the rise of institutions in the marketplace or content to let institutions go to the OTC market.[67] Precisely because the NYSE was worried about the growth of institutions, Exchange leaders viewed the retail investor as an important counterbalancing force. Since the big institutional investor was starting to come more frequently to Wall Street (and without much prodding), the Board of Governors concentrated most of their energies on wooing the small retail customer.

By 1953, after just two years with Keith Funston at the helm, the NYSE had made progress identifying the composition of the shareholder base and also assessing solutions to increasing shareownership. In 1953, the Exchange's efforts increased, as the NYSE organized and staffed a Market Development Department devoted to expanding retail shareownership.

Creation of a Market Development Program

Organizing a Market Development Department was important in the NYSE's efforts to lead an industry-wide mass merchandising effort. In June 1953, Stewart Dougall recommended the creation of a department dedicated to "planning, coordinating, and following through on all merchandising activities." The department should have a "strong staff of skilled specialists in merchandising and sales know-how who can concentrate on contacting, and collaborating with, those responsible for merchandising activities among the various elements of the Exchange community, including member firms, listed companies, banks and other institutions, as well as industry, trade, and other associations."[68] Receptive to the idea, Funston petitioned the Board to act upon the recommendation. In a June 1953 memorandum, Funston made his case: "There are an estimated 21,000,000 families who are able financially to buy shares, and only 18 percent of them are present owners. In tapping this market the Exchange community can increase volume on the auction market at the same time it accomplishes a worthwhile social gain through broadening the base of share ownership." He added, "Seldom does a community have such an opportunity to help itself and the nation at the same time. Seldom has a community such a chance to build good public relations through doing what is also best for itself."[69]

In 1938 the SEC had stated that the "interests of the Exchange are not incompatible with the national interest," but now, in 1953, Funston argued that the two interests were mutually reinforcing. He emphasized the importance of the NYSE Board Governors helping its member firms to market to the American public. Funston noted that the Big Board's "strategic position at the center of the securities industry enables the Exchange to carry on various types of sales promotional or merchandising activities better than could any individual Member." He concluded, "I believe it would pay dividends in improved public relations and in increased morale and business for our Member Firms if a Market Development Department were established in the Exchange."[70] The Board agreed, and the Market Development Department amalgamated under one umbrella existing committees and departments, including public relations, advertising, and investor relations.

A search commenced for an executive to head the Market Development Department, a quest almost rivaling the effort three years earlier to find a new Big Board president. An executive search firm, Ward Howell, screened applicants: the "prime" characteristic they sought was an "attractive personality" and only after that, "broad administrative experience." Ward Howell compiled a list of the strongest candidates, and President Funston and the Board interviewed the final contenders.[71] They chose a gregarious and ambitious young man named Ruddick ("Rud") Lawrence who, like Funston, was an outsider to Wall Street who had never worked in the securities industry. Lawrence's expertise was in advertising and marketing. He came to the NYSE after serving for eleven years as an advertising manager for *Fortune* and then as the director of promotion planning and development for NBC. Like Funston, Lawrence also had served as a lieutenant in the U.S. Navy during the war. He had worked in logistics, attached to the office of Secretary of the Navy James Forestall and to the chief of naval operations. Now Rud Lawrence had a new job, which *Business Financial News* classified as "Exchange promoter."[72]

After hiring Lawrence and creating a Market Development Department, the NYSE retained the services of BBDO. Moreover, the NYSE president remained the organization's chief spokesman. Lawrence insisted on it, later explaining "I felt very strongly that Keith Funston should be the spokesman for the Exchange. We couldn't control an organization with as many diverse factors in it very effectively if we didn't have a spokesman. And Keith was not only qualified and eager but fully agreed with that; he was an outstanding spokesman. He was articulate and had a winning way about him. . . . He had a great smile. . . . He could remember everybody's name, he was a wonderful asset for the Exchange." Lawrence added, "I insisted that Keith Funston . . . be our spokesman. Not the chairman, not the governors. We had to speak with one voice and, in those years, we generally did."[73] Unlike President Whitney in the 1920s, President Funston, however, did not enjoy full discretion for the content of his speeches. The Market Development Department carefully worded the public addresses, helping Funston communicate Board policy.

Lawrence assumed his post in the autumn of 1953. The Korean War ceasefire had recently been declared, and Wall Street looked favorably upon the cessation of hostilities. The stock market rallied—but only for a short time. By the time Lawrence began his job, the market already had retrenched. Even when stock prices began to rise again, trading volume remained relatively flat. More small brokerage firms closed, while other firms survived only by merging. "Amidst the greatest prosperity in U.S. history," wrote Robert Bleiberg in *Barron's*, "Wall Street has become a depressed industry."[74] In 1953, trading volume amounted to less than 355 million shares, roughly 100 million less than in 1925, even though the average number of shares listed had grown to 2.8 billion from 462.5 million during the same period. By inspiring Americans to become shareowners in American enterprise, Lawrence and his colleagues at the NYSE were going to help turn around these statistics and end Wall Street's long depression.

CHAPTER FOUR

Courting Retail Investors during the Cold War

You won't find the ad in the "Help Wanted" columns of your local paper nor will the job recruiters lurking the halls here at the Business School mention it to you, but American industry has a special "Help Wanted" sign out today. The ad, if printed, might read as follows: "Wanted—New Owners to join in growing enterprises. High pay. Good prospects. Only those with surplus savings should apply."

NYSE PRESIDENT KEITH FUNSTON, HARVARD BUSINESS
SCHOOL LECTURE (APRIL 1954)

You may not feel like rebels tonight, but you are part of an economic revolution that is important to all of us . . . [a] revolution against restricted capitalism—[against the] philosophy that owning securities is the privilege of a few.

NYSE VICE PRESIDENT RUD LAWRENCE, ADDRESS TO THE
AMERICAN INSTITUTE OF ACCOUNTANTS (APRIL 1954)

In late 1953, the NYSE Board of Governors boldly authorized Rud Lawrence's Market Development Department to launch Own Your Share (OYS), a multifaceted marketing campaign that included institutional advertising. The program aimed to promote the stock market to a mass audience. The Big Board hoped average Americans would become more actively involved in the stock market by opening brokerage accounts and at least sporadically making trades. Moreover, they wanted Americans to open accounts not just with any retail brokerage firms, but with "NYSE member" firms such as Merrill Lynch.

Own Your Share was a risky move on the part of the NYSE. While Board members expressed optimism about the economy and the vitality of listed companies, they worried that they might be inviting the public into the market at a bad time, such as before a prolonged downturn. In retrospect, OYS's timing was impeccable, as the stock market was on the verge of one of the longest bull periods in its history. OYS promoters were enabling those who heeded the message to get in on the ground floor of a major market upswing. The OYS campaign may have been partially responsible for creating a climate conducive to a bull market. Those approving the marketing campaign believed in the common stock theory of investment—the idea that stocks, over the long term, constituted the best possible investment. Therefore, even if the market fell, Exchange leaders believed it eventually would rebound, and investors who stayed the course would be rewarded. Still, marketing OYS on the eve of a market correction obviously would not reflect well on the NYSE nor serve the cause of expanding the shareowner ranks. As much as they feared action, the Board of Governors feared inaction more. They were keenly aware of the poor financial shape of many small- to midsized retail-oriented brokerage firms. Not benefitting from economies of scale like the larger firms, these firms struggled to maintain profitability, even after the Board in 1953 had authorized a rise in minimum commission rates. (Charles Merrill, incidentally, did not support this rate increase; he believed that the NYSE's fixed commission levels already were too high, and simply enabled inefficient firms to stay in business.)[1]

The Exchange Board decided they needed to intervene by providing members with marketing assistance. In commencing OYS, the Board was essentially helping smaller firms advertise and market themselves in ways similar to those pioneered by Merrill Lynch and other large brokerage firms. Far from lamenting any loss of a "first mover advantage," Merrill Lynch executives were gracious about OYS, taking the view that any promotions of the stock market's virtues would benefit their own company's business.[2]

The OYS Slogan

In the winter of 1953, in an old office that once belonged to former Exchange president Emil Schram, Rud Lawrence sat at his desk, pondering the best slogan to invite the American public into the market. Lawrence crumpled papers as he repeatedly devised and then rejected various slogans. Finally, he jotted down one phrase that he did not throw away: "Own Your Share of American Business," which became sometimes abbreviated as simply "Own Your Share" (OYS). Lawrence read the slogan again with satisfaction. That was precisely the gist he wanted to convey, the idea of "*own*"ership of a "share" of stock, a personal invitation ("*your*" share), and a sense of civic patriotism ("*American* business"), all rolled into six short words.[3]

"Own," the first word, reflected the Exchange's desire to have Americans conceive of equities as personal possessions, and, therefore, the act of investing as a purchase, not a gamble. The use of the second person possessive ("your" share) conformed to an emerging copywriting trend—giving the audience a chance to participate by wording the advertisement in such a way that "it leaves room for [people] to put themselves into it," as one marketing professional noted.[4] Instead of writing "Buying Stock is Easy," Lawrence tried to engage his audience with the words "Own *Your* Share." The third word, "share," reflected the business community's campaign to popularize the word "shareowner" instead of "stockholder." Three years earlier, financial news editor B. C. Forbes had advocated the use of "shareowner" because "Sharing, from Biblical times, has been advocated, lauded." Forbes contended, "The greatest sharers of today are our corporate enterprises and institutions. The American Telephone & Telegraph Company alone shares its profits with fully one million part-owners. If popularizing the use of the term 'share owner' does even a little to better the atmosphere, to inspire individuals and families to invest their savings in shares, it will be very much worthwhile."[5] For this reason, the NYSE campaign encouraged Americans to own "shares" not "stocks." Finally, the words "*American* Business" reflected Lawrence's desire to tap into the upsurge in patriotism and civic pageantry that accompanied the Cold War.[6] The rival Curb Exchange recently had heightened its own prestige, playing the patriotism card by changing its name to the "*American* Stock Exchange." Now, the NYSE, with the Own Your Share of American Business campaign, also attempted to drape patriotism around its image.

Invoking citizens' sense of patriotism proved to be a smart idea. Citizens at the time were rediscovering their national heritage, resurrecting and commemorating key events and documents. As President Truman said in an August 1947 radio address, "It is a good thing, on occasion, for Americans to look into their past." Truman encouraged citizens to remember the "well-springs" of the country's strengths, the memories of which would inspire them to rededicate themselves to American principles.[7] Truman believed that such rededication to the country's founding principles was critically important at a time that the United States was assuming a greater role on the world stage, and as the Soviet Union was quickly expanding into many countries that had been recently liberated from fascism. In 1947, Truman approved Attorney General Tom Clark's idea of a "Freedom Train" tour across the United States. Aboard the train were more than one hundred historical documents, such as the Mayflower Compact, the Declaration of Independence, and the Gettysburg Address.[8] The Buttonwood Agreement, which established the NYSE in 1792, was not among the pieces in the traveling exhibition, but the Exchange, too, wanted to show that it was pivotal to the nation's history. As OYS's architects maintained, the Big Board not only had grown up with the country, but had helped corporations to grow and thrive and had therefore enabled the nation to rise to its current status as a world leader.[9] The NYSE viewed the cultivation of economic, not just political, citizenship as essential to keeping the country strong.

Funston and the Board approved the carefully crafted OYS slogan, which went on to succeed "In the National Interest" as the NYSE's motto. In fact, the motto was not entirely original. Just a few years earlier, the U.S. Treasury Department had used an almost identical slogan ("Own a Share in America") to promote war bonds.[10] The Exchange now sought to align equity investing with an act of civic duty, akin to buying government bonds.[11] At the outset of the campaign, therefore, "Own Your Share" already struck a chord of familiarity with American citizens. The OYS campaign consisted of a series of institutional advertisements, investor education programs, and a host of other initiatives, all designed to make the NYSE and equity investing in general more appealing to the public. As OYS commenced, economist John Kenneth Galbraith dryly remarked that "Wall Street . . . has become, as a learned phrase has it, very 'public relations conscious.'"[12] That was true, although the Exchange Board, in their efforts to expand shareownership, was motivated by more than just a desire to serve the interests of Wall Street and boost the NYSE's image.

Immediately after the Board approved the campaign's launch, Exchange officials began promoting the OYS concept internally to members and their corresponding firms, making sure that they, along with the public, understood the theme of the program. In early 1954, the Board of Governors distributed to Exchange members an informational kit explaining the campaign and its objectives. NYSE officials also emphasized the importance of the campaign in numerous speeches to industry groups and associations. For instance, on April 20, 1954, the day after the program's official start, Rud Lawrence told the American Institute of Accountants that a revolution was taking place in which securities ownership no longer was the "privilege of a few."[13] While Lawrence spoke at the American Institute of Accountants, President Funston delivered the prestigious Dickinson Lecture at his alma mater, the Harvard

School of Business. Funston told them that "American industry has a special 'Help Wanted' sign out today." The sign read: "New Owners to join in growing enterprises."[14] No NYSE president had ever laid a welcome sign on the Big Board's door. In prior years, it would have been inconceivable for the NYSE to have made such an explicit overture to the public to enter the stock market. But Funston was now putting out that very sign, and explaining its necessity. Fond of analogies, he likened equity capital to being the foundation for a house, with the house serving as a metaphor for the nation: "Equity capital, the ownership capital provided by common and preferred stock, is the foundation upon which our entire corporate financial structure rests. And the size and permanence of the national economic structure we are building will be determined by the dimensions and strength of that foundation." He asserted, "The degree of expansion we can finance and the amount of debt we can safely add to our corporate structure depend directly on our equity capital base." Funston then asked, "How strong is this foundation, this base, that we have been creating in recent years? Is it strong enough to support the kind of house we must have to meet the needs of our growing national family?"[15] Funston concluded that the country's equity base needed to be strengthened, and contended that OYS intended to do just that.

Campaign Objectives and "Tie-In" Structure

In devising this campaign, Big Board officials wanted to make the NYSE appear friendly to individual investors. If Americans were less intimidated by the investing process, they would be more inclined to patronize member firms. Investing needed to seem easy, legitimate, and patriotic, which is why the Exchange launched "the broadest, most intensive public relations program in [NYSE] history."[16] An article in *Media/Scope* magazine explained why the OYS campaign was a milestone: "Before 1954, the New York Stock Exchange had advertised. So had many of its member firms. . . . But there had been no theme connecting the messages of Exchange advertising, no concerted effort to tell the public a basic story about an institution which was shown by its own research to present a confused image in the minds of many persons."[17] Now the connecting theme was "Own Your Share," and the campaign also had subthemes, like "Democratic Capitalism." The Exchange Board hoped that member brokerage firms would also spread these messages. Having member retail brokerage firms all expounding identical themes as the NYSE Board would create a memorable repetition effect.

Despite the large task of OYS, the Exchange's advertising budget was only $500,000 in 1953, and never exceeded $1.5 million annually in the 1950s and 1960s. By comparison, Merrill Lynch alone spent roughly $500,000 for advertising in 1950 and, by the end of the campaign, was spending $17 million annually. Though he complained often to the NYSE Board about the inadequacy of the Exchange's advertising budget, Ruddick Lawrence later said, "We had a small budget but we had imagination." OYS's architects needed imagination to inspire the financial and business community to spend their own money, not just the Exchange's, to promote the market. OYS's success depended on the extent to which the NYSE management could enlist the cooperation of member firms and listed companies as well as groups outside the business community.

Developing Own Your Share as a "tie-in" program was the answer. The Exchange's Market Development Department, collaborating with advertising agencies and marketing consultants, designed the campaign's themes and promotions. They then distributed the finished advertisements to member retail brokerage firms and listed companies who, rather than spending their own time and money creating promotions, simply affixed their names to these boilerplate ones and paid for the running of the advertisements. The NYSE followed the same pattern in other public relations initiatives, developing, for instance, standardized speeches about the stock market for distribution to member firms. The idea was to make it easy for the Exchange community at large to propagate a uniform, memorable "buy stock" message. Moreover, the NYSE Board would not be paying for all aspects of the promotions—it would be responsible mainly for development costs, not publication expenses. The cost of running the advertisements in print, radio, and television was considerably higher than the cost of making the advertisements, so the greater financial burden of the campaign fell upon participating member firms. With its relatively large advertising budget, Merrill Lynch consistently tied into the Own Your Share campaign, and in the process, benefitted not just themselves but also their retail competitors.

Own Your Share also dovetailed with programs administered by other organizations, outside the Exchange community, that possessed a similar agenda of spreading confidence in capitalism and the American way of life, if not the stock market specifically. The NYSE's Market Development Program worked to make sure its advertisements coincided with themes being promoted by various Ad Council campaigns, such as Miracle of America (1954), Confidence in a Growing America (1958), and Democratic Capitalism (1956–1959). Some of the Exchange governors such as Charles Wilson and Charles Francis (both public governors) were involved with the Ad Council, and therefore in a good position to facilitate the exchange of ideas between the NYSE and the Ad Council. In addition, the Big Board worked closely with other groups "selling free enterprise" such as the National Association of Manufacturers (NAM) and the Committee for Economic Development (CED).[18]

NAM, the country's largest industrial trade association, founded in 1895, sought to educate and inform the public about the critically important role that manufacturing plays in the U.S. economy. Several Exchange members belonged to NAM, including Exchange governor Robert Boylan. Beginning in the 1930s, NAM embarked on periodic public relations campaigns, dedicated to the "dissemination of sound American doctrines to the public."[19] Not enamored with the New Deal, NAM worked with Edward Bernays to try to stymie President Roosevelt's agenda. In the 1950s and 1960s, NAM was strongly anticommunist and was active in promoting the idea of free enterprise.[20]

The NYSE also benefitted from the activities of the Committee on Economic Development (CED). Formed in 1942, the CED, according to its mission statement, is "an independent, nonpartisan organization of senior corporate executives and university leaders dedicated to policy research on major economic and social issues and the implementation of its recommendations by the public and private sectors."[21] In the mid-twentieth century, the CED sponsored many workshops on economic education and fostered school programs devoted to promoting an understanding of the capitalist system.

Department Store Common Stock Displays

In the spring of 1954, the NYSE worked with retail member firms to bring the "Own Your Share" message to R. J. Goerke's Department Store in downtown Elizabeth, New Jersey.[22] No one in the Goerke family was affiliated with the NYSE, but the store sponsored the OYS message in the belief that providing customers with information about stocks (much like government bonds during the war) was a civic-minded gesture that would generate goodwill for the business. At the time, the business community was becoming increasingly aware that it paid to act as "Good Citizens."[23] NYSE leaders hailed Goerke's Department Store for making a small but important step in the direction of publicizing the merits of the market. Visiting Goerke's display, Lawrence declared, "May I offer congratulations to the progressive spirit of Elizabeth, to Goerke's, our listed companies and the Member Firms in . . . pioneering such a worthwhile effort. . . . We hope that this event will serve as a pattern for joint efforts among merchandisers, listed companies and our members in many other communities across the country."[24]

In sponsoring OYS, Goerke's transformed its store for a week. In the store's windows, large banners proclaimed the words "New York Stock Exchange" and "Own Your Share of American Business." Mannequins, delicately holding ticker tape and stock certificates in their porcelain hands, beckoned passersby to enter the store. Inside, standing beside a towering replica of a stock trading post, a friendly retail stockbroker fielded questions and distributed business cards of local NYSE member brokerage firms. Meanwhile, upstairs in the rug department, a short film about securities trading entitled "What Makes Us Tick" continually played. The film emphasized that a stock purchaser acquired not just a mere piece of paper, but also an important interest in a tangible company that provided the nation with needed goods or services. In addition to supporting a specific company, a stock buyer also bolstered the free enterprise system. Reinforcing the film's message, a display featured products manufactured by local companies listed on the NYSE, such as Allied Chemical & Dye as well as Standard Oil (then also known as Esso). Signs in the store windows proclaimed that buying a share of stock, a "share in America," fueled a vibrant "people's capitalism."[25] ("People's capitalism" was a phrase currently being promoted by the Ad Council.) For the exhibit, the NYSE's Market Development Department gladly loaned Goerke's promotional materials, from the stock trading post to the "What Makes Us Tick" film to the "people's capitalism" window signs. After Goerke's Department Store used them, the NYSE dispatched these materials to other businesses that were willing to sponsor the OYS message. Commenting on these stock exhibits cropping up in other stores and venues across the country, *Sales Management* magazine noted, " 'To sell, you must display.' But it might seem, at first glance, that if you sell securities, you have as merchandise just pieces of paper, not lending themselves to display. Until recently, dealers in investments accepted this circumstance as inevitable, but times are changing."[26]

OYS Advertisements: Style, Content, and the Four Cautions

While the traveling exhibits capture the flavor of the OYS campaign, newspaper print advertisements were a larger feature of the program. Anticommunist messages are evident in some of these promotions. An OYS advertisement in *Life* magazine, for instance, was entitled "What Every Russian Ought to Know about Owning Stocks in America." The copy began: "Before the Revolution, Russia had a national securities market in the city of Petersburg (now Leningrad). But it isn't open anymore. For that reason, the facts below about stock ownership in America might come as a surprise to the Russian people today." The advertisement proceeded to inform "Russians"—and actually, also the American public—that here in the United States anyone could buy stock, and America's stock owners were a diverse lot. The copy emphasized, "There's nothing mysterious about buying or selling stocks in America. The practice is as old as the nation itself, part of the fabric of capitalistic democracy and one of the reasons for its success." According to the advertisement, "Americans invest in stocks because they believe in the future of American companies and want to share in their growth and any profits that may be paid out in dividends."[27]

Such OYS advertisements carried an ideological message, promoting the virtues of the Exchange and capitalism. But most OYS advertisements were subtler and tended to focus on the practical benefits of stocks to individual investors and their families. In this regard, the Big Board imitated the style and copy of Merrill Lynch promotions.[28] "If you're concerned about tuition costs and such—here's how investing may help," began one of the Exchange's advertisements. "If your family's needs are increasing, consider these facts about investing" was another common headline. Usually reinforcing the copy were pictures and images, once considered taboo. In the advertisement entitled "This is the music that dividends pay for," a boy played a trumpet as his proud father watched. In "This is the smile dividends are helping to pay for," a cute little girl with braces flashed a smile at her birthday party. Such advertisements depicted the stock market not as a gambling den where speculators sought dramatic short-term profits, but as a reputable place for families to acquire extra income—and not so much from trading stocks, but from simply accumulating dividend checks. OYS advertisements often featured the postal worker delivering dividend checks to investors' doorsteps. At the time, many common stocks often yielded 4 to 6%, so dividend yields were an important investing consideration.[29]

Advertisements implied that people could enjoy a more comfortable lifestyle by investing in stocks, but never suggested that everyone could become millionaires in the market. Flamboyant appeals were conspicuously absent. By making a "soft sell," the Exchange hoped to avoid the charge that it played upon people's emotions to encourage blind investing. For this reason, OYS advertisements always featured "the four cautions." As Ruddick Lawrence explained, "We said, 'First understand the risk. Don't invest if you can't afford it. Second, have a cash reserve for emergencies. Don't put the rent money or the insurance money in the stock market. Third, get good advice, go to a broker or your banker or somebody who can help you and who can make sure— check it out.' And finally we said, 'Get the facts. Buy stocks on which you can get information. And understand the facts, try to learn the facts.'" Disseminating the four cautions required "an enormous educational program." Lawrence insisted, "We wanted people to be educated, we wanted them to be informed." Only on that basis could the NYSE "proceed soundly to develop this nation of stockholders."[30]

Pollster Alfred Politz tried to dissuade the Exchange from this timid strategy. He especially recoiled against advertisements that advised investors to make sure they possessed life insurance before buying stocks. "Perhaps," Politz said, "the risk connotation can be reduced by a more or less saying something that one has profit and losses, or gains and losses, and that is the kind of news they will always put together, which is ethically correct."[31] The Board of Governors, however, disregarded Politz's advice, preferring to err on the side of caution. For their own interests as well as those of investors, NYSE officials aimed to create advertising that was "conservative rather than daring," featuring copy that would "read just as well even though the market should drop next year." Pursuing this strategy, they aimed to create a "nation of sound investors."[32] As a newspaper article commented in 1954, "Uninhibited advertising will not do for the NYSE. . . . Even though research studies indicate a huge market of potential investors, the NYSE will continue to use the proper restraint in its advertising."[33] In an internal memorandum on advertising copy in 1955, Lawrence emphasized, "In our advertising and public relations, we have stressed repeatedly how important it is for investors—and especially new investors—to have a cash reserve for emergencies and some insurance, to get the facts and good advice, and to buy stocks in well-known and established companies." He added, "We have carefully avoided suggesting what to buy and when to buy. Since we can't foresee tomorrow's headlines nor tomorrow's stock prices, and since the general level of the market has experienced such a consistent rise, we believe that the Exchange advertising copy should increase its emphasis on ownership on a sound basis rather than putting the stress on the ownership—that for the time being we should put even more emphasis on education—how to invest soundly—and less on dividends and profit possibility."[34]

By this time, the NYSE had replaced BBDO with another agency, Calkins & Holden, which had been cofounded in 1902 by Earnest Elmo Calkins and Ralph Holden. Well-respected for its work, including its pioneering use of art in advertisements, Calkins & Holden enjoyed a strong reputation for design. The agency boasted such clients as Beech-Nut, H. J. Heinz, Pierce-Arrow, and now, the NYSE.[35] Michael Carlock, head of the NYSE account at Calkins & Holden, commented on the four cautions strategy: "The Stock Exchange is probably the only advertiser who offers his wares and then tells the customer to think twice before buying." At a time when warning labels on products were uncommon, the NYSE's cautious strategy was a departure from typical marketing practices. As Lawrence told *Editor & Publisher Magazine*, "Suppose you came across an ad for cookies and read: Remember the risk—our cookies are fattening. Or an automobile manufacturer who told you: Don't buy an automobile until you have taken care of your bills, and paid up your mortgage and have a fat reserve in the bank. Or a soap ad that urged you: Get expert advice. Don't use our soap until you check with a top-flight dermatologist. I suspect the thought of being hedged about with such inhibitions in marketing would give most advertising people nightmares." Yet, as he explained, "in the Exchange's literature, films, lecture courses, advertising—in every medium we use to reach the public—we post these warning signs that start off with a vital 'DON'T':

DON'T buy stocks—unless you understand the risk.
DON'T buy stock unless you can really afford to . . .
DON'T buy stocks on tips or rumors.
DON'T buy stocks without obtaining sound investment advice."[36]

Lawrence concluded, "In short, while we want everyone to understand the opportunity for investing, we don't want shareowners who can't afford to invest and who don't know what they are doing."[37]

The Exchange's "think twice" advertising strategy was an early example of what became known as "contra-marketing"—a tactic in which advertisers voluntarily include warnings in their promotions that the product is not designed for everyone. The tactic is most useful in advertising "socially unacceptable products," which marketing expert D. Kirk Davidson defines as products that lack a certain measure of legitimacy, such as cigarettes, alcoholic beverages, and gambling. These products, though legal, "elicit widespread disapproval. . . . Certain segments of the public find them offensive or inappropriate or harmful for a variety of reasons." Consequently, as Davidson notes, whereas "the marketing of most products and services takes place within a positive, or at least a neutral, environment," these products pose special marketing problems. To overcome them, some promoters engage in "something quite extraordinary in the marketing profession: they expend some effort and money to urge some of their customers *not* to buy their product."[38]

Contra-advertising did not become a popular marketing tactic until the late 1960s and 1970s, when new federal advertising regulations went into effect. (For instance, the passage of the Trade Regulation Rules on Cigarette Labeling and Advertising in 1965 meant that all cigarette packages in the United States henceforth had to display health warnings.[39]) Using contra-advertising in the mid-1950s, the NYSE was ahead of its time. Management realized that the "four caution strategy" reduced the likelihood of the SEC, Congress, or the public blaming the NYSE for encouraging improper consumption of a potent product. For critics who believed that stock buying was immoral at all times by all practitioners, contra-advertising did not alleviate their issues with Exchange promotions of the market. But for those who believed that stock buying was an improper activity for some of the people some of the time, the NYSE's contra-advertising strategy might allay their concerns. The Exchange was not encouraging everyone to come into the market—only "sound" investors who had analyzed and understood the risks. If the "wrong sort" of people became shareowners—those who, for instance, could not afford the losses—the Big Board could defensively argue that it had warned them about the hazards of equity investing.

The message of caution resounded not only in print promotions, but also in Big Board speeches. For instance, when interviewed by radio host Don Gardiner, Rud Lawrence refuted the idea that most people could make a quick fortune in the market, even though Gardiner led him in this direction. Knowing that Lawrence wanted to disseminate the OYS message, but evidently not understanding the campaign's cautious nature, Gardiner opened the interview with a tantalizing question to his audience, "How would you like to make a million dollars? Doesn't it sound wonderful? Rud Lawrence, do you think people can make a million dollars?" Gardiner apparently thought he was giving the NYSE official a golden opportunity to extol equity investing, but Lawrence did not want to promote the market in that way. Lawrence was a salesman, but a salesman who preferred to err on the side of underselling his product. Therefore, Lawrence responded, "I suppose it's possible [to make a million] but I certainly wouldn't suggest that they try to do it through the medium of stocks."[40]

Gardiner seemed not to hear. "Well, that's what we're going to talk about today, the possibility of making a million dollars in stocks. I think that there's a lot of interesting things that we can find out about the New York Stock Exchange." Introducing his guest, Gardiner told his audience that they were in the studio to have "a little chat about making a million dollars." Again, he asked Lawrence, "Do you think it is at all possible to make a million dollars today in the stock market?" Lawrence again hedged his response: "Well, Don, I suppose it's possible, but I certainly think it would be a grave mistake for the average investor to approach the stock market with the idea of making a killing. We feel that that's the wrong approach, and as a matter of fact, most stockholders and most investors are interested in supplementing their incomes with a dividend check or in increasing their capital as the country and the particular business they've invested in continues to grow; but to set out to make a killing, no. I think that would be definitely a mistake." Lawrence warned that an unrealistically optimistic expectation of quick and dramatic returns "would be an unfortunate handicap for anyone starting out" in equity investing. Gardiner finally dropped the subject of making a million in the market, asking Lawrence instead to explain to the listening audience what it meant to own a share of common stock, who should buy stock, and how they should do so. Lawrence took the opportunity to discuss the stock market's "democratic" nature, emphasizing that "the old idea that stocks were for the rich has certainly gone by the board." He also delved into ways, such as diversification, that investors could minimize the hazards of equity ownership.[41]

The NYSE waited to see if the public would appreciate its conservative advertising strategy and buy stock, or whether this new campaign, like those of the 1930s, would backfire. As the Board recognized, to a large extent, the reaction would depend upon the direction of the market—if people bought stock and the price of the stock rose, new shareowners would be pleased that the Exchange had given them a nudge. If stock prices fell, the NYSE feared that even its issuance of the four cautions might not protect the institution from charges that it seduced people into the market.

The advertising campaign was well timed, which makes it hard to determine its efficacy. Yet the very fact that the NYSE was promoting stocks may have contributed to the rising market. In 1954, the market began the ascent that *Forbes'* columnist Lucien Hooper had predicted at the beginning of the year. On the basis of rising dividend rates, promising technological innovations, and a group of burgeoning young consumers, a new generation who "knew not 1929!," Hooper had been hopeful that "the long period of chronic undervaluation of common stocks [was] coming to an end."[42] In fact, 1954 turned out to be one of the Dow Jones' top ten years in the twentieth century. A temporary reduction in Cold War tensions helped propel the bull market; the reduction in defense spending was more than offset by a surge in consumer spending and a construction boom.[43]

A bull market developed in full force. Between September 15, 1953, and December 31, 1954, the Standard & Poors (S&P) 500 index rose 65%.[44] At the end of 1954, Hooper, along with many other prominent market analysts such as B. C. Forbes and Michael Kourday, forecast an equally rosy 1955. Kourday perceived that the stock market could be positively affected by the implications of the ongoing baby boom. Noting the postwar rise in fertility rates as well as the simultaneous decline in infant mortality, he recommended stocks that catered to this growing market—like manufacturers of infant formula, baby food, and milk.[45] Fulfilling these analysts' expectations, 1955 would be another banner year on Wall Street.

The Fulbright Test of 1955

The NYSE was relieved to find itself promoting the market at a time of rising stock averages. Yet some observers, led by Arkansas Senator J. William Fulbright, grew concerned about the raging bull market and what they perceived to be a return of excessive public speculation in the equities markets. Overspeculation purportedly had led to the 1929 Crash, and the Great Crash, many wrongly believed, caused the Great Depression. (It was not until 1963 that Milton Friedman and Anna Schwartz advanced their monetary explanation of the Great Depression.[46]) Worried about the "suspiciously frothy" market, the Senate Banking Committee launched a study of the securities markets in January 1955. Senator Fulbright, who chaired the study, asserted that the public was entitled to know "the forces" that had caused stock prices to climb to the highest levels in twenty-five years. The committee noted, however, that it "was not motivated by knowledge or suspicion of widespread frauds, manipulations, or wrongdoings." Rather, it was "fully confident that legislation which had been enacted in the Nineteen Thirties with respect to the securities markets, including the exchanges, had provided its basic soundness."[47]

In fact the SEC was not very robust in the 1950s. Ironically, at the same time that involvement in the stock market was expanding, the SEC's roster of employees had diminished, owing to budget cuts. In 1955, the SEC had a little over 650 workers, much reduced from the 1,683 employees it had in 1941. Moreover, the SEC no longer had an aggressive, reform-minded chairman like William O. Douglas or James Landis. The agency's head in 1955 was Paul Windels Jr., who zealously pursued peddlers of fraudulent penny uranium stocks, but did not see the need to intently probe the exchanges. As regulatory historian Louis Kohlmeier wrote, the SEC "slept for most of the decade of the 1950s."[48]

Trying to fill a perceived void created by a seemingly too complacent SEC, the Senate Banking Committee, in the spirit of Carter Glass (the cosponsor of the Glass-Steagall Act), decided to conduct the first government study of the stock market in roughly twenty years, with the aim of examining the factors underlying the "continuous rise of stock prices from September 1953 to January 1955, and the acceleration of the rise in later months." The Committee sought to discover, in their words, "What did this dramatic sixteen months' stock-price rise mean? . . . Did the magnitude and persistence of the rise represent mainly a belated recognition of basic economic developments since World War II, which for various reasons failed to have their impact before? . . . Or did the continuation and acceleration of the rise denote that conditions were developing uncomfortably reminiscent of those in the late Nineteen Twenties?"[49] Fulbright and a majority on the Committee wrongly believed the latter. Yet the investigation became known as the "Friendly Fulbright Study," in part owing to investigators' noninquisitorial demeanor and also due to the NYSE's cooperative attitude.[50] Among the 21 witnesses appearing before the Committee were several Wall Street executives, including NYSE president Keith Funston and Winthrop ("Win") Smith Sr., one of Merrill's senior partners. When Funston appeared before the committee in March, he was forth-coming in his testimony, outlining, as requested, Exchange regulations and carefully explaining his answers. Funston politely but firmly insisted that the NYSE had made every reasonable effort to protect small investors. The Senate study, in its final report, found little to contradict Funston's contention. Ab-staining from criticizing the NYSE for the recent allegedly "unhealthy specu-lative developments," the Fulbright report instead blamed the Federal Reserve Board for not quickly raising margins sufficiently high enough to dampen speculation. (In fact, the Federal Reserve Board in the prior year had raised margin rates twice—first, from 50 to 60%, and then to 70%.)[51]

The NYSE community reacted to the findings with a mixture of annoyance and relief. On the positive side, they hailed the fact that the Banking Commit-tee had found nothing substantially amiss. As one member broker said, "The report gave the New York Stock Exchange and other registered exchanges a clean bill of health."[52] He was correct, although the Fulbright report did rec-ommend that 12 follow-up studies be undertaken in order to control "stock market abuses and difficulties." Since they had detected no such abuses at the NYSE, the Fulbright Committee was primarily worried about other markets, such as the over-the-counter (OTC) markets. The NYSE community lamented the Committee's loose use of the word "stock market." As one Exchange mem-ber complained, "To most readers 'stock market' means the New York Stock Exchange, so the [unintentional] effect of the report is to criticize us in the eyes of the hasty reader."[53] Exchange brokers also bristled at the contention that the Fed's 70% margin level had been too low. As the *New York Times* ex-plained, "Brokers naturally would prefer margins to be no higher than what is necessary to protect them, because high margins dry up market turnover and trim their commissions."[54]

The Exchange Board deeply resented what they perceived to be two key assumptions underlying the Fulbright investigation, namely that the recent bull market unhealthily resembled the speculative situation in the 1920s and that this market, too, would end in a crash. The Senate Banking Committee's final report devoted significant space to exploring the general characteristics of speculation, identifying evidence of speculation in the 1950s market, and essentially invoking the Shadow of 1929 that the NYSE had fought so hard to put aside. The Committee noted, "Speculative activity becomes evident when businessmen and the public generally become unduly preoccupied with the stock market and stock prices, new highs in stock-price averages are front-page news, the tipster increasingly flourishes, flamboyant advertising keyed to the lure of quick profits becomes more widespread, and there is a rush of security offerings of dubious merit. The expansion in the volume of short-term trading is facilitated by an increasing use of bank credit for stock speculation." Much to the Exchange's frustration, the Committee concluded that such signs of rising speculation "have been apparent in the recent bull market. They are not nearly as conspicuous as was the case in 1929, but this is not justification for ignoring their existence. Complacency in the earlier stages of the development of an unsound speculative psychology is likely to result in actions at a later stage which can only have harmful effects on the entire economy."[55]

Joseph Livingston, financial editor of the *Philadelphia Bulletin* and frequent critic of the Exchange's efforts to popularize the market, testified before the Fulbright Committee. Emphasizing the speculative character of the current market, Livingston disapprovingly noted, "More and more people are turning to the stock-market pages before turning to the comics. They want to figure out their winning[s] at the end of the day. That is not a good sign. People are no longer buying for [dividend] income alone, but for capital appreciation. They are not investors; they are speculators."[56] Livingston's comment reflects a different outlook on speculation than today, when many individuals and institutions buy stock for price movement, regardless of the time frame. In the 1950s, Livingston was castigating people for thinking more of long-term capital gains, not dividends. Another witness called before the Fulbright Committee echoed Livingston's pessimistic appraisal: John Kenneth Galbraith, whose book *The Great Crash of 1929* recently had debuted, invoked memories of 1929 and warned against a repeat of a dangerous boom and bust cycle. Galbraith's comments stung NYSE leaders, who feared that the fruits of their advertising efforts were about to dissolve.

Several Republican senators serving on the Fulbright Committee objected to the way the report focused on speculation as the fuel igniting the rise in stock prices. Filing a Minority Report, Republican Senators Homer Capehart (Indiana), John Bricker (Ohio), Wallace Bennett (Utah), and J. Glenn Beall (Maryland) claimed that the Fulbright study largely ignored "the principal factor affecting . . . [recent] price levels—the health of the economy." They claimed that that the Democrats on the Committee did not want to give credit to the real reasons underlying the rise in stock prices; the stock market, far from being primarily fueled by "iniquitous speculation," was simply responding positively to higher rates of production and growing international political stability engineered by the Eisenhower Administration.[57] As the Minority Report contended, "The stock market always reacts favorably to peace. The American people have great faith in President Eisenhower. They are confident of the success of his efforts to achieve lasting peace and without appeasement of the Russians. They are confident his program will result in maximum employment with a continued high purchasing power in the consuming public."[58] The dissenting senators criticized the study on several grounds—for portending that there would be an impending "bust," claiming that "a rapidly rising stock market was likely to threaten economic stability," and suggesting that the public had "become unduly preoccupied with the stock market." Finally, they noted, "And of course, there are frequent references to the 1929 crash. That theme runs through the report."[59]

While not appreciating some of the innuendoes in the Fulbright report, the NYSE was quite pleased that it had passed Fulbright's "test" with flying colors. Indeed, the NYSE's *1955 Annual Report* boasted that the Exchange was "found to measure up to the highest standards of public responsibility." The study of the securities market had "resulted in a wider and better appreciation by the public of the functions and operations of the Exchange." Funston remarked that the NYSE felt it "gratifying to receive the commendation of several top government officials and much of the nation's press."[60] In November 1955, Funston made the cover of *Time* magazine for his work popularizing the market. Hence, with the completion of the Fulbright study, Own Your Share continued uninterrupted.

The Growth of Mutual Funds: "Everyman's Investing Media"

While not being promoted by Own Your Share, mutual funds in the mid-1950s were experiencing strong growth; the difference from fifteen years earlier was enormous. In 1940, less than 300,000 mutual fund accounts existed in the United States, and assets under management (AUM) for the entire fund industry (both closed- and open-funds) amounted to only $450 million. By 1955, the number of mutual fund accounts had ballooned to more than two million, and AUM for the industry had grown to more than $7.8 billion.[61] Two key developments during the New Deal planted the seeds for growth in the fund industry: the Revenue Act of 1936 and the Investment Company Act of 1940.

The 1936 Revenue Act ended a big disadvantage to mutual funds: the fact that fund investors faced an onerous double layer of taxation on dividends. The mutual fund industry had long maintained that it was unfair that shareholders in the fund be taxed upon receipt of their dividend distributions when the fund already had been taxed on the same monies. Merrill Griswold, head of Massachusetts Investors Trust ("MIT," the first mutual fund, founded in 1924), argued that a mutual fund should be conceived as a "conduit" between investors in the fund and securities in the fund's portfolio. Therefore, according to Griswold, shareholders should be treated as if they directly owned the stocks, and so mutual fund dividend distributions should be taxed only at the personal level. The "conduit" line of reasoning proved to be a compelling one, as the Revenue Act of 1936 exempted mutual funds from tax, provided a fund met certain tests such as adequate diversification.[62]

Four years after the passage of the Revenue Act of 1936, the Investment Company Act of 1940 went into effect. In the aftermath of an SEC study examining abuses in the closed-end investment company industry, the Act tightened regulation on all investment trusts. In a strategic move that stood in contrast to the NYSE's defensive reaction to the creation of the SEC in 1934, many in the fund industry assisted the SEC in designing this legislation.[63] Likewise, they generally welcomed the Investment Advisors Act of 1940, which subjected fund managers to registration and regulation. The mutual fund sector realized that investment companies needed to regain popular trust if they hoped to make a comeback, and protective legislation could help boost that much-needed investor confidence. As the *Wall Street Journal* reported in a headline in August 1940: "Many Investment Trust Firms Feel Regulation Is a Constructive Move."[64] Mutual funds initially favored the idea of regulation more so than closed-end funds, but the latter also eventually supported the enactment of the Investment Company Act once the SEC agreed to extend the tax relief in the 1936 Revenue Act to all funds, closed and open.[65]

With the resolution of dividend taxation issues and the implementation of external regulations, the mutual fund industry was poised to reap renewed public confidence and enjoy rapid growth. As disposable personal income levels rose in the 1950s, a bull market emerged, and mutual fund promoters began actively proselytizing Americans on the benefits of these investment vehicles. Funds exploded in popularity, stoked by novel distribution methods and new types of funds, such as balanced funds, bond funds, and international funds.[66] While many new firms, such as Dreyfus, Franklin, and Neuberger & Berman, launched funds during this period, several of the mutual funds founded in the 1920s also boomed. In fact, as of the late 1950s, MIT, Wellington, Fundamental Investors, and Affiliated Fund were four of the five largest funds in the United States. The other mammoth fund, Investors Mutual, belonged to Investors Syndicate (which later became Investors Diversified Services, or IDS).[67]

One factor not contributing to fund industry growth was advertising. Mutual funds at the time fastidiously refrained from running the types of fund advertisements ubiquitous in today's newspapers, magazines, television, and other media. Fund advertising was illegal, under a strict interpretation of the Securities Act of 1933, which was aimed at regulating offerings of new securities. Section 5 stipulated that a company wishing to sell securities could not "transmit any advertisement or other communication offering such securities unless the communication meets the requirements of a full statutory prospectus or is preceded or accompanied by the full prospectus." Tombstone advertisements were permitted, but these types of advertisements merely identified the security being advertised and offered a copy of the prospectus.[68] While most companies rarely issue new securities, mutual funds continually issue new shares. Due to their redeemable nature, mutual funds always would be constricted by Section 5, with their shares never being able to be advertised.[69] While the SEC conceded in the 1950s to expand the scope of acceptable tombstone advertising, mutual funds remained seriously limited in their advertising methods. For instance, they could not even mention a fund's past investment performance in an advertisement.[70]

Thus, while the NYSE's Own Your Share promotions flourished, mutual fund advertisements did not. In the 1950s, the mutual fund industry agitated for relaxation of the curbs on advertising. Addressing the annual mutual fund convention in 1955, Herbert Anderson, the president of Group Securities, Inc., complained, "While our industry wants and must have regulation, our insurance and banking friends have it to a sound degree, without the restrictions we face on advertising—on telling the story of their service. Costs to the public can only be reduced through volume, which can be achieved only as our story can become known." Anderson called for major revisions to Section 5 of the Securities Act of 1933.[71] Until that happened, the fund industry had no choice but to channel its marketing efforts in other directions, including sending hordes of salesmen door-to-door.

How did the NYSE and large retail member brokerage firms in the OYS years react to the rise of mutual funds? A precedent did exist for securities firms being involved in the fund business. During the Roaring 1920s, investment houses like Goldman Sachs, along with banks, had dominated sponsorship of closed-end funds.[72] However, they had left the business in the aftermath of the Great Crash, with banks having no choice but to exit due to the separation of commercial from investment banking mandated by the Glass-Steagall Act.[73] The question at midcentury was whether securities firms would become immersed again in the investment company business, and if so, on what terms. In the late 1940s and early 1950s, a handful of investment banks, including Lazard Freres and Lehman Brothers, decided to sponsor mutual funds. Around the same time, some brokerage firms like Smith Barney debuted their own mutual funds.[74] Investment houses were attracted to the relatively high fees associated with mutual fund sales. The upfront fee to buy a mutual fund was approximately 7–8% of the net purchase amount.[75] Facing weak commissions from stock sales at a time of low trading volume, Kidder Peabody, a white-shoe investment house founded in 1865, was one firm that decided to tap into the mass market for mutual funds. The *New York Times* noted in 1949, "Whether the move [toward an emphasis on mutual fund sales] will turn out to be a mere stop-gap expedient of a harassed industry or a long overdue and permanent bid of the financial center for the savings of the middle-income masses remains to be seen."[76]

While some securities firms were climbing aboard the mutual fund bandwagon, several of the nation's leading retail brokerage houses, including Merrill Lynch, Dean Witter, E. F. Hutton, and Paine Webber firmly resisted sponsoring or underwriting mutual funds.[77] In the 1940s and 1950s, Charles Merrill was emphatic about not getting his firm ensnared in the mutual fund business. His vehement avoidance of funds stemmed in part from a near-disaster two decades earlier when he had nearly promoted a closed-end fund that later imploded. Merrill sincerely wanted to protect small investors from harm (although mutual funds were quite different from closed-end funds). He also wanted to protect his firm's reputation.[78]

Merrill had additional reasons for eschewing mutual funds. Merrill Lynch had built its reputation in part on the wisdom of its carefully assembled team of securities analysts ("the thundering herd"). The company advertised itself as the place where ordinary Americans could get the facts on stocks and deal directly with analysts to develop portfolios based on their specific needs. Now, expert mutual fund managers could provide that same service. The mutual fund model posed a threat. Taking a long-term perspective, Merrill worried that while initial sales of mutual funds might be profitable for his firm, mutual fund clients at the time rarely made changes to their investments; their buy-and-hold philosophy might endanger the firm's revenues as transaction volume might decrease.[79] Not until the late 1960s, long after Charles Merrill's death in 1956, did the firm, under the leadership of Don Regan (later Treasury Secretary under President Ronald Reagan), begin to distribute mutual funds sponsored by other firms as well as underwrite some of its own mutual funds. During the 1960s, mutual funds had grown so popular that even Merrill Lynch could no longer ignore the profit inherent in the industry.[80]

Despite its proclaimed interest in cultivating small investors, initially the NYSE Board of Governors did not embrace the mutual fund trend. In fact, for a time, the Own Your Share creators, along with Merrill Lynch and other retail brokerage firms and some listed companies, promoted a different investment vehicle that competed with mutual funds. In 1954, the Big Board introduced an innovative stock purchasing program called the "Monthly Investment Plan."

CHAPTER FIVE

Selling Stocks on the Monthly Plan

> Wall Street has the red carpet out for Joe Doakes and his missus. If he has as little as 50 cents a day to invest, all the research facilities and the best minds of the nation's financial headquarters are at his disposal. And nobody is going to sneer at old Doakes or give him the brush off because he hasn't got a million bucks. Instead he will be called Mr. Doakes and is likely to be told he is the backbone of America.
>
> DAILY NEWS, DECEMBER 14, 1954

Advertisements constituted an integral part of the Own Your Share campaign, yet NYSE executives understood that it was not enough simply to generate popular interest in the market; interest needed to translate into action. Those contemplating buying stocks after seeing OYS advertisements needed to understand how to take the next step, and be comfortable taking that step. Exchange leaders realized that many Americans had never visited a retail broker's office, often due to the perception that brokers were only interested in big customers. Americans of modest means frequently deferred purchasing stocks until they had accumulated enough funds to buy in "round lots" (one hundred shares of a stock at a time); otherwise, if they just bought a few shares of a stock at a time (an "odd lot"), they incurred a higher commission fee.[1]

To overcome these obstacles to potential investors buying stock in small share increments, the NYSE in January 1954 inaugurated an innovative stock-purchasing program called the "Monthly Investment Plan" (MIP). Explicitly designed to appeal to little investors, MIP was the culmination of several months' intensive work by the Big Board in collaboration with retail member brokerage firms and odd lot houses. It enabled an individual with modest savings to open an account in a stock of a listed company of his or her choice, and then arrange to buy small amounts of shares by mailing to the MIP-sponsoring broker or employer a prearranged monthly contribution to the account. (A larger investor simply could buy one hundred shares of a stock outright through a broker and bypass opening a MIP.) As financial reporter Sylvia Porter emphasized, the NYSE tailored MIP to "the littlest of the little investors," that is, those who were unlikely to have sufficient money to buy one hundred shares at a time and who did not want to pay an odd lot premium every time they purchased fewer shares.[2] The architects of OYS hoped MIP would be an economical and practical way for a small investor to accumulate a significant position in a particular stock over time. At any time, the investor could open an additional MIP account to start building a position in a different stock. Exchange officials hoped that small investors gradually would open multiple MIPs and therefore achieve the benefits of diversification.

At the time MIP debuted in 1954, mutual funds were beginning to gain in popularity. But this was not a mutual fund: MIP was, in a sense, the Big Board's alternative offering. An individual who purchased a MIP owned shares in one specific NYSE-listed company; in contrast, an individual who bought a mutual fund owned shares in the fund itself, and hence indirectly owned many securities. A mutual fund holder was not a shareholder of any of the companies in that fund's portfolio and therefore was not entitled to exercise shareholder rights, such as voting rights on issues that affected the company. Conversely, a person who owned a MIP was a bona fide shareholder in that company, and thus eligible to participate in shareholder governance, including attendance at shareholder annual meetings. In the Cold War years, the NYSE Board of Governors reveled in how MIP allowed citizens of modest means to participate in "shareholder democracy." This was a powerful reason why the Board preferred MIP to mutual funds and chose not to promote mutual funds, though many retail member brokerage firms eventually would enter that lucrative business.

In the 1950s, the NYSE did not even list shares in mutual funds, even though three decades earlier, it had listed shares in closed-end investment trusts.[3] Following the implosion of many highly leveraged closed-end investment trusts after the 1929 Crash, the NYSE wanted to stay away from mutual funds.

The Big Board also feared institutional domination of the stock market. Hence, most mutual fund salesmen in the 1950s and 1960s were over-the-counter (OTC) brokers.

MIP was the NYSE's answer to a problem that Stewart, Dougall & Associates had identified in their 1953 consulting work for the NYSE. After interviewing numerous potential investors, Stewart Dougall concluded that a major impediment to broader individual shareownership was that Americans of modest means could not easily and economically purchase small amounts of stock. In its June 1953 report, the consultants recommended that the NYSE develop "a plan for the convenient purchase of listed securities." Stewart Dougall envisioned something akin to an installment plan, whereby investors could purchase as many shares of stock as they desired over a designated time period on a fixed payment schedule, much like life insurance or a car loan. Americans had become accustomed to settling their bills and their installment payments on a monthly budget basis, and so the NYSE had to find a way to fit stocks into those buying habits.[4] As Stewart Dougall stressed, "The American public has been steadily conditioned to think in terms of purchase plans which require payment out of income. In such ways, Federal [income] taxes are paid; government bonds are bought; life insurance premiums are paid; homes, automobiles and numerous types of consumer goods are bought. The one opportunity the public has not had is free choice of *any* individual corporate stock or stocks they might prefer to buy through an easy purchase plan." The firm optimistically predicted, "If such a method of buying is made available, and is adequately publicized and merchandised, a reasonable assumption can be made that it will be a powerful force in broadening shareownership and contributing to market liquidity." Stewart Dougall added: "We do not believe any organization other than the New York Stock Exchange can develop such a plan effectively."[5]

In June 1953, at the time Stewart Dougall made this recommendation, the NYSE had, in fact, been working for a few months on developing just such a plan. The report provided an added impetus to finalize it. The program that ultimately developed, MIP, was not an installment purchase plan; rather, it was, more accurately, "pay-as-you-go-investing." Unlike enrolling in an installment plan, an investor who purchased a MIP would own as many shares of stock as he or she had purchased to date; the MIP customer did not incur any debt, in part because MIP did not permit margin accounts. Giving great thought to MIP's design and structure, NYSE executives hoped that the program would become the cornerstone of the broader Own Your Share campaign.

Launching MIP

In early January 1954, shortly before MIP became available to the public, the Big Board publicized the impending program, disseminating information about it to the Exchange constituency as well as the public. In a speech to the Association of Customers' Brokers in New York City, Lawrence explained that MIP was not just "a new way to buy stocks," it was "also part of an idea that is big enough to help create hundreds of thousands of new investors." He continued, "That idea of course is Democratic Capitalism—the conviction that Americans everywhere should have the opportunity to own their share of American business." The Exchange's conception of "democratic capitalism," of course, was much broader than what Lawrence briefly had described in his speech. It involved the idea that capitalism, as opposed to communism, was quickly dissolving class differences, as everyone shared in the fruits of growing prosperity under this economic system. Broader shareownership helped spread the wealth, and hence the NYSE saw the Own Your Share campaign, including MIP, as a way to speed the progress of capitalism becoming ever more democratic. By explicitly connecting MIP to democratic capitalism, Lawrence essentially was arguing that MIP would help make the United States stronger and more resistant to communism, as MIP would give its purchasers a vested interest in not just a particular listed company, but also in the country in general. Talking to retail brokers, Lawrence also explained how MIP could benefit the Exchange community: it could bring more business to retail member brokerage firms, higher volume to the Exchange, and better public relations for the securities industry. Broadening the market, Lawrence contended, was in everyone's best interests.[6]

Lawrence and his colleagues in the Market Development Department cultivated the press, issuing a myriad of news releases that explained the importance of the NYSE's new stock purchase program. In response, many newspapers published favorable editorials about MIP, even before the program officially debuted. Praising MIP, the *Boston Herald* argued, "This is the age of the little financier, not the mogul, and we're proud to be part of a nation where the common man can also be a capitalist." The *Chicago Sun-Times* was equally ebullient, noting, "Public response indicates that the new Monthly

Investment Plan for buying common stocks on the NYSE is one of the greatest forward steps ever undertaken by the 'Big Board.'"[7] In a theme that other newspapers also emphasized, the *New York Daily News* lauded MIP for its role in keeping the country strong in its fight against communism: "We hope this plan will meet with every success, and will spread stock ownership among Americans far more widely than it is spread now. One reason for this hope is that we don't like to see a lot of our fellow citizens missing chances to invest in sound, productive and profitable American industries and businesses. Another is that we'd like to see the greatest possible number of Americans become vitally interested in maintaining and improving the Capitalist system, and in fighting all persons or groups that want to tear the system down."[8] Pleased, Lawrence informed the Association of Stock Exchange Firms that "the press reaction has been strongly in favor of the Plan, and the public's response to the publicity and advertising is astounding."[9]

Member Firms Marketing MIP

While newspapers extolled MIP's promise, the plan's success hinged in large part on the willingness of retail member brokerage firms to market the product. Merrill Lynch eagerly embraced MIP from the start, immediately recognizing that MIP could dovetail nicely with its long-standing efforts to cultivate small investors. Shortly after the program's launch, Merrill Lynch ran an extensive advertising campaign encouraging customers to buy MIPs. Given that financial advertising still was not widespread, the breadth of Merrill's advertisements was impressive: Merrill Lynch ran advertising in 170 newspapers and ten magazines.[10] "At Last, You Can Be an Investor for Only $40 a Month!" proclaimed the headline of one advertisement. The copy continued, "That's right. You can start buying stocks on our 'pay-as-you-go' plan for just $40 a month—or even $40 every three months." (In fact, in 1954, $40 was not an insignificant regular contribution: $40 translates to approximately $320 in inflated-adjusted dollars).[11] Merrill Lynch advised readers who wished to get started on an MIP account to "Just fill out the coupon below, and we'll send you a membership blank together with our booklet which gives you complete details on the Monthly Investment Plan."[12]

Within the first few weeks of advertising MIP, Merrill Lynch received some 12,000 responses from individuals who mailed in the coupons. In addition, Merrill Lynch offices were flooded with drop-in visitors, and their phone lines were inundated with callers seeking more information.[13] Buoyed by the interest generated, Merrill Lynch continued to aggressively market MIP through a variety of media, not just print advertisements. For instance, Merrill Lynch advertising manager Louis Engel featured MIP in his popular book, *How to Buy Stocks.*[14] In special public investment lectures, radio spots, and other venues, Merrill Lynch disbursed information about MIP. Not surprisingly, Merrill Lynch quickly became the largest MIP provider of all member brokerage firms and remained in this leadership position during the entire life of the program. At the conclusion of MIP's first year, Merrill Lynch accounted for approximately half of all MIP business. This percentage grew to 65% by 1966, and almost 90% by the time the program concluded in 1976.[15] One reason for Merrill's dominance of the MIP business may have been related to the company's unusual compensation structure: salesmen operated on a fixed salary, not a commission basis. MIP was fundamentally a "buy-and-hold" strategy with only modest prospects for trading and generating perpetual commission income, but this was not as problematic for Merrill Lynch retail brokers as it was for many brokers at other houses who still relied on commissions.

A handful of other large brokerage firms, such as Bache and Company (previously known as J. S. Bache), also promoted MIP; however, many brokerage firms were less than enthusiastic.[16] As Lawrence lamented early in 1954, "The people who seem to be the least enthusiastic about the Plan are some of our own Members and registered representatives, and in my travels I have found that their lack of interest is due largely to lack of understanding" about how the program worked. In truth, an unclear understanding of the program was not the biggest reason why many brokers were reluctant to sell MIP. More compelling was the widespread perception among commission-dependent retail brokers that MIP had little profit potential for them and therefore was not worth their effort. Lawrence, however, initially attributed broker reluctance to market MIP to other factors, noting, "Any new product or service usually has problems in getting distribution and in educating the trade." Therefore, he urged member firms to take "the time to hold meetings and educate their [account] representatives on how the plan works and how to sell it."[17]

While many member retail brokerage firms educated their salesmen on the program's nuances, some also tried to educate their sales force on their vested interest in selling MIP. They pointed out that MIP commissions could be substantial if taken in the aggregate. To help illustrate that point, Bache and

Company devised a chart that showed its brokers what they could make if they sold just one $100-a-month MIP plan each month. In that hypothetical example, the commission earned would have been $2,300 a year, or approximately $18,440 in inflation-adjusted dollars.[18] Some MIP accounts, however, involved smaller sums. Some investors subscribed to a $40-a-month plan, and others committed an even smaller amount: the minimum plan on offer entailed payments of only $40 per quarter. In the first six months of operation, the average MIP monthly payment was $70 a month, which was somewhat less than Bache's example, but more than the minimum plan.[19]

While the broker who sold a large volume of MIP accounts theoretically could be moderately successful, the hope was that some of these numerous small accounts would eventually mature into more profitable, full-fledged trading accounts. This required patience from retail brokers and their firms. Merrill Lynch again led the way. Since the 1940s, it had adopted a long-term strategy, focusing on small brokerage accounts, and the strategy ultimately paid off.[20] But other brokerages were ambivalent about waiting for small accounts to mushroom into bigger ones. A key question was whether a broker could make easier, faster, and bigger money elsewhere, such as by cultivating wealthier clients who opened regular brokerage accounts or by selling mutual funds. With regard to the latter option, mutual fund commissions were substantially higher than MIP's rates. Given these circumstances, many members' initial reluctance to aggressively market MIP was understandable. Anxious to get more retail member brokerage firms on board selling MIP, Exchange leaders decided to provide them with a helping hand. Just as they had worked on making MIP easy for customers to buy, NYSE executives now worked on making MIP easy for brokers to sell.

To encourage retail member brokerage firms to market MIP, the NYSE provided them with "merchandising kits," replete with sample brochures, which firms could reproduce to give to prospective clients.[21] Brochures such as "How to Invest on a Budget" explained MIP in easy-to-understand language.[22] Giving member brokers merchandising kits and other sales aides was a major departure from Exchange practices. In February 1954, Rud Lawrence told a gathering of Exchange governors, "As you know, we are feeling our way in this [marketing] area." He explained, "Traditionally, the Exchange has not been active in helping our members sell stocks. Obviously the Exchange should never attempt to tell the public what stocks to buy or when to buy them. That is the job of the Member Firms. However, we have a deep conviction that if our objective is actually to broaden the market we must work much more closely with our Member Firms on their sales problems."[23] Throughout MIP's life and the life of the greater OYS program of which MIP was a key part, the NYSE Board remained committed to teaching retail member brokerage firms how to market more effectively to Main Street. Simultaneously, they sought to educate the public about the fundamentals of finance as well as disseminate specific information about programs like MIP.

MIP Fundamentals

So how exactly did MIP work, and to what degree did it constitute an innovative program? MIP allowed an individual to invest a fixed sum in a stock on a periodic basis, but for this to be feasible, an investor needed to be able to buy fractional shares of stocks—something that the NYSE historically had not offered; the smallest amount of stock that anyone could purchase had been one share. However, in the early 1950s, the NYSE, working with member firms, including odd-lot dealers, devised a way to overcome this obstacle, thus opening the path for MIP's creation. Noting that as of January 1954, an investor could "buy a fractional share of stock . . . figured out to the fourth decimal point," Merrill Lynch's Lou Engel commented, "The [MIP] plan wasn't formulated, of course, for that reason—just to permit an investor to buy part of a share. It was designed to permit people to invest a set sum of money every month—or every quarter if they preferred—and to acquire for that money full or fractional shares of any stock listed on the New York Stock Exchange, except those sold in ten-share units."[24] As Engel pointed out, MIP allowed an investor to accumulate gradually "a worthwhile interest" in a company's stock, without having "to wait to become an investor until he had acquired several hundred dollars, enough to buy five or ten shares of some stock." He added, "MIP is a method of buying stock by the dollar's worth, regardless of how the price may change from month to month, just as you buy $2.00 or $3.00 worth of gasoline, regardless of what the per-gallon price is."[25]

In addition to surmounting the obstacle of fractional shares, the Exchange's Market Development Department addressed other issues to implement MIP, such as the type of contract buyers would need to open an account. How flexible should the contract be? On the one hand, a rigid contract, under which buyers had to make their periodic payments or else face stiff penalties for early withdrawal, would enable member brokerage firms to count on a certain amount of money routinely flowing into their MIP accounts. Yet the NYSE had pioneered MIP to appeal to the masses, and they feared that rigid contracts might prove intimidating to the very people the Exchange hoped to entice into the market. As a result, the Big Board decided to enact a flexible MIP contract. Merrill Lynch executives, writing about MIP, often used the word "contract" in quotes, suggesting that it was hardly a contract in the binding sense of the word. As Lou Engel explained, the "'contract' . . . is actually nothing more than a declaration of intent," adding, "Since M.I.P. contracts can be canceled by the buyer at any time and are so drawn that the buyer can skip payments without penalty, they are in no sense of the word binding or obligatory."[26]

When MIP debuted, the NYSE ultimately decided to call the agreement a "purchase order." In the first full sentence of the order form, the text begins "IT IS MY PRESENT INTENTION." The wording is revealing, suggesting that intentions can change. The NYSE understood that fact of life, and wanted to make sure prospective MIP purchasers also understood it. The form also stated, "I [the buyer] reserve the right to cancel this order at any time, without penalty or charge, by written notice to you."[27] MIP enrollees' ability to discontinue their scheduled payments for any reason, and at any time, without suffering a penalty differed from more strict insurance contracts. MIP's flexible nature more emulated bank savings accounts, which required neither periodic contributions nor any suggested deposit amounts (the exception being Christmas club accounts).[28] The MIP purchase order also gave an exit clause for the brokerage firm selling the plan. "You [the seller] also may cancel this order at any time by written notice to me [the buyer]."[29]

An investor who opened a MIP was loosely agreeing to buy at regular intervals a standard dollar amount of one particular stock, like American Telephone & Telegraph (AT&T). If the investor wished to purchase shares in another company, such as General Electric (GE), he or she needed to open another MIP account. In contrast to mutual funds, an MIP investor accrued the benefits of portfolio diversification only if he or she owned multiple accounts. The NYSE tried to deflect criticism by noting that many corporations offering MIPs (like General Electric) were well diversified, having a wide range of product offerings, but this was a weak defense.[30]

Since portfolio diversification, unfortunately, was not an embedded feature of MIP, the Exchange Board and retail member brokerage firms hailed MIP for other reasons. MIP helped Americans cultivate healthy habits of thrift and also enabled customers to take advantage of automatic "dividend re-investment." As dividends became due and payable to the MIP holder, the broker arranged to have the dividends automatically applied to the purchase of additional shares for the customer's account. That the client did not incur any commission fees for shares acquired through dividend reinvestment enhanced his or her potential return on the investment. Another major benefit of MIP was "dollar-cost averaging," the practice of consistently purchasing the same dollar amount of a particular stock on a systematic schedule, whether it be monthly, quarterly, etc. As MIP advocates emphasized, dollar-cost averaging reduces the risk of an investor buying a considerable amount of stock at a bad time, such as right before the stock's price falls. With dollar-cost averaging, an investor spreads over time his or her purchases of shares in a particular listed company. Since the dollar amount per period is fixed, the investor acquires more shares when the stock price is low, and buys fewer shares when the stock price has increased. Therefore, over time with dollar-cost averaging, the average cost per share declines. As Merrill Lynch's Lou Engel emphasized, regular, systematic purchases of stock, such as MIP provided, helped protect stock buyers.[31]

One downside to the dollar-cost averaging technique, however, was the somewhat significant commission fees involved with buying small shares of stock in frequent intervals (versus a large amount of stock at one time). At the time, the brokerage commission fee on transactions of one hundred dollars or less was 6% (as compared to 3.1% on transactions between two hundred and three hundred dollars, and 1.5% on transactions of $1,000 or more). Therefore, if an investor set aside $50 a month towards a MIP plan in GM, he was not actually buying $50 worth of shares in that company every month because the broker first deducted his standard commission. To help investors reduce their transaction costs, MIP promoters frequently advised potential investors to buy shares not on a monthly, but on a quarterly, basis.[32]

In a pamphlet about MIP intended for public consumption, the NYSE included a chart on commission amounts (see table 5.1).[33] Clearly, the NYSE was not hiding the requisite fees. At the same time, the NYSE did have a vested interest in being transparent about the commission schedule: educated investors who realized the relatively steep 6% commission associated with payments of $100 or less might be more inclined to periodically invest a greater sum in order to qualify for the reduced rates. But small investors did not typically have large amounts to invest. Member retail brokerage firms tended to

Table 5.1   NYSE commission rates, circa 1950s

Payment	Amount invested at odd-lot prices	Commission amount	Percentage
$40.00	$37.74	$2.26	6.0%
$60.00	$56.60	$3.40	6.0%
$80.00	$75.47	$4.53	6.0%
$100.00	$94.34	$5.66	6.0%
$200.00	$194.00	$6.00	3.1%
$300.00	$293.14	$6.86	2.3%
$500.00	$490.10	$9.90	2.0%
$1,000.00	$985.15	$14.85	1.5%

Source: How to Invest on a Budget (NYSE: 1967), 6, Publications Box, NYSE Archive.

justify the relatively high commission fees on the basis of the work involved maintaining these accounts. Summarizing the situation, Lou Engel said, "Buying stocks in small units is expensive—expensive for the broker and expensive for the customer."[34] When it debuted, therefore, MIP was an unusual stock purchase plan, one that offered several potential benefits to investors, such as dollar cost averaging and dividend reinvestment. But it was also a plan that was far from ideal for the very small investor, due to the relatively high transaction costs and the plan's inherent lack of diversification. Therefore, how would the public receive MIP?

MIP's Early Results

During the first six months of MIP's operation, NYSE officials constantly pointed to the progress being made, highlighting the number of customer accounts opened while at the same time candidly acknowledging that they wished brokerage firms would spend more time and energy marketing MIP. In late July 1954, *Barron's* reported that more than 19,000 MIP plans had been opened since the program began in January and suggested that this number indicated MIP's vitality. Arguably, however, an average of a little over 3,100 plans a month for six months was not particularly impressive, especially given that millions of Americans at the time owned no stock, and hence a potentially very large market existed for the product. Moreover, some individuals who enrolled in the program owned multiple MIP accounts, so 19,000 plans did not equate to 19,000 individual buyers. Nevertheless, *Barron's* seemed pleased by MIP's progress and noted that new accounts currently were being opened "at the rate of 100 to 150 a day."[35] Initially, the most popular listed securities among MIP investors were Radio Corporation, Dow Chemical, General Motors, AT&T, Standard Oil of New Jersey, General Electric, Tri-Continental, Long Island Lighting, U.S. Steel, International Nickel, DuPont, and Socony-Vacuum Oil.[36]

While many analyzed MIP's progress on the basis of enrollment statistics, Rud Lawrence focused on the bigger picture. In February 1954, Lawrence explained that MIP is "helping to change the public's thinking about stocks—who can buy them and how to buy them." He extolled MIP for "changing the traditional marketing patterns of our Member Firms." As Lawrence noted, some member firms, in promoting MIP, had been "experimenting already with new advertising techniques—cooperative newspaper advertising, radio, direct mail and television—with Saturday openings, with booths in public places, with investors' clubs." He concluded, "Some [member firms] are finding out what it means to come face to face with large numbers of the public and are organizing to sell and to service the small investor at a profit." Lawrence pronounced this to be a "healthy" development.[37] Lawrence also realized that promoting MIP might encourage some people to open regular brokerage accounts. What Lawrence and other MIP proponents did not seem to envision was the possibility that their work also unintentionally may have been helping to convert people to the benefits of mutual funds, as much of the small investor rhetoric surrounding Own Your Share and MIP could easily be applied to buying a mutual fund.

In April 1954, Lawrence told the American Institute of Accountants that they were all engaged in a "Fight for Democratic Capitalism" and needed to be propelled by the "conviction that Americans everywhere should OWN THEIR SHARE OF AMERICAN BUSINESS." Lawrence explained to them how the NYSE intended to "create millions of new investors," in part by applying "weapons and methods of modern merchandising." Lawrence pointed to MIP as a "good illustration of the application of modern merchandising techniques to our business." As Lawrence went on to explain, the "sale of defense bonds and insurance as well as automobiles and real estate has taught two basic principles of large scale merchandising: (1) Purchase must be easy and painless [and;] (2) Payments must be systematic." He added, "Moreover, in business with low margins cost of handling each unit must be low and therefore, if possible, mechanized." MIP, Lawrence asserted, satisfied these specifications.[38]

Mutual funds, of course, also were simple to join, and investors who routinely contributed to such funds also reaped the benefits of dollar cost averaging. Mutual funds and MIPs were competing products, but the NYSE adamantly denied this was the case. When Rud Lawrence served as a guest on the popular radio show *Let's Find Out* on WCBS, moderator Martin Weldome directly asked Lawrence, "Is this plan in any way . . . in competition with the Mutual Fund Plan?" Lawrence replied, "I would not say so. Of course, I suppose you might say that any plan that invites investment . . . competes with all kinds of other types of investments—but actually the MIP serves quite a different purpose. It permits an individual to invest in specific stocks—a specific stock, one stock for each plan; whereas, in Mutual Funds, of course, you buy a share in a portfolio, which includes many stocks that are managed."[39]

MIP possessed different strengths and weaknesses than mutual funds. While a MIP account was not a diversified investment, it did allow the holder to exercise shareholder rights at that company. Also, the NYSE believed that the problem of lack of diversification could be overcome if MIP holders opened multiple accounts in different stocks. In the 1950s, focusing on MIP's strengths, the NYSE latched onto the program as another promising way to broaden shareownership and reinvigorate the securities industry.

The Benson & Benson Survey

Seeking to merchandise MIP more effectively, the NYSE commissioned the Princeton consulting firm of Benson & Benson to conduct a series of interviews with two hundred MIP investors, chosen out of a pool of the first 3,000 MIP subscribers.[40] Unlike the Brookings study, the survey's design was not very scientific, nor did the consulting firm claim it to be. As the agency explained, while the interviewees were "not purported to be representative of the total population," they were thought to be "reasonably characteristic" of investors who opened monthly investment plans.[41] Conducting field interviews seven months into the program, Benson & Benson asked survey participants to explain what prompted them to enroll. Frequently, MIP investors responded with comments such as the program "makes me save," requires only a "small investment," and promotes "periodic savings."[42]

Trying to discern whether MIP buyers were predominantly first-time equity investors, the survey asked, "Did you already own stock at the time you first began buying through the MIP? Did you ever own stock?" According to the survey results, a majority (60%) already owned stock when they began MIP, 31% had never owned stock until then, and 9% had once owned stock.[43] Judging from this sample, MIP was not primarily appealing to Americans totally new to the stock market: roughly 70% already had had some experience owning equities.

OYS officials were interested in the extent to which people owned multiple MIP accounts, as this would give investors diversification. The survey inquired, "Are you buying more than one stock through different MIP orders? How many different stocks are you buying?" In response, eight out of ten interviewed said they were signed up for only one monthly investment plan. However, the NYSE took solace that this sample group had only been enrolled in MIP for seven months. The survey did find that "nearly half" of those interviewed were contemplating buying additional MIPs "in the near future."[44]

The NYSE also approvingly noted that 90% of those interviewed indicated that a "drop in stock prices would not make them inclined to give up MIP," even though they were not contractually obligated to continue buying shares. Only 5% said that they would not continue to invest in the plan; the remaining 5% said that they didn't know. Exchange officials interpreted the high willingness to continue investing in a downturn as evidence that retail member brokerage firms had well educated MIP purchasers on the benefits of dollar cost averaging. When asked why they would continue investing in the event of a market decline, the majority (61%) responded that they would do so in order to "get more shares at lower prices."[45]

Funston, Lawrence, and the Board of Governors hoped that MIP would serve as an entry point into the market for new investors, hopefully stimulating them to make additional forays into equity investing. To gauge whether this was happening, the survey asked MIP investors, "Since the time you became interested in the Monthly Investment Plan, have you considered buying, or have you bought any stock other than through MIP?" The response was somewhat less desirable than the NYSE had hoped: the majority (56%) indicated that they had not considered buying other stocks. Yet 29% said that they had bought other securities since becoming involved with MIP and 12% indicated that they had considered buying other stock. In discussing the survey results, Benson & Benson concluded, "MIP stimulates stock investment in general."[46] Exchange officials found encouraging interviewees' answer to a simple question: "Would you recommend MIP to other people or not?" An overwhelming percentage (95%) said they would recommend the plan to their friends. The Big Board hoped that word-of-mouth marketing by MIP customers would boost the number of individuals subscribing to these plans.[47]

In addition to interviewing two hundred MIP subscribers, Benson & Benson interviewed two hundred individuals who had not enrolled in the plan. The survey found that 74% of those who had heard of the plan but not participated in it nevertheless praised MIP as "a good idea." Most frequently, non-subscribers cited "other financial commitments" as the primary reason why they had not invested in MIP.[48] Reviewing the results of the Benson survey, the Exchange Board was optimistic that MIP, given time, would be successful. NYSE president Keith Funston looked upon this plan for small stockholders as his "special pride and joy."[49]

Celebrating MIP's Milestones Despite a Slow Takeoff

As MIP concluded its first year, the NYSE's *1954 Annual Report* did not hint at any problems with the plan's popularity, highlighting the positive reception accorded it by both investors and member brokerage firms. Photographs in the Annual Report featured happy MIP investors, often with their spouses and children. The NYSE endeavored to portray MIP as something like life insurance, embraced by responsible adults seeking more secure futures for themselves and their loved ones. One picture showed a husband and wife sitting down with an investment counselor to review MIP's key features. Another picture showcased Mr. and Mrs. William Reinhardt of Oakland, California— a purportedly average, middle-class American couple that just happened to open the 25,000th MIP plan. In subsequent years, the NYSE frequently would celebrate MIP milestones—such as the 50,000th MIP plan, the millionth plan, and so on—and would widely publicize these events as signs that MIP was working.[50]

Besides hailing MIP's growth among the masses, the NYSE's *1954 Annual Report* also claimed that member brokerage firms greeted "with enthusiasm" the Exchange's "pioneering effort" to help them market MIP. As evidence of this enthusiasm, the *Report* noted that, in 1954 alone, member firms "ordered at their expense a total of two million pieces of promotional material prepared by the Exchange."[51] Many retail brokerage firms, however, were not as active at selling MIP as some of the larger houses like Merrill Lynch. As well, MIP enrollment was proceeding at a slower pace than the NYSE had originally anticipated—a fact Funston admitted in an interview in late 1955. While

Lawrence initially blamed the slow start on retail brokers' lack of familiarity with MIP, it gradually became obvious that there were other reasons why the program was not more popular. Some retail brokers worried that the market had risen too high for investors to buy into such a plan, especially one, like MIP, that only built up shares in one stock. They contended that their customers would be better served by "buying into a mutual plan with its diversified holdings, instead of concentrating on a single company." (By the mid-1950s, popular participation in open-end mutual funds was surging.) Funston disagreed, arguing that dollar-cost averaging minimized MIP's risks. Funston also refuted the contention that a bull market was an inopportune time to start such a plan. He pointed out, "When we started the plan in 1954, industrial averages were at 290, and everyone said it was too high. Now [approximately a year later] the averages are at around 470." While Funston refrained from prognosticating as to the market's direction, he clearly (and correctly) believed that the market still had strong upward potential. Funston continued to work tirelessly to educate the public about MIP's advantages. As *Time* reported, Funston traversed the United States and Europe making speeches "to plug MIP and the Exchange."[52]

Big Board officials were growing more cognizant of the Exchange's role as a model for stock exchanges around the world, and they utilized MIP as "a symbol of the desire of [the securities] industry to serve the average investor."[53] While extremely aware of MIP's value as a symbol of their interest in small investors and democratic capitalism, they also wanted MIP to succeed in terms of actual participants. Exchange officials continued to encourage member firms to merchandise the MIP concept in creative and more aggressive ways, such as through the use of direct mail advertising.[54] At the conclusion of 1956, however, only 54,000 MIP plans were in effect. Since the plan had debuted, MIP investors had placed a total of just $49 million in the market, albeit spread over 1.2 million shares.[55] While these levels were relatively small, the NYSE nevertheless hailed them as progress.

In the autumn of 1956, the NYSE celebrated the millionth share of stock sold under MIP's auspices. In the NYSE's words, "a capitalist from Moscow" purchased the millionth share.[56] Actually, the capitalist who bought that share was an American, though she was working in Moscow. A disbursing officer at the United States Embassy in Moscow, Constance Stuck, had opened a MIP account with Merrill Lynch approximately a year after the program debuted. In September 1956, she had the good fortune of buying the millionth share of stock sold through MIP, and NYSE leaders, along with Merrill Lynch, did their best to maximize the story for public relations purposes. Merrill Lynch flew Stuck to New York where partner Winthrop ("Win") Smith Sr. along with NYSE President Funston welcomed her on the Stock Exchange floor and gave her a tour of the financial district. Win Smith explained to the press why his firm did not hesitate to fly Stuck to Wall Street. As he said, "She epitomizes everything that we and other member firms of the New York Stock Exchange hoped to accomplish when the monthly investment plan was launched two and a half years ago. We wanted to put investments within the reach of more and more people of moderate means, and we wanted to broaden the base of stock ownership."[57]

Besides tapping into the obvious publicity value inherent in the millionth share holder being a "capitalist from Moscow," the NYSE also hailed Constance Stuck as being a shining example of a successful MIP investor. When Stuck opened her first MIP account, she chose Dow Chemical, which just happened to be the best-performing MIP stock since the NYSE initiated the program in 1954. At the time (late January 1955) that she began her $40 periodic investments in that stock, Dow Chemical was selling at $47 3/4 a share. By the time she bought the heralded millionth MIP share, Dow Chemical had risen to $77 per share, which meant that Stuck had reaped an unrealized gain (after brokers' commissions but before taxes) of roughly 35% in less than two years. Constance Stuck also exemplified the NYSE's hope that an individual opening one MIP account gradually would open additional accounts as well. She recently had opened her second MIP account, this one in Safeway Stores (Charles Merrill's former employer) and that stock, too, had performed well since her initial purchase. Between Safeway Stores and Dow Chemical, Constance Stuck had been investing $100 per month in the stock market. When the *New York Times* reporter asked how she managed to routinely save that much to channel into the market, Stuck replied, "It's not too difficult to save money if you're stationed in Moscow. A foreign service officer there doesn't find too much to spend money on." She added that she put her savings "directly to work in American business," because she was confident that the American economy "was going to grow and prosper."[58]

For those who were also convinced that further economic expansion and a strengthening bull market were on the horizon, there were, of course, other ways besides MIP to invest in American enterprise—like directly buying stocks or buying mutual funds. MIP suffered from this competition for investors' dollars, even with some brokerage firms, like Merrill Lynch, heavily promoting the program and even as some listed companies began to offer MIPs to their employees.

Corporations Offering MIP to Employees

One of the first NYSE listed companies to embrace MIP for its employees was American Motors Corporation (AMC), established in May 1954 by a merger between Hudson Motor Company and Nash-Kelvinator. George W. Romney, chairman and CEO of AMC from 1954 to 1962 and an active Republican, became an ardent MIP champion. Not only did he make the program easily available to his own employees through automatic payroll deductions, Romney also worked with the Big Board to proselytize MIP's benefits to other corporate executives.[59]

Employee stock purchase plans (ESOPs), of course, were not new. During the early 1900s, such plans had begun to gain momentum. In the 1950s, as the market recovered, ESOPs began to attract renewed attention from employers and employees alike. As *Management Record* reported in 1959, the "vast majority" of these plans, typically were "designed to help employees acquire only the employing company's stock." However, as the article noted, "More recently, a few companies have departed from this conventional practice; they permit employees to invest their savings in any listed stock" through utilizing MIP. In 1957, AMC became one of the first companies to envision MIP's possibilities as an alternate type of stock acquisition plan that a company could offer to its employees.[60]

In a four-page pamphlet that the NYSE made widely available to listed companies and member brokerage firms, Romney explained why "A Motor-Maker Embraces MIP" and, implicitly, why other companies should do likewise.[61] He related how, upon the inception of AMC in 1954, many employees expressed a desire for an employee stock ownership program. While some executives might have been pleased with employee interest in the company's stock, Romney was initially perplexed, as he worried that an ESOP might pose "decided disadvantages" to his employees. The short-term prospect of dividend payouts on American Motors' stock was rather "bleak," as Romney realized that his company would need to make considerable capital expenditures to compete effectively against the Big Three (GM, Ford, and Chrysler). Besides the dividend situation, the company's stock price, Romney feared, might not appreciate as well as management hoped, precisely due to the same problem of intense competition in the automotive industry. During the course of the next decade, American Motors would carve out a profitable niche in the realm of small cars, such as its Rambler line. At the onset, however, it was not clear if the company would prosper. Given this uncertain environment, Romney wondered whether management should be encouraging employees to buy the stock and making it so easy for them to do so.

Romney also appreciated the counterargument—that if a company did not offer some sort of ESOP, it might have trouble sustaining employees' "morale and confidence." Since at least the 1920s, it had been accepted dogma in corporate America that employees who owned shares in the stock of the company where they worked were apt to be more loyal and dedicated to the enterprise. Romney, however, challenged this idea: "Whether or not an employe [sic] chooses to invest in his own company's securities is no valid criterion of his loyalty to management—nor of his worth to the business." "In fact," Romney continued, "a cogent case can be made for the employe [sic] who adheres to the sound economic principle of spreading the risk." Ideally, to protect themselves, investors should own stocks in multiple companies, not just their own company's stock.[62]

Romney was not the only corporate executive reevaluating management's traditional interest in getting employees invested only in their own company's stock. Charles Wilson, chief executive of rival General Motors (GM), had similar ideas and incorporated them into his company's revolutionary new pension plan. While many corporations wanted their private pension funds to be invested in their own company's stock, in no small part to heighten worker loyalty, some executives, like Romney and Wilson, saw the issue in a broader light, believing, just like the NYSE, that employees who owned stock in any company were invested in capitalism writ large. Besides desiring employees to be both loyal to the company and loyal to capitalism, they wanted workers, for their own sake, to be well-diversified.[63]

Like Wilson, Romney was sensitive to the fact that a company's stock could go down as well as up, and that therefore, it was risky for management to push workers toward putting most of their savings into predominantly one stock. Romney concluded, "to advise—or to refrain from advising—an employe [sic] on the purchase of company stock was a type of responsibility that no director, officer or responsible supervisor should assume." With these beliefs, Romney sought to find an employee investment program that was not tied exclusively to stock in American Motors Company, and that would place the full responsibility for investment choices on employees not managers. Romney turned to MIP, praising the idea that employees could open an account in any one (or more) of an array of 1,200 stocks. He noted that "the company's long-established payroll deduction service could be put at the disposal of employes [sic] who wanted to earmark a portion of their salaries on a systematic basis for investment purposes." Motivated by a self-professed desire to "help minimize the employe's [sic] chance of getting seriously hurt financially," Romney embraced MIP rather than a standard ESOP that only offered the company's own stock.[64]

The NYSE helped American Motors launch MIP and made available to Romney's employees a 16-page leaflet that explained in simple language "The Story of the Monthly Investment Plan." A representative from a NYSE member retail firm also came to the company's headquarters to answer questions from potentially interested employees. To participate, employees had to complete two forms—a MIP purchase order form and a payroll deduction authorization agreement.

Romney placed enormous faith in the power of MIP, and not just in its ability to increase participants' wealth. As Romney said, "It is my personal belief that MIP—applied on a company-wide basis—could prove a more effective way to further the economic education of industrial employes [sic] than any amount of 'free enterprise' literature made available on reading racks."[65] Romney continued, "First hand experience with risks and rewards involved in our profit-and-loss system is a useful form of adult education. The spreading of stock ownership as broadly as possible through our industrial society should heighten the public's appreciation of the function of profits—and perhaps in time help strengthen the bond between management and employes [sic]."[66]

After the NYSE widely disseminated to the Exchange community Romney's article, "A Motor Man Embraces MIP," both the NYSE and AMC received many inquiries from listed companies about the program. At least initially, however, few listed companies formally adopted MIP, in part because larger, well-established companies like AT&T and General Electric already had ESOPs in place. (Investors could purchase a MIP in a listed company through any NYSE member retail broker, but they could not purchase one directly from the listed company unless it had initiated a MIP program.) By late 1959, only nine companies had embraced MIP, and most of them had not done so in the way Romney had envisioned. Seven of the nine companies offered their employees only the opportunity to invest in one MIP—namely, their own, contrary to Romney's emphasis on portfolio diversification and employees' freedom to choose their own investments.[67]

By the mid-1960s, however, several more corporations had begun to offer MIPs. In part, this owed to retail brokerage firms' efforts in "pushing MIP as a means by which listed companies—and some unlisted ones too—could initiate employee stock purchase plans on a voluntary, payroll-deduction basis." As Merrill Lynch's Lou Engel reported, "Hundreds of companies have now joined forces with brokers to promote such plans, and tens of thousands of their employees are now becoming stockholders in their companies for the first time." While noting that company-sponsored stock purchase plans had a long history, Engel explained that "the M.I.P. angle is new and attractive to many managements because the broker carries the onus of selling the plan, and management feels less responsible for the price action of its stock." Likewise, Engel emphasized, "The plan is attractive to the employee because he acquires his stock commission-free; the company picks up the commission tab." Thus, as Engel noted, "the employee escapes payment of virtually all the odd-lot differential on the stock he acquires, since the company purchases the stock for all the employee accounts monthly in a single block and hence acquires virtually all the stock at the cheaper round-lot rate." This was a key difference between an individual participating in a MIP account on his own versus participating in a MIP account sponsored by his employer: MIP plans offered at places of employment were more economical for investors wary of large commission fees.[68]

According to Engel, "If it were not for these corporate stock purchase plans, the Monthly Investment Plan could not claim much of a record of success in the first dozen years of its existence."[69] A major problem was that the loose nature of the MIP contract made it easy for individuals to stop their monthly payments and opt out of the program. Indeed, in the first fifteen years of the program, investors closed more than 540,000 MIP accounts. Sometimes, individuals closed accounts because they no longer could afford to set aside a monthly amount to invest. However, others cancelled their MIPs because they preferred to invest in the market through other vehicles, such as their own brokerage accounts or, increasingly, through mutual funds. The future did not appear to be rosy for MIP, as mutual funds, not MIP, were the chief success story of the period. By the mid-1960s, mutual funds had 6.7 million

Table 5.2   MIP summary,
January 25, 1954–June 27, 1969

Plans	No.
Started	846,361
Terminated	532,904
In force	313,456
Shares purchased	15,241,513

Source: Monthly Investment Plan Quarterly Report,
July 1969, Research Department, MIP Folder, Box 22,
NYSE Archive.

active accounts at a time when only a little over 300,000 MIP accounts were
in effect (see table 5.2).[70]

Still, NYSE officials took heart in their belief that MIP promotions also indirectly helped to spread shareownership in many forms by educating the
American public about investing fundamentals like dollar-cost averaging and
criteria for stock selection. Fully aware that the government, regulators, and
the public all were closely watching their efforts to expand shareownership,
Exchange executives understood well that their ultimate goal was not just to
create a nation of investors, but a nation of sound investors. The OYS campaign thus prioritized education—both education about capitalism as well as
education focused on the practical aspects of equity investing.

CHAPTER SIX

Creating a Nation of "Sound" Investors

> In a quiet and utterly peaceful way, America's middle income millions have
> come to hold the real balance of economic power, and this silent revolu-
> tion has been accomplished without anybody's head falling into the
> basket. . . . The financial community and the New York Stock Exchange
> have played a major role in helping to bring all this about. Through a
> number of broad new educational programs launched in recent years, we
> have tried to bring much greater understanding to what had been—for too
> many people—a baffling and mysterious area—the world of investment.
> RUD LAWRENCE, REMARKS TO SETON HALL UNIVERSITY (1957)

During the Own Your Share years, the NYSE energetically endeavored to spread not just shareownership, but also economic education. In Exchange leaders' eyes, the two tasks—"democratizing" the stock market and financially educating the public—went hand-in-hand. Broadening the nation's shareowner base, Funston and his colleagues realized, would mean bringing into the market many individuals of modest means—and probably also of only modest education, including of finances. Presumably, novice investors would benefit from being taught some investing basics as, for example, how to read financial statements and how to minimize risk through portfolio diversification. The NYSE broadly construed "economic education" to also include the dissemination of material on the benefits of capitalism, the role of the Exchange as a bastion of capitalism as well as the critical functions of stock exchanges in general and their essential contributions to keeping countries (not just the United States) strong and free of communism. Big Board officials believed it was necessary to tutor investors and noninvestors alike on the importance of stock markets. If people appreciated stock exchanges' functions and the way in which equity investing promoted individual and national prosperity, those who were not currently shareholders might want to become equity investors.

To build the shareowner ranks, the Big Board wanted to improve popular perceptions of Wall Street. Since the early 1900s, Exchange leaders had believed that if they could get the public to understand how the securities markets worked, popular attitudes toward Wall Street would improve, and more people would want to invest in the market, and also to support the NYSE against additional external regulations. As NYSE president Seymour Cromwell said in 1923, "The Basis of Cooperation is Understanding."[1] Similarly, another NYSE president, Charles Gay, had averred in 1935, "There is no mystery about the Exchange. We want the public to know just how we handle the orders entrusted to us and discharge the responsibilities placed upon us. Such a campaign of education will necessitate patience on our part. . . . Thus the Exchange will regain the confidence of the public because it is entitled to it, because it deserves it."[2]

In the Own Your Share years, Exchange leaders' commitment to investor education also emanated from a desire to protect themselves from the charge of enticing unsophisticated shareowners into the market. Yet the architects of the OYS message seem to have been motivated not just by self-interest, but also a genuine, altruistic desire to help shareowners avoid common pitfalls and increase their chances of investing success. They also wanted shareowners to understand the personal and national importance of "owning a share of America." Funston, Lawrence, and the Exchange Board believed they had a profound responsibility to create not just a nation of investors, but also a nation of "sound" investors. They wanted this round of mass investing, unlike the 1920s, to be a success story for both the NYSE and the small investor, and they saw investor education as key.

In their work disseminating information about how stock markets truly worked, NYSE officials in the mid-twentieth century resurrected tactics that their predecessors had used, such as tours of the NYSE's Exhibit Hall and Visitors' Gallery, seminars and speeches, brochures and pamphlets, as well as educational films.[3] These tactics, however, had not been terribly effective in the past. Despite the sporadic efforts of the Exchange to dispel popular misconceptions about the stock market, erroneous ideas persisted in the early 1950s, such as the widespread notion that the NYSE controlled stock market prices and owned the stocks listed on the Exchange. In terms of basic investing knowledge, Americans at midcentury were woefully deficient. Few adults could define even rudimentary terms, like "common stock" or "stock market." According to a 1954 poll of 3,000 individuals conducted by the Politz Group, fewer than one in four adults surveyed could define the NYSE's purpose, which was to raise capital, provide liquidity, and create a "fair and orderly" marketplace. To the chagrin of Exchange executives, a common wrong answer was that the institution "set" stock prices. Equally disappointing was the fact that only one in four adults could define accurately the meaning of a share of common stock.[4]

The Big Board concluded that they needed to enlighten the public about the "virtues" of stock markets and the nuances of investing. They now were better positioned to do this, for by the 1950s, the NYSE was on a firmer financial footing than it had been during the dark Depression days; the organization, therefore, could afford to devote more time and money to an effective educational strategy. For the first time, the NYSE boasted a dedicated Investors' Information Department. The Exchange also was now open to utilizing institutional advertising. Every OYS advertisement was in a sense a piece of economic education, as these promotions taught viewers a range of investing lessons, like the wisdom of buying stock only after putting aside money for emergencies. In their mission to educate Americans on the stock market, the NYSE executive organization also collaborated to an unprecedented extent with member firms, such as Merrill Lynch. As well, the NYSE was able to "piggy-back" the economic education efforts of a host of organizations like the Committee for Economic Development (CED) and the Ad Council, who were working in a similar vein promoting free enterprise.[5] The NYSE also took cues from Merrill Lynch's success in the realm of economic education. So the NYSE's educational efforts during the Cold War years were more robust than ever. As NYSE president, Funston helped the cause of economic education. An educator at heart, he recognized from the beginning of his tenure the need for investor education. Throughout his long stint as Exchange president, Funston supported the Big Board sponsoring a wide range of educational measures.

Educational Films

Funston and his colleagues improved the quality and effectiveness of films as educational and promotional tools for the Exchange. In earlier decades, the Exchange's films tended to be dry, overly technical, and uninteresting. For instance, according to the *New York Times*, the NYSE's 1930 film "The Nation's Market Place" was "not notably successful" in enlightening the public.[6] Moreover, the films were not widely distributed, and hence they had a negligible impact on educating the public and stimulating equity investing. As the Great Depression deepened, the NYSE Board retrenched on many activities that they deemed discretionary, including film-making. In 1946, finally recognizing the need to replace "The Nation's Marketplace," the NYSE Board authorized "The March of Time," a newsreel series created in 1931 by Roy Edward Larsen at Time Inc., to develop a short film about the stock market. The new film was entitled "Money at Work." With wide play in movie theaters across the country, "Money at Work" was a step in the right direction, yet the script still did not bring the discussion about investing down to the level of personal experience.

Funston and the Board took cues in film content and advertising techniques from Merrill Lynch. In the 1950s, Merrill Lynch, with the assistance of its advertising manager Lou Engel, had hit upon a successful film formula. The firm's films featured prominent themes like "investigate before you invest" that echoed the same themes that Merrill Lynch was highlighting in its print advertisements. Merrill Lynch's films, like their advertisements, carried a light, conversational tone that had been conspicuously missing from the NYSE's heavily didactic films. Merrill Lynch's films sought to educate the public about the stock market, but their executives believed they could accomplish this in film without being boring and losing viewer interest.

Among Merrill Lynch's popular releases from this era was "Fair Exchange," a short film that debuted in April 1951. The *New York Times* praised the brokerage firm for making a simple but informative investing film geared toward ordinary people. The newspaper summarized the plot: "A husband comes home with a wonderful tip on Supersonic Dishwasher, Inc., and an urge to sink all the family savings in its stock. The wife disagrees, wanting to play [it] safe, but he dashes off for a Merrill Lynch office. She chases after him. Together they get a fair education in the advantages of investigating before investing."[7] In the first year and a half, more than 1.2 million viewed this movie—a high number at the time for a film about the stock market. The film aired in a wide variety of venues, such as Merrill Lynch offices, men's and women's clubs, industrial and business groups, corporations, community organizations, church groups, as well as high schools and colleges. Dedicated to market research, the brokerage firm not only kept assiduous records of viewing statistics but also periodically interviewed viewers to learn their reactions. A common comment was that "Fair Exchange" helped take "some of the mystery out of the stock market."[8]

Wishing to duplicate the success of "Fair Exchange," Merrill Lynch developed another short film, "How to Invest," and arranged a grand debut of the six-minute program at New York City's Armory on May 24, 1955. Billing it as the "Country's First 'How to Invest' Show," the *New York Times* reported on the day before the show began that "Rather amazingly, nothing will be sold. Charles E. Merrill, directing partner of Merrill Lynch, Pierce, Fenner & Beane, the New York Stock Exchange house that is sponsoring the event, has emphasized that the aim is education rather than quick returns." Admission was free, and while the six-minute film played continuously in the background, Merrill arranged for visitors to see a large exhibition glorifying American business. As the welcoming exhibit explained at the Armory entrance, "Since America began, our industrial system has depended for its driving force on one primary source of power—invested capital. And people have invested their capital in business because it promises to pay them a good return. This is a story of how that promise has been fulfilled and how you can share in the promise of tomorrow." To tell that story, Merrill Lynch enlisted the aid of prominent organizations—American Gas and Electric, General Foods, General Motors, IBM, New York Telephone Company, Manufacturing Chemists Association, and American Iron and Steel Institute. As the *New York Times* reported, "With mechanized dioramas, brilliantly lighted tableaus, action films and animated puppet displays, they will show how their industries have developed and the direction they seem to be taking for the future."[9]

NYSE executives wanted to make their own such films to take the mystery out of the market. In 1952, the Board discontinued showings of the NYSE's old "Money at Work," and replaced it with a new animated short film, "What Makes Us Tick," produced by John Sutherland. Sutherland had gained positive attention during World War II for his live-action training films for the U.S. military. After the war, he focused on documentaries and short industrial films for companies such as General Electric, DuPont, and U.S. Steel, garnering a reputation for effectively featuring companies "with subtlety and style."[10] With Sutherland's help, "What Makes Us Tick," like Merrill Lynch's "Fair Exchange" and "How to Invest," conveyed stock market operations to a mass audience in easy-to-understand language.

Later NYSE films such as "Working Dollars" (1957) also adhered to the formula established by Merrill Lynch, a formula that included a crucial ideological component, hailing the NYSE as an equitable marketplace and the bastion of capitalism. For example, the NYSE's "Working Dollars" did not just explain investing facts (including the new Monthly Investment Plan) but also highlighted the nation's stock exchanges as places where people were "free to invest" however they pleased: the film cast "freedom to invest" as a key American freedom, along with "freedom to work," "freedom to dream," "freedom to compete," and "freedom to advance."[11] The NYSE, thus, was putting forth its own version of the famous Four Freedoms, "essential human freedoms" set out by President Franklin D. Roosevelt in his annual message to Congress on January 6, 1941: freedom of speech and expression, freedom to worship, freedom from want, and freedom from fear.[12] Moved by President Roosevelt's speech, artist Norman Rockwell depicted these freedoms in four poignant paintings that the *Saturday Evening Post* featured in its magazine in successive issues, beginning on February 20, 1943. In order to sell more war bonds, the U.S. Treasury Department arranged to showcase these popular paintings on a nationwide tour entitled "The Four Freedoms War Bond Show" and the Office of War Information (OWI) disseminated approximately 2.5 million copies of the images.[13] When less than a decade later, the NYSE promoted "freedom to invest," along with three other freedoms, the idea of four freedoms, however defined, resonated with the American public.

Perceiving the emotional and educational value of *Working Dollars*, Merrill Lynch began showing this and other Exchange films, along with its own films, at many of the firm's branch offices. Merrill Lynch did not seem to resent the NYSE copying its film format, as the primary intention of such films was to help investors become better educated. Therefore, Merrill Lynch executives felt it did not matter who in the Exchange community was sponsoring the films, as long as they were effective.

A Formal Position for Education at the NYSE

In the early 1950s, it was not clear the extent to which the NYSE executive organization would dedicate resources to promotional activities and investor education initiatives.[14] Exchange officials came to realize that broadening the nation's shareowner base and increasing popular participation required educating a whole new class of investors. The NYSE Board viewed economic education as beneficial for the public, the nation, and the nation's securities markets.

Not long after Own Your Share commenced, NYSE President Funston recognized the need for a formal department for investor education. In an internal memorandum in October 1954, Funston requested that the Board of Governors authorize a new position of Education Director. Carefully articulating why such a position was necessary, Funston emphasized that "Lack of economic education in our schools and colleges presents a serious problem for both educators and the Exchange community." As he pointed out, "Most students—the voters and investors of tomorrow—have little opportunity to learn about common stocks and corporations, the profit system and the role of the investor."[15]

Funston continued, "many teachers welcome educational material about business and finance—especially if it fits into the curriculum and is suitably prepared for classroom use." To combat financial illiteracy, the NYSE needed, among other actions, to get material into educators' hands. Funston urged the Board of Governors "to undertake a long-range program to build understanding and wholesome attitudes toward investing." He outlined such an investor education program: "The program will make available to educators literature (including descriptive booklets, research studies, teaching guides and vocational guidance brochures), visual aids (including posters, charts, displays and films), tours and speakers. It will also bring educators and investment men together to work out mutual problems and encourage investment men to take a more active interest in their local schools and colleges. The program will also encourage students to consider opportunities for careers in our business." Funston recommended that the Board approve the addition to the public relations staff of "a man who can concentrate on these activities for schools and colleges."[16] Funston saw economic education as part of public relations, as did the Board, who authorized the position in that manner. In 1955, Dr. Allen Felix, who received his doctorate in education from Teachers College of Columbia University, became the NYSE's first Director of Education.[17] By the late 1950s, the NYSE had also organized an Investors Information Program, headed by William Kendrick. In preparing educational materials and activities, Kendrick worked closely with Dan Woodward (Director of Advertising and Promotion), John Brown (Director of Research and Statistics), and Charles MacCoy (Vice President of Public Relations). Kendrick, like Woodward, Brown, and MacCoy, all reported directly to Rud Lawrence, who in turn reported to Funston. By the late 1950s, therefore, a formal team was in place at the NYSE, committed to the task of educating current equity investors and potential investors. They all supported Funston's vision of a nation of shareowners and viewed their educational task as urgent and important.

The Committee for Economic Development (CED) also was dedicated to economic education. In a 1949 speech, W. Walter Williams, Chairman of CED, explained the organization's philosophy: "If education is the means which we must use to learn how to appreciate our own country, its problems, and the dangers and pitfalls which it faces—then by all means let us increase our education processes. Let us sharpen our educational tools. . . . Let us all learn as students—then let us teach what we learn with all our might. . . . This is not 'selling' America to Americans. It is teaching Americans the practical understanding of the problems they face as a people." He explained that he meant more than "the formal type of education."[18] In the opinion of Williams as well as NYSE leaders, school curricula needed to be adjusted to include material about stock markets and investing. Students also needed to learn first-hand about Wall Street by getting out of the classroom and seeing how Wall Street worked. The NYSE encouraged school classes to take field trips to the Exchange, and many member firms (particularly Merrill Lynch) welcomed visits from student groups. Exchange officials and many member firm representatives volunteered to go to local schools to bring the language of equity investing into the classroom.

School Trips and Lectures

The NYSE Board encouraged brokerage employees to give talks on investing at local schools (generally, junior high schools, high schools, and colleges, and occasionally grammar schools). Keith Funston and Rud Lawrence traveled to many schools to lecture on the stock market's importance to national prosperity and democratic capitalism. In November 1957, just a month after Russia's Sputnik satellite blasted into space, causing Americans to fear that they were losing in the space race, Lawrence gave an optimistic address about America's strengths to students and faculty at Seton Hall University in South Orange, New Jersey. Lawrence told the assembly, "Spread of shareownership in America brings about a silent revolution, and this people's capitalism is given impetus by the Stock Exchange." He continued, "The most dramatic feature of this free-enterprise system has not erupted in newspaper headlines. Nor has it been squeezed into the small talk of ordinary parlor conversation. It has, in fact, come about within the past few years quietly—and with large numbers of people failing to observe it. The phenomenon I'm talking about is the gradual emergence of what we have come to call a People's Capitalism— the ownership by millions of people everywhere, through their stock investments, of our means of production." Building on midcentury cultural notions of "progress," Lawrence concluded, "This development, evolutionary in its progress, is likely to prove revolutionary in its impact as well. It will provide this country with the means of reaching the goals and broadly distributing the profits of an industrial system that is restlessly moving upwards." Lawrence credited the NYSE's multipronged educational initiatives for engendering greater public understanding of the investing world.[19]

Exchange officials believed in not just teaching students about the stock market, but also educating schoolteachers. For instance, Keith Funston and Director of Education Dr. Allen Felix eagerly cooperated with Teachers College at Columbia University when, in 1958, it began offering a one-credit course, "Resources of the Financial World for Teachers," featuring field trips to financial centers in the New York area, such as the NYSE and the American Stock Exchange (AMEX), Merrill Lynch's Manhattan headquarters, odd-lot dealers De Coppet & Doresmus, the Stock Clearing Corporation, and the Federal Reserve Bank of New York. "Sandwiched between these trips," reported the *New York Times*, were "more talks and workshops conducted by officials of the New York Stock Exchange." Teachers who took the course praised it for giving them practical knowledge about equity investing as well as a deeper appreciation for the importance of the securities business to the country's well-being. As 23-year-old David Kendig explained, after only the second class, he had relinquished "some negative attitudes" he had entertained about Wall Street.[20] Anxious that educators be more knowledgeable about the stock market and hold more favorable opinions of Wall Street, in the 1950s, NYSE officials began holding workshops for teachers. Exchange executives brought teachers on private tours of the trading floor. At the same time, the Exchange (like the CED) strived to get educational materials for classroom use into teachers' hands, such as the Big Board's in-house publication the *Exchange Magazine*.[21]

The NYSE also liked the idea of teachers conducting mock or actual stock investing exercises in class, believing that such experiential learning would boost students' interest in equities and encourage them later in life to get involved in the market. In some high school economics classes, students, supervised by teachers, pooled their money and bought a few shares of a stock, the performance of which they then tracked for the remainder of the semester. In some instances, even grammar school classes engaged in similar exercises. When a class of sixth-graders in Hamden, Connecticut, wanted to buy stock as part of a class exercise, the schoolteacher contacted three brokerage firms to come to class and make a recommendation for a stock. As the *New York Times* reported, two of the firms "demurred on the ground that the children were too young to understand finance, but a presentation was made by the third company." The firm that agreed to come into the school was Merrill Lynch, and the representative who came recommended that the class purchase a local company listed on the NYSE, Scovill Manufacturing. With each student contributing two dollars, the class of forty-four was able to purchase two shares of Scovill. The students watched their investment for the remainder of the school year and even attended the corporation's annual shareholder meeting.[22] While the Hamden sixth-graders monitored their fledgling investments, NYSE executives were in turn watching over these experiments in economic education, initiatives that received media coverage. Rud Lawrence fastidiously kept a clippings folder of such reports, and tried to get other schools to emulate these exercises.

Investment Clubs

Also committed to fostering investor education among adults, OYS officials looked favorably on grassroots investment clubs as opportunities for neighbors to be teaching neighbors about the market as they invested together. These clubs, which had to register with the National Association of Investment Clubs (NAIC), typically met weekly or monthly to discuss existing and potential investments. Each individual made a set monthly contribution, and owned a certain percentage of the portfolio. The group voted on the merits of the stocks under consideration and decided how to invest the pooled funds. For novice investors who were not sure how to analyze a financial statement or perhaps were intimidated about visiting a broker, investment clubs were an easy introduction to the market and also a way to achieve portfolio diversification. Sophisticated investors also participated in these clubs, often additionally investing on their own. While the famous Beardstown Ladies Investment Club drew attention to investment clubs in the 1980s, in fact, it was during the 1950s that such groups first began to proliferate.[23] Exchange officials hoped that these organizations might help invigorate trading, but investment clubs never became heavy transactors.

The NYSE came to view investment clubs' primary importance to be "a new educational tool for people's capitalism," in Rud Lawrence's words.[24] The NYSE also hoped that the clubs, by teaching people about the market, would help bring more people into the shareownership fold. Noting in 1956 that approximately "100,000 people are group-investing every month" (which Lawrence construed to be a large number), Lawrence observed, "They have, quite literally, come from almost everywhere. No single organization or individual has promoted them. Instead, they have spread largely by word-of-mouth, feeding on the increased interest in periodic investing, especially for retirement, and on that strong social flavor of their makeup. And in a way, that social base is part of their charm. Almost all these clubs have something in common beyond a desire to learn about investing—jobs, neighborhoods, clubs, something. Any sampling illustrates a fundamental togetherness."[25] NYSE officials and member firm representatives often visited investment clubs to give lectures. The Big Board created pamphlets on investment clubs for member firms, explaining the movement and how they could tap into the trend.

While supporting the investment club trend, NYSE executives strove to prevent potential abuses. They warned investors to form clubs "only among friends," not to allow officers of the clubs to receive any compensation, and to limit the amount of monthly contributions to the clubs, the last point illustrating the NYSE's desire to have mass investing unfold in a restrained manner. Far from encouraging small investors to put large sums into the market, OYS architects wanted club members not to be pressured to invest more than they could afford. This pressure likely would have backfired, reinforcing the bad images from the Depression years of the NYSE as insensitive to the fate of the small investor. Lawrence explained, "We believe that the amount of the monthly contribution in any club should have some reasonable limits. The limit would naturally depend on circumstances of the membership." Lawrence added, "Until now few of these considerations [officers' compensation, too high monthly contributions, etc.] have come to our attention as problems. Yet the great challenge for our community is always to look ahead."[26]

In the 1950s, the NYSE also established Investors Information Committees in more than one hundred cities scattered across the country. These committees, composed of representatives of Exchange member firms, coordinated adult education courses for schools, libraries, and other organizations, and often delivered guest lectures in these courses. By 1963, the Investors Information Committees were delivering thousands of lectures a year, which together reached approximately one million Americans annually.[27] It was a grassroots strategy. As Funston and Lawrence well understood, even if NYSE executives spent all their time delivering informational lectures on the stock market, they could not make a dent reaching the vast number of Americans needing a primer on the market. Tapping into brokers' extensive branch networks through Investors Information Committees, however, was a possible solution. Merrill Lynch alone had a plethora of branch offices in numerous cities and towns, large and small, across the country. NYSE executives, therefore, asked representatives of these offices to volunteer to deliver investing lectures. Thousands of brokers responded to the call. OYS officials were more than willing to give these brokers a helping hand, providing them with sample lectures as well as speaking points. Broker representatives, however, always retained the freedom to craft the content of their talks. The lectures were typically free, although some groups, like local YMCA's, sometimes charged nominal amounts.

By the 1960s, the educational workshops, which by now the Exchange referred to as "investment seminars," were attracting considerable attention and patronage. As *New York Times* reporter Robert Cole advised his readers, an investment seminar was a "simple way to learn how [the] stock market works." Explaining that it was "not too difficult" to enroll in a how-to-invest class, Cole noted, "Courses are offered in dozens of cities and are promoted widely. You can probably find one in your area through your broker, adult evening school, public library or local 'Y.' You might also find one on the job—many of the big corporations arrange them—or through your civic, fraternal, or service clubs." He added, "Good courses also are available in a wide variety of other places: military bases, resort hotels, department stores and even ships at sea."[28] Investment seminars ranged in level of difficulty, with some aimed at beginner investors, others at more advanced investors, and still others at "the semipros and pros." Cole explained, "In some cases, as in Merrill Lynch's, the broker sponsors the seminar. In others, a local group may arrange it and call on the New York Stock Exchange to supply speakers." The NYSE, noted Cole, "stands ready to provide volunteer speakers to organizations within 65 miles of New York City. Outside that area it works through committees in 100 cities across the country."[29] Cole urged his readers to take action. "Dozens of courses are under way right now, probably in your area, and this is as good a time as any to learn about investing. If you don't have the time during the summer, dozens of courses will be starting in the fall. Now would be a good time to investigate the subject."[30]

Investing Pamphlets and Books

Investors could also "investigate the subject" by reading investing manuals on their own, rather than taking a class or seminar. For many years, high-ranking NYSE officials had written books explaining how the stock market functioned, such as *The Work of Wall Street* (Sereno Pratt, 1903), *The New York Stock Exchange* (Edmund Stedman, 1905), *The Stock Exchange from Within* (William Van Antwerp, 1913), and *The Stock Exchange* (Henry Noble, 1933).[31] Many of these books sought to combat rumors about Wall Street and put forth the NYSE's story about how the stock market really worked. Yet most of these books were not accessible to the layman. The NYSE needed to disseminate books and pamphlets that the public would want to read and would be able to understand.

Merrill Lynch, as was often the case, provided the template. In 1948, the firm published an easy-to-read investing booklet, "How to Invest," and made it available to their clients free of charge. The *New York Times* highly recommended the booklet, saying that it "strips away much of the mystery that surrounds investments in the minds of many Americans but it makes no effort to paint investments as a sure road to riches." The *Times* also praised the booklet's brevity, promising readers that it would only take two hours to digest, time well spent.[32]

The success of the "How to Invest" booklet encouraged Merrill Lynch advertising manager Louis Engel to embark on a full-length book about the stock market, directed at a mass audience. In 1953, Engel's book debuted, simply entitled *How to Buy Stocks*. Readers could buy a copy of the 252-page book for only $2.95, and it quickly became a bestseller.[33] Burton Crane, the *New York Times* reporter who a few years later would write the classic, *The Sophisticated Investor* (1959), favorably reviewed Engel's book. Crane heralded its simplicity and clarity: "At last there is a book—a two-plus-two-makes-four kind of book—for incipient investors. . . . It is written in such straightforward non-technical language that even a moron could understand it. Parents with normally-bright six-year-old children could give it to them with no fear except that they might grow up to be investment buyers."[34] Engel proffered advice on subjects such as how to digest financial news, how to open a brokerage account, and whether to buy on margin. He explained complex topics like investment banking in clear, simple prose. Engel used the device of a hypothetical company (Rod and Reel Company) as an example to illustrate his points. Crane applauded the way in which Engel "in the simplest of language, gets down to the material that usually fills books on investing."[35]

Noting Engel's success, the NYSE's Investor Information Department quickly developed dozens of investing pamphlets. One of their most popular was "Investment Facts about Common Stocks and Cash Dividends," which highlighted the average dividend return on equities listed on the NYSE in the prior eight years.[36] In the early 1960s, the NYSE and member firms gave away an estimated 8.5 million educational pamphlets, many of them donated to schools.[37]

In October 1960, the NYSE arranged to have a special educational advertisement placed in the *Reader's Digest*, which, at the time, reached an estimated 12 million American homes and offices. This special advertisement was a full 16-page insert, a pullout investment guide aimed at a mass audience. Entitled "How to Invest for Growing Income and Family Security," the guide delved into a range of entry-level information about the stock market. Some subject headings included, "Just What Are Stock and Bonds?," "What Investing Can Mean to You," "Rules for Wise Investors," "How to Choose Your Broker," and "How to Read Newspaper Stock Tables." As Funston explained in the introduction, "The purpose of this guide is to try to answer your questions about investing and to point out some of the reasons why millions of Americans own securities today." He insisted, "Investments in stocks and bonds give added vitality to our economy, for it is only by plowing some of our savings and earnings back into business that we can help make possible more growth, more production, more jobs." Funston recognized, though, that "Not all of us, of course, are in the position to invest, nor should invest, for there is risk whenever money is put to work." Yet he urged people "to read this guide to investing and keep it for future reference," asserting that "Every American has a responsibility—to himself, his family and his country—to know how our free enterprise system works and how to share in it more directly if he so desires."[38] The NYSE was pleased with the public's favorable reaction to the

Digest insert, and many readers contacted the Big Board with requests for reprints.

With new and improved stock market films and pamphlets, a stronger network of Exchange speakers, and various other educational initiatives, the NYSE made progress in the Own Your Share years toward spreading an ideology of shareownership, as well as imparting practical information about the investing process. The precise effects of these educational activities are impossible to quantify, but the NYSE, together with member firms and other allies, had made inroads in the late 1950s and 1960s in terms of ameliorating the large-scale ignorance about the stock market that the Politz poll had revealed in 1954.

While Funston and his colleagues focused on educating investors and potential investors of all ages, shareownership continued to spread, especially dramatically among the nation's youth. For a time in the 1960s, minors became the fastest-growing segment of the shareowner base. The rise of young shareowners was no accident, for the NYSE had targeted certain groups, especially children. They also, for a time, had targeted women. The 1952 Brookings Report was always Funston's benchmark for measuring later improvement in shareownership among the population as a whole as well as gains in specific groups. Brookings had established that the number of women shareholders (not shareholdings) had been roughly equal to the number of men. As the NYSE worked to expand the country's shareownership ranks, the leaders of OYS tried to increase women's participation in the stock market, particularly as they realized the rising number of women in the paid workforce. As for children in the market in 1952, the Brookings Report had determined that very few of the existing shareowners were children, teenagers, or young adults. Out of 6.5 million Americans in the market, less than 200,000 minors (under the age of twenty-one) owned stock. OYS sought to change that statistic. Increasing shareownership by minors was challenging, given legal obstacles, yet the Exchange proved quite successful.[39]

Making Children Shareowners

It is not surprising that so few minors were in the stock market in the early 1950s. The problem was that even if a parent or relative had been interested in giving a child stock, doing so was tricky for both the gift-giver and for the retail broker. As Merrill Lynch's Lou Engel described it, opening an account for a child "always presented a thorny problem." He elaborated, "In the absence of state legislation specifically authorizing such gifts to children, brokers incurred a measurable risk in selling stock that was registered in the name of a minor; a minor is not legally responsible for his acts, and if brokerage transactions were carried out in the name of a minor, he could, on coming of age, repudiate them, and the broker would have no redress."[40] Stock transactions made for a minor might not always turn out favorably. If a stock increased in value, the minor, of course, would be pleased, but if a stock soured, he might be tempted to try to disassociate himself from responsibility for the original transaction conducted on his behalf. Brokers feared such a scenario and worried that they would be held accountable.

While some states allowed a gift of stock to be registered in a minor's name, ownership of the stock was typically frozen until the minor reached 21 years of age. As Philip Keuper, an employee of the NYSE's Department of Public Information, recalled, "This meant that even a parent couldn't sell a declining stock to save the child financial loss and reinvest the proceeds in some other security unless a legal guardian was . . . appointed."[41] As reporter Elizabeth Fowler lamented, gifting stocks was a "complicated business" not just for brokers, but also for parents and other prospective gift-givers.[42] Parents or relatives wishing to open a brokerage account for a child could do so, but in most states, the process was expensive, time-consuming, and arduous. A formal trust fund needed to be established, along with a court order that officially designated the parents as trustees legally empowered to buy or sell stock for their children.[43]

Early in the OYS years, the NYSE began lobbying legislators to make it easier for adults to gift stock to children, forming in 1954 a National Committee dedicated to that task. In 1955, eight states enacted Securities Gifts to Minor legislation (Connecticut, New Jersey, Ohio, Wisconsin, Colorado, California, Georgia, and North Carolina), followed by three states early in 1956 (New York, South Carolina, and Virginia). While pleased that these eleven states had acted, the NYSE realized the importance of getting the legislation passed in all states. Though a tedious process, by 1961, all states had enacted a so-called Model Law "permitting an adult, acting as a custodian without court appointment, to handle investment for a child."[44] By the mid-1960s, 48 states and the District of Columbia had put into effect a Uniform Gifts to Minors Act (UGMA), which expanded the former Model Law "to permit gifts of money as well as securities and a larger choice of custodians."[45]

Under the new law, as a NYSE official explained, "the security is registered in the name of the adult, or the giver, as custodian for the child." The wording on the stock certificate might read, "John Smith, as custodian for Mary Jones, under the New York Uniform Gifts to Minor Act." By the late 1960s, in almost every state, a custodian now possessed the authority "to act for the child in the management of the securities—to sell them, reinvest the proceeds in other securities, collect dividends, and generally manage the investment until the minor is 21."[46] No longer did a custodian have to powerlessly preside over a frozen account until the child came of age.

Giving stocks to minors also created tax benefits. According to an Internal Revenue Service ruling, securities gifts to minors qualified for the annual gift tax exemption, which at the time was $3,000. As the NYSE was quick to note, "This means that up to $3,000 in stock ($6,000 for a married couple) can be given under the new statute each year to a child without incurring a gift tax. It also means that income from gift securities is taxable to the child, so that no income tax will be payable up to the child's $600 exemption."[47]

While many states were still in the process of adopting the UGMA, in 1962, the NYSE made a concerted push into the children's market with their "Gifts to Minors" program.[48] By the mid-1960s, children shareowners had become the fastest-growing age segment within the shareowning population. By 1965, the number of minors owning stock had risen to approximately 1.3 million from 450,000 in 1962, and 192,000 in 1948. Given that the total number of shareowners in the United States was approximately 20 million individuals, 1.3 million child shareowners represented approximately 6.5% of the shareholder nation.[49]

In the late 1960s, the NYSE sought to penetrate the children's market even farther. Tax incentives built into the legislation governing securities gifts facilitated their marketing efforts. Other factors, such as rising disposable income, helped make stock gifts to minors attractive. As NYSE official Philip Keuper emphasized, "In the ten years from 1956 to 1966, families with incomes of $10,000 or more increased by almost 300 percent—disposable income by more than 60 percent." Keuper also credited a boon in "stock splits" by large listed companies as being a factor in encouraging stock gifts to minors.[50]

In a stock split, a company decides to divide its existing shares into more shares.[51] The impetus for a stock split often stems from the perception by management that the stock price has risen to a point that it impedes the ability and willingness of investors, particularly small investors, to buy it in round lots. For instance, taking commission fees out of the picture, an investor who wanted to buy 100 shares of a stock valued at $50 would need $5,000. But if the stock splits "2-for-1," the investor who wants to buy 100 shares would only need $2,500. The total dollar value of the shares has not changed in a stock split, although many investors view a split as a sign that the company is doing well. The Exchange's Market Development Department looked favorably on stock splits, and encouraged companies to engage in them. The Big Board thought stock splits fostered broader shareownership in two ways: first, it made the share price more accessible to investors who wished to save on commissions by buying in round lots; second, and generally less appreciated, a stock split could prompt parents and other adults to gift children with some of the split shares on such special occasions as birthdays.

For adults to gift children with shares required a broad awareness of the Uniform Gifts to Minors Act, and Exchange officials needed to disseminate information about the new legislation. The Department of Public Information sent press releases and other correspondence to the Associated Press and other reporters, detailing the nuances of the statute. Also, the NYSE's Market Development Department carefully tracked which reporters were covering the gifts to minors story, and they meticulously saved clippings of articles that appeared in local and national newspapers.

Like virtually all the reporters who described UGMA, *New York Times* reporter Elizabeth Fowler did so in glowing terms and noted that the NYSE "deserves much credit for making it possible to make securities gifts to children both easy and rewarding." Fowler also contended that gifting a minor with stock could be an effective way to help pay for college tuition. "How in the world will I ever be able to put Johnny through four years of college?" Fowler rhetorically asked. She elaborated, "Many parents of modest means are probably asking themselves this question as recent reports show that college tuition has soared to the $1,500 a year mark or more at leading schools. With on-campus living expenses going up at a comparable rate, the financial outlay for four years could easily run to $12,000—at today's prices." But Fowler told her readers not to fear: "Actually, there is a relatively painless solution to what appears to be an overwhelming problem. It consists of making a gift of securities to a minor, something which has only become practicable in recent years." Fowler explained that the original gift, plus additional shares of stock gifted at other junctions, combined with the reinvestment of dividends, over time would result in a "tidy nest egg ready and available to send Johnny on the way to ivy halls." Fowler emphasized that "The proceeds of course, can be used for any purpose, not only to finance a college education."[52] Yet the image of being able to pay for college through stock gifts must have been powerful for many American parents. The NYSE's OYS campaign advertisements in the 1960s also used the theme of Johnny in college, with his tuition being taken care of by prudent long-term stock investments. Under the new law, a minor did not have to come of age (21) before becoming eligible to receive a direct benefit from stock gifted to him. As most students started college at age 18, age 21 would have been too late to receive a financial boost from stocks toward all four years of higher education. Consequently, the legislation allowed the custodian for the minor to "pay over to the minor or expend for its benefit any or all of the custodian property he deems advisable, for the support, maintenance, and education of the minor."[53]

Gifting securities to anyone (a minor or an adult) also could be an effective tax strategy, a way to "reduce normal income taxes, since it shifts some income away from the donor," as Fowler noted. Of course, this would be particularly helpful to donors in a high tax bracket. As Exchange officials as well as reporters carefully explained to potential gift-givers, the minor would have to pay tax on any income from a gift, but the minor would be taxed at a lower rate. This did not preclude parents who gave their child (or children) gifts of securities from taking the standard exemption for each child— $600 in the mid-1960s.[54]

The Big Board worked hard to explain the many facets of the legislation and neutralize concerns. In the 1960 *Reader's Digest* insert "How to Invest for Growing Income and Family Security," the NYSE included a section on "A Growing Gift for a Growing Child."[55] The Market Development Department also created educational kits for member retail brokerage firms to help them promote Gifts to Minors to prospective customers. The kits included various brochures to encourage parents and relatives to give children "securities . . . the gift that can grow as they grow." Legislation had, in fact, made it easier for people to gift anyone with stock, regardless of their age. Hence, the NYSE plugged the idea of stocks being a great gift for other groups, such as college graduates and newlyweds. Many Exchange brochures depicted various groups (not just children) receiving "the gift they'll never forget." But the NYSE particularly favored promoting stock gifts to minors, especially babies. According to the NYSE's logic, the earlier one became initiated into the world of share-owning, the better. Young shareholders, they assumed, hopefully would be lifelong, loyal equity investors.

The OYS campaign also designed radio commercials promoting securities gift-giving. In the autumn of 1965, the NYSE distributed this sample master commercial to member firms: "When your child or grandchild—or your favorite niece or nephew—has a birthday, one present you might not have thought of is a share of stock. Strange idea? (YOUR FIRM NAME), members of the New York Stock Exchange, doesn't think so. For today, there are more than one million young people under 21 who own shares in public corporations." The commercial emphasized, "Birthday, Christmas, graduation—they're all fine times to give stock to minors under your gifts to minors statute. The value of the stock may grow as the child grows. . . . And, of course, it's a wonderful way to help teach children about our free enterprise system and the uses of money."[56] The commercial did not state that the value of the stock also could decline, in which case gifts to minors could be a very bad idea. But the NYSE, so worried in the early postwar period about the market's direction, had begun to believe more ardently that common stocks, indeed, were the best long-term investment.

Promotional pamphlets prepared for the Gifts to Minors program tended to be less guarded in prognostications about the market than in the OYS advertisements targeted to a mass market. For instance, in a pamphlet, the NYSE optimistically noted, "American industry as a whole has been expanding. And there is every reason to believe it will continue to grow over the years—to develop new products, new industries, new markets and expand all along the growing edge of our economy." As the pamphlet pointed out, a gift of stock that appreciated in value could be used to help "pave the way for their college education and the realization of their life goals." The same pamphlet emphasized, "By giving your children their share in American industry now, you are making them partners in the future." In fact, the pamphlet was entitled, "How To Make Young People PARTNERS IN PROGRESS . . . with a Gift of Securities."[57] To foster more young "partners in progress," the Exchange also engaged in various publicity measures, for instance, inviting children to the Stock Exchange floor to be photographed holding their shares.

Funston, Lawrence, and the rest of the Own Your Share team took pride in the fact that more than a million minors owned stock by 1965,[58] although the rising bull market also created a favorable environment for people of all ages to join the market. However, the NYSE's role cannot be underestimated, as Big Board officials worked hard to facilitate the passage of Uniform Gifts to Minors legislation and then to market it.

Marketing Shareownership to Women

The Exchange's Market Development Department worked diligently to expand the number of women in the market. With regard to both women and minors, the Big Board seemed not as interested in the level of shareholdings as they were consumed with the number of shareowners. This focus on the number emanated in large part from the NYSE's emphasis on democratic capitalism, as the Exchange viewed rising numbers of shareowners as evidence of more people sharing in the fruits of capitalism (although obviously, larger shareowners shared more in those fruits).

While minors constituted only a small portion of the shareowner base prior to the inception of the OYS campaign, women, by contrast, were already in the stock market in considerable numbers. When President Funston commissioned the Brookings Report, NYSE officials were surprised to find that women stockholders in 1952 comprised almost 50% of adult stockowners in the United States (3.14 million women compared to 3.21 million men). While the NYSE had overestimated the total number of shareholders in the country at midcentury, they had underestimated the relative proportion of women.[59] Exchange officials reasoned that many women must have inherited stock from husbands who predeceased them. This explanation makes some sense, given that women indeed were likely to live longer than men—an estimated 5.5 years longer at the time.[60] But some of the woman stockholders had bought stock with their own earnings.[61] However, women on average did not have as many excess funds to invest in financial instruments as did men. Many women still did not work outside the home, and those who did have paid jobs generally earned substantially less than men.[62] It took only one share of stock to make a person a shareowner, however, and hence to appear on the Brookings list. A minimal amount of stock owned or infrequent trading may help explain women's low visibility in the market at midcentury.[63] Also, some of the women whose names were registered on stock certificates may have been shareowners in name only, as husbands sometimes put stock in their wives' names for tax or estate planning reasons.[64]

Many of the 3.14 million women investors in 1952 were not frequent trad-ers. But most male shareowners, though on average more active investors than women, also tended to follow a conservative buy-and-hold strategy. As the *Magazine of Wall Street* noted, the Brookings Report showed that the "great majority" of shareowners (male and female) "hold their securities on a per-manent or semi-permanent basis. This means that they are not as much inter-ested in active trading as in the accumulation of savings in investments of one kind or another."[65] Stock turnover statistics confirm this; in 1952, turnover was only 13%, in contrast to more than 100% at the height of the bull market in 1929.[66]

Reacting to Brookings' statistics on total shareownership, NYSE officials perceived an urgent need to expand the country's shareownership base. Yet the NYSE hierarchy initially displayed no strong interest in explicitly target-ing women to become shareowners, although they did recognize the value of courting women to bring their husbands into the market.

At the start of the Own Your Share campaign in 1954, the verdict was still very much out on Wall Street as to whether women, acting on their own, could be good rational investors. A marketing message that expressly invited women into the investing fold was considered risky. Although the Big Board hailed the Brookings findings about female shareownership, they merely were confirming an existing trend and not yet asking more women to join the market.

The NYSE's Market Development Program chose a safe route. Rather than making direct appeals to women to buy stock, they targeted married women for their power to influence their husbands. OYS advertisements frequently featured husbands and wives talking together about stocks, with wives explic-itly looking to their seemingly more knowledgeable spouses to make invest-ing decisions. Funston, Lawrence, and NYSE staff worked with a series of advertising agencies to develop campaigns that portrayed equity investing as a family-oriented activity—something that a responsible husband and wife discussed together in the interests of fostering their long-term financial health. Playing upon husbands' desires to be adequate providers, Exchange advertise-ments repeatedly featured the stock character of the supportive housewife, who admired her husband for his investing savvy.[67]

Other advertisements sought to portray conversations about investing as part of couples' daily household discussions, hoping to detangle stock invest-ing from its negative connotation as gambling. Investing, as portrayed in these advertisements, was not something that was done on the sly, behind a spouse's back. Investing, as the NYSE also hoped to convey, was not akin to betting on the horses: rather than being considering something that jeopardized the family welfare, investing purportedly protected the family's financial well-being. The title of a 1957 OYS insert in *Reader's Digest* magazine captured the message: responsible investing resulted in "Family Security." In the accompanying illustration, a husband in the living room pores over the newspaper's stock tables, while his children play in the background. His wife also appears interested in the market, as she holds an edge of his newspaper.[68]

OYS depicted equity investing as a key part of not just family life, but also the American way of life. Investing, as these advertisements conveyed, was a pivotal way families could grow their assets, thereby enabling them to finance worthwhile purchases, such as their children's college education or medical and dental bills. Moreover, advertisements emphasized that equity investing also advanced national security.[69] By buying a share in a company, an investor was supporting American free enterprise. OYS promotions thus tapped into the surge in patriotism that accompanied the intensification of the Cold War.[70] NYSE officials, though, were careful not to stress patriotism too heavily, as they wanted people to buy stocks for sound rather than purely emotional reasons.

As the Own Your Share campaign progressed, the number of shareowners in the country rose significantly. From 6.5 million equity investors in 1952 (4.2% of the population), the nation's shareowner base increased to 17 million investors (9.4% of the population) by 1962.[71] The NYSE's promotional campaign was one of many factors at work making shareownership attractive to Americans. Other developments included innovations in financial products like mutual funds, an expansion in independent advertising by member firms (like Merrill Lynch and Bache), the growth of investment clubs across the nation spurred by the National Association of Investment Clubs (NAIC), and corporations' rising propensity to engage in stock splits. Perhaps more than any factor, though, the rising bull market that began in 1953 enticed new investors to Wall Street. But with this overall growth in the number of new investors, were women in the 1950s and 1960s maintaining their proportional presence in the market? The answer is unequivocally yes. By 1962, women constituted 50.98% of all adult shareowners, a slight rise from 49.45% a decade earlier.[72]

Merrill Lynch Advertisements Target
Women in the Early 1950s

Merrill Lynch deserves credit for helping to expand the nation's share-owner ranks—male and female—in the 1950s and 1960s. While both the NYSE and member firm Merrill Lynch engaged in mass marketing in the early 1950s, Merrill Lynch took the lead in marketing to women. Beginning in the 1950s, Merrill Lynch ran a series of "ladies-only" investment lectures, the first set of which, given in 1950, ran in sixty-two cities before an audience of more than 30,000 women. Merrill Lynch also cultivated relationships with reporters, including several working at women's magazines like *Good House-keeping*, and encouraged them to persuade their readers to consider buying stock. To some extent, such marketing efforts on the part of Merrill contrib-uted to the Brookings' finding in 1952 that 25% of shareowners had joined the market in the prior three years.[73]

In 1952, prior to the Exchange's OYS campaign, Merrill Lynch debuted several advertisements that courted women. In a Merrill Lynch advertisement that ran in the *New York Times* in June 1952, a trim, neatly dressed middle-aged woman in a skirt and blazer proudly proclaimed, "I'm Shopping for Stocks!" The caption asked, "Sound strange? Well it's true. You do shop for stocks, very much the way you shop for a dress, or a hat or shoes. When you choose a new ensemble, you select very carefully, because the color, the fab-ric, the style of each item must complement the rest of the outfit. So, too, when you start an investment program, you select your purchases carefully to get the results you want." The advertisement continued to invoke the shop-ping analogy: "You weigh the advantages of one stock over the other just as you would with a coat or dress. 'What use will I get from it? How will it go with the rest of my investments? And why is this company's stock a better risk than another'—are all questions to ask when you go shopping for stocks." The advertisement concluded, "if you'd like to feel a bit more at home on your 'first trip to market'—just ask for our 4-page pamphlet called 'What Every-body Ought To Know about this Stock and Bond Business.' It won't cost you a thing. Simply address a letter or postcard to Mrs. Marion Nobbe, Dept. 1A, Merrill Lynch, Pierce, Fenner & Beane."[74] Notably, the advertisement directed interested women to contact a female Merrill Lynch account representative. Merrill Lynch, like other retail brokers at the time, often assumed that women customers would be more comfortable reaching out to women brokers, an assumption that was not always correct. Merrill Lynch, nonetheless, was trying to make the "woman customer" not feel intimidated by the world of investing.

Another Merrill Lynch advertisement, also featured in the *New York Times* in June 1952, depicted a young, fashionable woman who bore a striking resemblance to actress Audrey Hepburn. Wearing a black ensemble and sporting a thick strand of pearls, the woman appeared wealthy and sophisticated. Entitled "This Little Piggy Went to Market," the advertisement described a "smart little girl" who owned a piggy bank and then "grew up and put her nest egg where it would do the most for her." This woman understood that "extra money, wisely invested, could earn dividends. Dividends which made possible delightful little extravagances she hadn't dreamed she could afford." Wisely, she "went straight to a brokerage firm that's made a career of helping new investors. A specially trained account executive carefully discussed her particular problems . . . how much it was advisable for her to invest . . . the safest and best ways to do it. So, it didn't take her long to learn there's really nothing hard or complicated about investing." The advertisement ended, "her story could be yours—because the size of your account doesn't matter at Merrill Lynch. If you could use a little extra income . . . and what woman couldn't? . . . why not discuss it with us? Or, if you prefer, simply write a letter outlining your situation to Mrs. Marion Nobbe, Dept. 4A."[75]

Another advertisement, "Mama's Little Dividend," from the same campaign, read, "Yes, Mama's very happy she heard about Merrill Lynch. Now she *invests* her money intelligently . . . 'earns' 5 percent to 6 percent on her extra savings." As in other Merrill Lynch women's advertisements from this period, copywriters tried to convey the message that the woman who bought stock was sexy, sophisticated, and intelligent. Copywriters also emphasized that Merrill Lynch was a friendly place, where brokers would not mind answering the questions and dealing with the concerns of not terribly experienced investors. As the "Little Dividend" advertisement contended, it was natural that this woman should have selected "Merrill Lynch, Pierce, Fenner & Beane to 'do business' with . . . because that's a brokerage firm that does all it can to help investors—regardless of how much they can buy or sell. Her own account executive is never too busy to discuss her problems . . . gives her facts and information on particular stocks . . . carefully explains anything that she feels she should ask about. And he's never made her feel that her small account was just a 'nuisance,' either!"[76]

Targeting Women Investors in the Later Stage of the Own Your Share Campaign

In the early 1950s, while Merrill Lynch experimented with targeting the so-called woman market, the NYSE hesitated. Not until 1962 did they initiate their "Special Women's Campaign" under the auspices of Own Your Share. With this campaign, the NYSE moved from targeting women as influencers to targeting women as investors. Whereas the young modern housewife dominated advertisements in the Own Your Share campaign in its formative years, a different kind of woman—a career woman, more sophisticated and more independent—featured in advertisements from the 1962 OYS Special Campaign. The NYSE recognized that the growing legions of women in the workplace constituted a large and relatively untapped market for the securities industry.

Several beliefs and misconceptions inhibited most NYSE member brokerage firms from marketing to women: (1) women would lose their money and hurt themselves if they invested; (2) women would destabilize the market and spread panic, thereby hurting others as well as themselves; (3) courting women would somehow lessen a broker's prestige and respectability; and (4) women would not make lucrative customers. By the 1960s, however, with women's increased presence in the workforce, these arguments seemed less valid. Gender biases were diminishing. But Wall Street still questioned women's capacity as investors. However, NYSE executives and member firms did have rising faith in their own capacity to be competent financial educators: both women and men could be taught how to be good, responsible investors. Big Board officials also reasoned that the more people who joined the shareholder ranks, the less likely the market would be impacted by the panicky actions of a few unstable small investors. Therefore, with the significant rise in the number of investors, more emphasis on financial education, and a renewed belief in the common stock theory of investment, it seemed less risky to court average Americans of both sexes.

In the fall of 1962, the NYSE released several advertisements designed to appeal to career women. Campaign advertisements tended to flatter women's savvy, and in the process, reinforce gender stereotypes. For example, like the Merrill Lynch advertisements from a decade earlier, several Own Your Share promotions geared to women repeatedly conflated investing with the shopping experience, in the hopes that shopping would resonate with the female target audience. A "smart shopper [is] like a good investor," stated one NYSE advertisement: "The smart shopper never listens to fast 'sales talk.' She examines the merchandise, compares values, then buys what she needs and can afford. The good investor does the same." Similarly, a NYSE advertisement entitled "Who Said Investing Is a Man's World?" promised that "Investing can add an interesting new light to a woman's life, married or single, providing you use a woman's good sense to start out right."[77]

It is difficult to gauge women's reactions to these promotions, as the Exchange did not perform intensive market research on these advertisements as they had for other campaigns. Perhaps this was because the campaign was designed as a short-term marketing endeavor (the Special Women's Campaign ran for less than a year). The brevity of this appeal to women reflected not so much a lack of commitment to the female market, but the extent to which Own Your Share was losing support by the 1960s. Many members of the NYSE had come to feel that the program was a waste of money, as retail brokerage firms already had sufficient business. While Funston and Lawrence claimed that OYS promoted "democratic capitalism" and hence always would be valuable, others disagreed. In fact, some began to argue that OYS not only wasted the Exchange's financial resources, but also endangered the well-being of the securities industry, as it contributed to too rapid growth given the industry's worn infrastructure. As tumultuous events on Wall Street in the late 1960s soon would suggest, the OYS marketing campaign may indeed have outgrown its usefulness.

The Formal Demise of Own Your Share

From the very start of his tenure as NYSE President in 1951, Keith Funston always had been one of the strongest Exchange proponents of broadening shareownership. When he first assumed office, Funston resolutely stated, "I'll try to be a salesman of shares in America," and, as *Time* magazine later reflected, he "did splendidly as the No. 1 drummer of U.S. everyman's capitalism." In the fall of 1966, Funston surprised the Exchange community when he announced his intentions not to run for reelection when his term expired.

Explaining his decision, the 55-year-old Funston simply stated, "I think I deserve a rest." Funston's tenure had already been the longest in the Big Board's history, and Funston was considered to have done an exemplary job as NYSE president. *Time* magazine noted, "Throughout almost all the long postwar bull market, Funston has been the symbol and champion of the New York Stock Exchange's Corinthian-columned citadel, a man who helped change its image from that of a clubby, tricky place to that of a respectable and generally profitable market for everyman."[78]

Seven months after Funston's announcement, the NYSE's 33-person Board of Governors finally chose Robert W. Haack as their new president.[79] Haack, who received his bachelor's degree at Hope College in Michigan and his master of business administration at Harvard Business School, had more than a decade of experience on Wall Street. Since 1964, he had served as the president of the National Association of Security Dealers (NASD), a self-regulatory organization charged with the operation and regulation of over-the-counter markets.[80] In evaluating Haack's candidacy, the NYSE Board liked that he had been able to work harmoniously with the SEC, while not acquiescing to the agency's demands.[81] Haack assumed the Exchange presidency during a chaotic period, and would serve only one term.

Haack quickly had to contend with a major problem: although since 1954 the NYSE had promoted broader shareownership, ironically, many member firms were not prepared to handle the paperwork generated when millions of investors, both retail and institutional, began more active trading. As one of Haack's successors later recalled, "problems of prosperity" plagued brokerage firms by the late 1960s: brokers suddenly "found themselves wading knee-deep in a rising flood of paper—orders, confirmations, bills [invoices], stock certificates, transfer instructions, all the paraphernalia of ways of doing business that had been overtaken by the times."[82] The problem resided not with the Exchange trading floor, but with many member firms that had not yet automated their operations. Indeed, the apparatus for handling stock transactions was much the same as it had been in the early 1900s; no central clearing house for securities yet existed. The Board had not pressed member firms to modernize their clearing operations, recognizing that many houses could ill afford to update their operations. Consequently, when trading volume in the late 1960s spiked, brokerage firms' "back offices"—where ancillary and support services occurred—were overwhelmed.[83] In the ensuing "paperwork crisis," stock certificates were lost, misplaced, and stolen.

In response to the crisis, the Board of Governors decided to temporarily shorten the NYSE's trading hours to give member retail brokerage firms a chance to organize their records. Haack announced, "Firms with serious [back office] problems may be asked take steps to limit the growth of business or to reduce business."[84] The Own Your Share program was a victim, in part, of the difficulties in handling heightened trading volume. As Haack and a majority of the Board agreed, it hardly seemed wise to encourage more investors to open brokerage accounts at a time when stockbrokers could not reliably process existing orders. Some member firms, like Merrill Lynch and E. F. Hutton, disagreed, arguing that it was important for the NYSE to continue to promote the virtues of shareownership to the American public. According to their thinking, the value of advertising was cumulative, and the NYSE should not interrupt its Own Your Share message.

Rud Lawrence, still vice president of Public Relations and Investor Services, anticipated the demise of his beloved OYS program. Effective April 30, 1968, Lawrence resigned, so that, in his words, Haack could "have a free hand in public relations programs and policies." While Lawrence publicly described his resignation as "a friendly parting," Haack and Lawrence clearly had different ideas about where the Exchange's priorities should reside.[85] Haack was more focused on cost-cutting and automating the Big Board, whereas Lawrence remained wedded to courting the small investor. Noting Lawrence's pending departure from the NYSE, the *Wall Street Journal* wrote, "Mr. Lawrence presided over the exchange's public relations operations when the Big Board, under G. Keith Funston, Mr. Haack's predecessor, vigorously fostered the concept of broader shareownership by the American public." The *Wall Street Journal* lauded the "public relations landmarks" achieved during the Funston-Lawrence era. The report noted, among other accomplishments, the addition of 17.5 million individuals into the shareowning ranks during the prior fifteen years, the creation of a vibrant speakers' bureau with a roster of more than four thousand lecturers, and the nurturing of investment clubs. Yet the OYS campaign had also challenged Wall Street, and the *Wall Street Journal* noted, "Ironically, the exchange staff's energies nowadays are increasingly directed toward solving the problems of bigness . . . [including] the inability of many member firms to efficiently handle high trading volume."[86] Indeed, within the very success of OYS lay the seeds of its demise. Busy contending with "problems of bigness," the NYSE Board of Governors terminated the program. The "Help Wanted: New Shareowners" sign that Funston meta-phorically had put up in 1954 finally had been taken down.

A few years later, in 1976, the Board finally ended MIP, its flagship program to broaden shareownership. As the *Wall Street Journal* announced, "It's RIP for MIP." Sounding the "death knell" of the Monthly Investment Plan, the *Journal* noted, "Though the plan has been little used recently by investors, its end comes at a time when the Exchange is bewailing the shrinkage in the number of individual stockholders in the U.S."[87]

While shareownership had surged in the Own Your Share years, in the early 1970s, the situation had changed. As the stock market suffered a slide in 1970 and then a major bear market in beginning in 1973, many Americans branched out of stocks and into bonds, certificates of deposit (CDs), and other financial instruments.[88]

Institutional stock holdings and trading volume continued to gain major inroads over respective individual levels.[89] Whereas individual retail investors in 1961 accounted for 61% of the dollar trading volume on the NYSE, in 1974, they represented less than 30% of the trading volume. The *New York Times* emphasized, "As trading by individual investors has slowed, trading by huge financial institutions—bank trust departments, insurance companies, pension funds, mutual funds, foundations and the like—has increased dra-matically."[90] Newspapers and magazines across the country featured the per-ceived declining role of the "little guy" on Wall Street. Among the various headlines were pronouncements of the "disappearance" of the small investor, "the case of the vanishing investor," and the "death" of the small investor.[91]

Contrary to these reports, small investors were not abandoning the stock market. It was more of a migration than a withdrawal, and often a migration within the stock market from direct (retail) to indirect (institutional) invest-ing. The picture painted by the press looked worse than it was, in large part because both the media and the NYSE used too loosely the terms "small in-vestor" and "individual investors." By "individual investors," the NYSE really meant "individual retail" investors, not all investors (direct and indirect).[92] It would be more accurate to state that many Americans in the 1970s were broadening their horizons by shifting their preferred vehicle for investing. Many were investing their money outside the stock market, as bonds became glamorous and popular. Furthermore, more small investors were becoming involved in the market through institutions such as pension funds and mutual funds. The Own Your Share campaign can claim a good chunk of the credit for this development as well; at a time when mutual funds could not really advertise, MIP promotions inadvertently had helped promote mutual funds.

The impetus for the Board's decision to discontinue its sponsorship of MIP in 1976 was the announcement by Carlisle DeCoppet & Company, Wall Street's largest odd-lot dealer, that it was withdrawing from the business of specializing in small orders. Carlisle DeCoppet's departure from the odd-lot business dealt a major blow to MIP, because so many member firms (roughly two hundred) had used that dealer to administer their plans, as most other odd-lot dealers had already exited the business, finding it not sufficiently profitable.[93]

One of MIP's weaknesses, at least from the viewpoint of many Exchange members, had been the ease with which buyers could cancel their agreements. But the purchase contract also had included an exit clause to the brokerage firm selling the plan,[94] and this enabled retail brokers to quickly end their relationships with MIP buyers in 1976. As the *Wall Street Journal* reported that March, "plan members across the country began receiving computer-printed letters signed only by the Monthly Investment Plan, telling them the program is over." Investors were duly "informed that they will receive certificates for all full shares, plus cash for fractional shares and any dividends due them."[95] The abrupt manner in which the NYSE notified participants of the program's termination may have added to the public's rising perception that the Big Board now was more interested in institutional investors than small retail investors.

The international scene likewise was changing. In the 1970s, a period of "détente," or "friendly understanding" came to characterize relations between the communist world and the United States. In 1972, President Richard Nixon made an historic visit to China and met with the chairman of the Communist Party Mao Zedong. Shortly thereafter, Nixon and Soviet general secretary Leonid J. Brezhnev engaged in a highly productive superpower summit, marked by the signing of the landmark Anti-Ballistic Missile (ABMS) Treaty and the SALT Accord Interim Agreement on Strategic Offensive Arms. Détente, however, lasted just a short time. Not until 1991 did the Cold War end, with the dissolution of the Soviet Union, symbolized by the fall of the Berlin Wall two years earlier.

With the easing of Cold War tensions in the 1970s, the NYSE no longer emphasized the theme of the Exchange as a bastion against communism, nor

returns promised by the common stock theory of investment, long-term investors supposedly could beat inflation. However, Richard Cohn, a finance professor at the University of Illinois, noted in 1979 that "People no longer think of stocks as an inflation hedge, and based on experience [over the course of the past decade], that's a reasonable conclusion for them to have reached." Similarly, Alan Coleman, dean of Southern Methodist University's business school, observed, "We have entered a new financial age. The old rules no longer apply." Small investors seemed to be retreating en masse from the stock market.[100]

Some Big Board leaders, however, correctly appraised the situation. As NYSE President James Needham said, "It's much too early to write the individual investor's obituary." He later added, "To paraphrase Mark Twain's famous cable to the Associated Press, the demise of the individual investor has been greatly exaggerated."[101] Of course, Needham was right: public participation in the stock market tends to be cyclical, rising and falling with bull and bear markets. The activity of individual retail investors eventually accelerated again, along with institutional equity investing, the latter at a higher rate. Some of the factors stimulating expansion of shareownership were events of the 1970s whose effects were not fully felt until later decades: the passage of the Employment Retirement Income Security Act (ERISA) in 1974; commission rate deregulation in 1975, along with the development of the first index fund the same year; and the creation of 401(k) plans in 1978. Also, money market funds emerged in the 1980s and a prolonged bull market began in 1982.

The Long Bull Market

From August 1982 to March 2000, with only minor interruptions (such as in 1987), the stock market experienced a prolonged ascent. From August 12, 1982, to January 14, 2000, the Dow rose a spectacular 1,408% from 776 to 11,722.98.[102] It was a mutually reinforcing trend; the heightened interest and involvement in the stock market helped fuel the bull market. Americans during the 1980s and the 1990s became even more tied to the vicissitudes of the stock market. Not only did institutional investing continue to make inroads among the public, but also individual direct investing grew, particularly as online investing transformed the brokerage landscape. In 1994, E*trade became the first brokerage firm to offer a website dedicated to online trading. Suddenly, for those who had a computer with an Internet connection (ap-

did the Exchange prioritize the notion of "democratizing" the stock market. Although the objective of the Big Board's advertising still involved the idea of the NYSE serving a patriotic purpose, "the interest of the country" was no longer wrapped up in broadening the shareowner ranks to include many more small investors. In the wake of Own Your Share, Robert Haack and the Board of Governors approved a new plan for advertising and public relations, the aim of which was "to build public confidence in the leadership, integrity and skill of the Exchange and its members in operating this complex marketplace in the interest of the country."[96]

The new advertising plan stipulated that the NYSE would "concentrate [its] advertising on a new target—the upper income, well-educated investor and non-investor." The old OYS plan had never entirely neglected the affluent as a target market, but the program had been mainly directed toward the "Middle Majority." The new plan, therefore, represented a change in direction. The campaign's new slogan did not invite the public to join the market. Instead of "Own Your Share of American Business," the tag-line was "High Standards in the Public Interest."[97] D. H. Woodward, an advertising executive at the NYSE, recalled that advertising in the early post-OYS years aimed to "keep the confidence" of the investing public.[98]

As the 1970s drew to a close, the prospects of a vibrant, expanding pool of individual shareowners in the future seemed bleak to some professional observers. The cover of *Business Week* in 1979 wrongly predicted "The Death of Equities." Noting that more than seven million investors had left the stock market since 1970, the article contended that "this 'death of equity' can no longer be seen as something a [future] stock market rally—however strong— will check. It has persisted for more than 10 years through market rallies, business cycles, recession, recoveries, and booms." While not mentioning the Own Your Share campaign by name, the article referred back to it, noting, "The public was first drawn to equities in big numbers in the 1950s by a massive promotion campaign by Wall Street that worked because the economic climate was right: fairly steady growth with little inflation. To bring equities back to life now, secular inflation would have to be wrung out of the economy, and then accounting policies would have to be made more realistic and tax laws rewritten. But these steps may not be enough."[99]

Time and again in the OYS years, promoters of stocks and mutual funds had invoked the specter of inflation as a reason to participate in the market, not to avoid it. By being in the market and earning the purportedly superior

proximately one-quarter of U.S. households in 1999), purchasing stocks had become easy and convenient, not to mention cheap. E*trade challenged the industry by offering flat commissions of $14.95 on stock trades, regardless of size. To put that price in perspective, at Schwab, known for its low rates, the average commission at the time was $65.[103] Schwab quickly reacted by lowering its prices and also establishing online trading, as did other competitors such as Ameritrade and TD Waterhouse. By 1999, approximately 12 million households had online accounts from which they made a total of more than a half-million trades a day.[104]

In the late 1990s, Internet and technology-related stocks like eBay, Yahoo, and Amazon riveted investors' attention as these stocks began to soar, even though many of the new corporations had yet to show profits. While the NYSE conducted no Exchange-wide advertising program to boost shareownership like it did in the 1950s, individual retail brokerage firms aggressively mass marketed, encouraging the public to get a piece of the action.[105] In contrast with the heavy focus on investor education during the Own Your Share years, broker advertisements during this dot.com bubble period often oversimplified equity investing, sometimes making it seem almost a surefire route to instant wealth. In a 1999 television advertisement sponsored by the Discover Brokerage unit of Morgan Stanley Dean Witter, an average-looking guy named Al seems to be making a living driving a tow truck, but then it becomes clear that Al actually is just keeping his day job for fun. He already has made a fortune in the stock market—so much so that he has purchased his own tropical island—actually a "country," clarifies Al in the commercial. Disturbed by the commercial's message, the SEC faulted Discover Brokerage for making exaggerated claims about stock returns in their advertising. Discover Brokerage President Thomas O'Connell defensively contended that viewers understood that it was meant to be humorous, and that fictional Al's lucrative trading results were not typical of what most investors could expect.[106] While regulatory authorities tried to clamp down on potentially misleading brokerage firm advertising, particularly after the Discover Brokerage commercial, many brokerage firms, facing intense competition, continued to push the boundary of acceptable advertising practices.[107]

With stocks high, commission rates low, and trades easy to execute on a computer and without an intermediary, investors in the late 1990s began to increase the frequency of their trading, hoping to capitalize on rapid stock price fluctuations. Just as large institutional investors were now heavily turning over the stocks in the portfolios they managed, many small investors, too, were less inclined to "buy-and-hold" for the long term. The average holding period of stock sharply declined. Whereas in the 1950s, many individual investors bought stock intending to own it for decades, or perhaps even a lifetime, in the 1990s, according to former Labor Secretary Robert Reich, the typical investor held a stock for an average of approximately two years. The trend accelerated over the next decade, declining to just six months by 2004.[108] Since the 1990s, also, day trading by both amateurs and professionals has grown in popularity.

In October 1999, *Fortune* reporter Andy Serwer announced, "For better or worse (and for richer or for poorer), the US is fast becoming a nation of stock traders." Serwer further noted, "And while it is easy to get caught up in all the hoopla over deranged day traders and zany Internet IPOs, the real story runs much deeper than that. Power that for generations lay with a few thousand white males on a small island in New York City is now being seized by Everyman and Everywoman. In fact, it is no overstatement to suggest that this movement from Wall Street to Main Street is one of the most significant socioeconomic trends of the past few decades."[109] Similarly, another *Fortune* reporter, Joe Nocera, commented, also in 1999, "It is probably not too much to say that small investors have been the critical factors during this latest phase of the great 1990s bull market. Their 401(k) plans have supplied steady infusions of new capital. Their refusal to panic has steadied the market in rocky times. . . . But something else has been going on too." Nocera went on, "Slowly but inexorably, investing has become an integral part of everyday life in middle-class America. . . . Half the population, it sometimes seems, is in an investment club. There is a level of awareness—and a level of sophistication—about the market that is simply unprecedented. It has become part of the popular culture."[110] In the first decade of the twenty-first century, equity investing would remain part of the popular culture, though those participating in the stock market would endure a more challenging ride than so many had experienced during the exhilarating, long bull market of the late twentieth century.

Own Your Share in Retrospect

> Well, at the risk of dwelling too much on broadening the market, which by the way I think was one of the great ideas of our time—of course we have since gone to the moon—but in those days I thought that broadening the market perhaps would be one way by which our generation would be distinguished.
>
> RUD LAWRENCE, 1984 ORAL HISTORY

The Own Your Share campaign had a lasting impact on shaping the contours of this shareowner nation. During the Funston-Lawrence era, the Exchange promoted direct investing in the stock market. Yet the Big Board's campaign helped inculcate among the public a much broader message—that it was wise for average middle-class Americans to understand how to invest in financial instruments so they could take charge of their economic well-being. Just as Americans who were barraged with Liberty bond messages in World War I became comfortable with the concept of investing and later flocked into the stock market, people who were exposed to the NYSE's "buy stock" message eventually expanded into other investing vehicles. Benefitting from the economic education initiatives of the NYSE and other organizations, children in the OYS years grew up to be investors in the 1980s and 1990s who were willing to take advantage of opportunities to invest, often via new financial products. In the forty-odd years since the NYSE's Own Your Share promotional campaign concluded, the investing landscape has been completely transformed. Those seeking their slice of the American dream and looking to delve into the capital markets have a dizzying array of choices, and the list is long: not just equities (stocks) but also equity derivatives, simple ones like puts and calls or more complex ones like DECs, LEAPs, and the like; bonds, including Treasuries, Agencies, and Munis as well as Corporate; also commodities, whether they be agricultural products, precious metals, or industrial raw materials; not to mention real investment trusts (REITs), exchange-traded funds (ETFs), stock index futures, etc.[1] Today, many people involved in the market often invest through mutual funds and pension plans, that in turn look to these more esoteric and sophisticated products to further enhance returns while hopefully diversifying the risk.

Yet despite efforts to tame risk, the first decade of the twenty-first century proved to be a volatile one in the stock market. The decade began with the collapse of the Internet stock bubble. Between March 11, 2000, and October 9, 2002, the technology-laden Nasdaq Composite declined from 5,046.86 to 1,114.11. The terrorist attacks on September 11, 2001, profoundly shook the Dow, as well as investor confidence. According to a 2002 Gallup poll, two out of three Americans (68%) contended that buying stocks was more of a gamble than a true investment. Somewhat surprisingly, 63% of stockowners also felt this way. The poll also asked if respondents felt that the stock market favors the rich: 78% said yes, and 76% of stockowners also agreed. Certainly, the market's decline in the 2000–2002 period negatively affected the public's attitudes, although the poll actually was conducted immediately after the third biggest one-day gain of the Dow in history.[2] Nevertheless, the American public still largely espoused the belief that common stocks were the best long-term investment. And, despite often not following the practice, 63% of stockowners surveyed by Gallup revealed that they still believed that "buy-and-hold" was the smartest stock investment strategy.[3]

In 2004, President George W. Bush campaigned for a second term on the vision of an "ownership society" that was strongly reminiscent of the "Own Your Share of American Business" theme propounded by the NYSE during the height of the Cold War. Bush's "ownership society" drew upon the centuries-old concept of popular proprietorship. As President Bush phrased it, "If you own something, you have a vital stake in the future of our country. The more ownership there is in America, the more vitality there is in America, and the more people have a vital stake in the future of this country."[4] Besides advocating affordable healthcare and having homeownership within the reach of most Americans, Bush envisioned citizens having more options for managing their own retirement. He proposed privatizing Social Security, allowing a portion of each employee's payroll taxes to be placed in a personal account, which could be invested in stocks and bonds, if the employee so chose. While Bush's Social Security privatization plan encountered strong opposition and was never implemented,[5] the proposal illustrates the extent to which average Americans' welfare was becoming more and more intertwined with the gyrations of the stock market.

In 2006 and 2007, the stock market, fueled by solid earnings reports and other positive news, climbed upward. By October 9th, 2007, the Dow Jones Industrial Average had reached a new record level: 14,164.53. But problems in the economy would soon send the Dow spiraling downward. Indeed, in 2008 and 2009, the United States and global stock markets were sharply buffeted by the bursting of the housing bubble and the related subprime meltdown. On September 15, 2008, in the wake of Lehman Brothers announcing it was filing for bankruptcy, the Dow plunged more than 500 points. By March 9, 2009, the Dow closed at 6,547.05—a far cry from the high of 14,164. While the details of the massive recent financial debacle are beyond this book's scope, it is worthy to comment upon the fate of Merrill Lynch, a firm that has played a large role in the story of popular participation in the stock market.

Merrill Lynch, once the darling of Wall Street and the small investor, was devastated by the unraveling of the mortgage business, which began in late 2007. Under the reign of CEO E. Stanley O'Neal, the company had invested heavily in the mortgage industry.[6] Emboldened by lucrative returns in 2005 and 2006, Merrill Lynch rapidly expanded its presence in the mortgage business, acquiring a dozen companies in less than two years, including that of subprime lender First Franklin. Soon thereafter, however, a rising number of mortgages entered default, prompting rating agencies to begin to slash the debt ratings on collateralized debt obligations (C.D.O.'s). Hard hit, in 2007 Merrill had to take a $7.9 billion write-down related to its exposure to mortgage C.D.O.'s, causing Merrill to incur a staggering $2.3 billion loss for the year, the largest in the firm's long history.[7] In September 2008, Bank of America agreed to acquire Merrill Lynch, thereby saving Merrill Lynch from possible bankruptcy.[8]

Winthrop (Win) H. Smith Jr., son of one of the founding partners of Merrill Lynch, delivered an impassioned speech to shareholders as they reluctantly approved the merger with Bank of America. The speech actually was more of a eulogy, lamenting the death of the company and heralding the founders' core values.[9] As Win Smith recalled, from the day the company was formed on January 6th, 1914, Charles Merrill's first rule was that the "Interests of the Customer always came first." Merrill Lynch, as SEC chairman Arthur Levitt once said, had a "soul." Smith remembered fondly the days when "Merrill Lynch was a brand that we were so proud to wear on our heart and even our ties. We had a swagger, and we were damn proud to be part of 'The Thundering Herd.'" He berated CEO Stanley O'Neal for "throw[ing] our founding principles down a flight of stairs and tear[ing] out the soul of the firm," and he criticized shareholders for allowing O'Neal "to over leverage the firm and fill the balance sheet with toxic waste to create short term earnings." Smith concluded, "No wonder that the Main Street that learned to trust Merrill Lynch in the 1940's has lost faith in Wall Street in 2008. Merrill Lynch is not alone in this. But in the past Merrill Lynch rose above the crowd and distanced itself from the greed that brought others down. Our principled leaders steered us through many challenges, and we emerged stronger because of them."[10] He recalled the positive role played by Charles Merrill and his father, Winthrop Smith Sr., in helping Americans lose their wariness toward stocks and embrace equity investing.

In the mid-twentieth century, Merrill Lynch, along with a handful of other brokerage firms like Fenner & Beane, which Merrill Lynch later absorbed, had helped broaden shareownership, making progress toward achieving a "people's capitalism." Adept at advertising and marketing, Merrill Lynch employees like Louis Engel contributed direction to the NYSE's Own Your Share campaign. By the end of the first decade of the twenty-first century, though, many Merrill Lynch customers departed the company, after having lost substantial money in their brokerage and mutual fund accounts during the bear market. Many clients had also suffered serious losses in their supposedly safe money market funds, which actually had significant subprime exposure.

Own Your Share advertisements from the 1950s and 1960s had promised that a well-diversified portfolio of stocks was an effective way to ensure "Family Security," but during bear markets, investors can lose confidence. During and after the recent recession, many frustrated individual investors left the stock market, much as they had in the inflation-ridden 1970s. In August 2010, a *New York Times* headline announced, "In Striking Shift, Small Investors Flee the Stock Market."[11] According to the Investment Company Institute (ICI), in the first seven months of the year, domestic stock market mutual funds suffered redemptions of more than $33 billion. Scared investors withdrew some or all of their funds for a variety of reasons—some, struck by the hard times, now needed the money, while others simply were frightened by their existing losses and wished to limit them by moving their investments into presumably safer vehicles, such as bonds and bond funds. The ICI's figures on withdrawals, along with an ICI annual survey of 4,000 households, suggest that Americans may be losing their "generation-long love affair with the stock market," as *New York Times* reporter Graham Bowley notes. The ICI survey, taken every year, illustrates that U.S. investors' willingness to assume stock market risk has decreased consistently since 2001, most especially among younger investors (those under 35 years of age).[12]

While approximately half of U.S. households are now involved to some extent in the stock market (overwhelmingly, through the vehicle of stock mutual funds and pensions), it is questionable whether this widespread participation will continue. Given the amount of money in retirement plans, a key question is whether most Americans will continue to pour money earmarked for retirement primarily into equity mutual funds, or whether they will redirect their retirement money into other investments. While noting that investors quickly reentered the stock market after the technology and dot-com crash in the early 2000s, Bowley ominously warned that "bigger economic calamities like the Great Depression affected people's attitudes toward money [and the stock market] for decades."[13]

The Own Your Share of American Business campaign in the 1950s and 1960s played a pivotal part in Americans' overcoming their prolonged fear of the stock market—and investments in general—in the long wake of the 1929 Crash. At the height of the campaign in the 1960s, a variety of surveys and polls indicated that most Americans believed that investing in the stock market was a prudent strategy. Undoubtedly, the majority of average-income Americans who joined the stock market in the flush Own Your Share years and stayed the course made handsome profits over the years. Despite occasional scandals, the playing field on Wall Street is exponentially more level than it had been in the Roaring 1920s. As Americans recently have come to realize anew, however, common stock investing is far from a foolproof road to riches. Then again, the architects of Own Your Share of American Business, trying to manage investor expectations and avoid excessive optimism concerning big quick returns, had never promised this.

So how should the OYS program be remembered? Was it a success in either the short or the long term? What is success, and how should it be defined? On

Table E.1   Selected highlights from NYSE shareowner census reports, 1952–1990

Year	No. of individual shareowners*	Shareowner incidence in adult population	Median household income	No. of adult female shareowners*	No. of adult male shareowners*	Median age
1952	6,490	1 in 16	$7,100	3,140	3,210	51
1956	8,630	1 in 12	$6,200	4,260	4,020	48
1959	12,490	1 in 8	$7,000	6,350	5,740	49
1962	17,010	1 in 6	$8,600	8,290	7,970	48
1965	20,120	1 in 6	$9,500	9,430	9,060	49
1970	30,850	1 in 4	$13,500	14,290	14,340	48
1975	25,270	1 in 6	$19,000	11,750	11,630	53
1980	30,200	1 in 5	$27,750	13,696	14,196	46
1981	32,260	1 in 5	$29,200	14,154	15,785	46
1983	42,360	1 in 4	$33,200	20,385	19,226	45
1985	47,040	1 in 4	$36,800	17,547	27,446	44
1990	51,440	1 in 4	$43,800	17,750	30,220	43

Source: New York Stock Exchange, Highlights of NYSE Shareowner Census Reports (1952–1990), accessed August 8, 2008, nysedata.com/factbook, NYSE.
*in thousands

one level, success could be measured by the growth in the number of retail shareowners, which climbed significantly during the OYS years, rising from only 6.5 million Americans in 1952 to 24 million Americans in 1968, as table E.1 illustrates. With few interruptions (the 1970s being one), the number of shareowners in later years continued to expand. Of course, the OYS program was not the only catalyst for rising shareownership, and certainly not everyone exposed to an Exchange advertisement bought stock. With regard to advertisements in general, *Fortune* correspondent William Whyte once skeptically asked, "Is anybody listening?"[14] According to tests conducted by Daniel Starch and Associates, a pioneer in evaluating audience recall of advertisements, people tended to listen to and remember the Own Your Share message. One evidence of reader engagement was that thousands clipped OYS "coupons" that appeared with advertisements, which they then sent to the NYSE requesting additional information on equity investing.

The power of Own Your Share's "buy stock" message should not be underestimated, nor should it be measured primarily by the rise in direct individual investing. Admittedly, the NYSE in the 1950s and 1960s measured OYS's success by gains in the number of individual stockowners. Yet OYS, unintentionally, also helped spread the appeal of indirect institutional investing. OYS helped inculcate in Americans the importance of being involved in the stock market, and many of those who heard that message went on to participate in the market, often through vehicles such as mutual funds and pension funds rather than the OYS's preference for the direct route. OYS fell short in its goal of ensuring a "balance" between individual and institutional investing. As table E.2 indicates, individual trading as a percentage of total trading volume on the exchanges declined in the period from 1950 to 1975 and continued to decline thereafter. Likewise, as illustrated in table E.3, individual holdings as a percentage of total outstanding equities also declined during the same period, as the percentage of institutional holdings correspondingly grew.

OYS leaders did not, however, ultimately fail in their broader and more important quest to foster a nation of many small (along with some big) shareowners. Without a doubt, OYS can claim part of the credit for providing an environment conducive to the growth in the number of direct and indirect shareowners. In addition, the OYS campaign succeeded in helping to restore profitability for many business-starved retail member brokerage firms. OYS taught member retail brokerage firms how to employ mass marketing more

Table E.2   Institutional versus individual
trading volume on the exchanges

	% of trading volume	
Year	Institutions	Individuals
1950	20	80
1961	33	67
1971	60	40
1975	75	25

Sources: Marshall E. Blume and Irwin Friend, *The Changing Role of the Individual Investor* (New York: John Wiley and Sons, 1978), 105, and James J. Needham, *The Threat to Corporate Growth* (Philadelphia: Girard Bank, 1974), 11–12.

Note: The 1950 and 1975 statistics (from Blume) include trading volume on all exchanges. The 1961 and 1971 statistics (from Needham) include trading volume on the NYSE only. If all exchanges were taken into account in the 1971 statistic, the institutional trading volume is likely to be slightly higher than 60%.

Table E.3   Institutional versus individual holdings
as percentage of total outstanding (O/S) equities

Year	Institutional	Individual
1950	6%	94%
1960	13%	87%
1970	19%	81%
1980	37%	63%

Source: Adapted from Carolyn K. Brancato and Stephan Rabimov, the Conference Board Governance Center, *The 2007 Institutional Investment Report*, table 10, p. 2, accessed April 15, 2009, www.conference-board.org/pdf_free/IIRCharts0107.pdf.

effectively. The OYS program helped improve the Exchange's profile: the message resonated with many Americans.

The OYS campaign, though, was not just about increasing the shareowner ranks in order to improve the Exchange's image or even to boost member firms' profitability levels. The creators of OYS also adamantly believed that having more of the public involved in the stock market would help stop the spread of communism. Were they right, and did OYS succeed in this regard? Certainly, communism in the United States never took hold like it did in other countries where equity cultures were not in place. It cannot be denied that communism around the world grew weaker during the late twentieth century, during precisely the time when shareownership in both the United States and around the world was growing at its fastest pace.

In promoting a philosophy—indeed, an ideology—concerning stockownership, Own Your Share affected not only buyers, but also the sellers.[15] As historian Marvin Meyers once observed, "With talk begins responsibility."[16] His point regarding the potential self-transformative power of public relations applies here, as the NYSE took seriously its responsibilities to spread "sound" shareownership. The Own Your Share program propelled the securities industry to broaden their conception of who should be shareowners: in the 1950s and 1960s, the NYSE came to believe that most people could and should be shareowners.

In the mid-twentieth century, the Big Board realized that broad shareownership was good for investors and good for the country. In their internal correspondence, not just their public speeches, President Funston and his colleagues referred to the OYS campaign with quasi-religious fervor. Funston glorified it as a "crusade"; Lawrence hailed it as a mission akin to getting a man on the moon.[17] Alfred Fuller, the highly regarded door-to-door salesman who founded the Fuller Brush Company in 1906, remarked, "The successful seller must feel some commitment that his product offers mankind as much altruistic benefit as it yields the seller in money." He continued, "The salesman is an idealist and an artist; in that respect he differs from the huckster, who is just out for profit." The lesson, Fuller said, was that "those who thought only of financial return failed promptly, while those who, like myself, were enthused with mission as well prospered materially far beyond their dreams."[18]

NYSE President Funston and his Own Your Share team had that critical sense of mission that had been absent from the Exchange in the early 1900s. As *Forbes* magazine remarked in 1951, "To the Old Guarders on the Street, stocks [were] a way of making a living." In contrast, Funston and his followers perceived stocks as "a means to a way of life."[19] Specifically, the OYS team viewed stocks as a means of preserving the *American* way of life, the free enterprise system, as well as capitalism. Interviewed in 1984 after he had retired, Lawrence also emphasized that same theme of mission. He declared, "In broadening the market, we found that an important dividend was that it gave the industry and individual brokers a sense of mission. No longer were they just selling stocks and bonds; they were creating a nation of informed investors. They were helping to raise equity, to create jobs . . . build plants and provide money for the tools. They were helping to keep the enterprise system strong, and, in doing so, helping to keep America strong."[20]

Inspiring Wall Street's faith in Main Street, not just Main Street's faith in Wall Street, Own Your Share's zealous architects deserve credit for diminishing the long-lingering "Shadow of 1929." They helped illuminate to the retail brokerage community that the business of small investors was worth cultivating. They contributed to remaking equity investing into a practice that most Americans viewed as acceptable and desirable. While popular attitudes about Wall Street would endure cyclical changes, the legitimacy of stocks as part of an investment strategy has become widely accepted. OYS transformed many citizens' image of equity investing from a sinful, foolish pursuit, akin to gambling, to a wholesome, quintessentially American activity. In retrospect, due in no small part to the OYS marketing campaign, the 1950s and 1960s proved to be critical decades for reestablishing an equity culture—one that would prove far stronger and enduring than that of the 1920s.

Notes

INTRODUCTION: **Sowing an "Equity Culture"**

Epigraph. New York: NYSE, 1951, 12.

1. According to a NYSE report, in 1998, 84 million people owned stock in the United States. This statistic represents both direct and indirect stockowners, the latter reflecting institutional holdings. *Shareownership 2000 Highlights,* NYSEData.com Factbook, 2002, accessed June 6, 2011, www.nyxdata.com/nysedata/asp/factbook/viewer_edition.asp?mode=text&key=51&category=11. By 2001, 51.9% of U.S. households owned stock, and in 2007, 49.1% owned stock. See Sylvia Allegretto, "The State of America's Wealth, 2011," Economic Policy Institute, Briefing Paper no. 292, March 23, 2011, esp. table 7, p. 13.

2. Allegretto, "The State of America's Wealth," table 7, p. 13.

3. The top 5% of households in 2007 owned 69.2% of common stock. That figure includes stock owned directly and stock owned indirectly, the latter through mutual funds, trusts, and retirement accounts such as IRAs, Keogh plans, and 401(k) plans. Allegretto, "The State of America's Wealth," table 6, p. 11. In terms of the richest 1% of households, in 2007, they held stock holdings, on average, worth $4.2 million (in 2009 dollars) (Allegretto, 15). See also Aaron

Brenner, "The Myth of the Shareholder Nation," *New Labor Forum* 13, no. 2 (Summer 2004): 20–35, esp. 24.

4. The term "equity culture" comes from B. Mark Smith, *The Equity Culture: The Story of the Global Stock Market* (New York: Farrar, Straus and Giroux, 2003). Smith does not precisely define the term, but I use the phrase here to encompass the idea of participation and interest in the stock market going mainstream.

5. See, for instance, Adam Shell, "Invest in Stocks? Forget about It," *USA Today*, May 8, 2012, 1A, 2A.

6. According to the Investment Company Institute (ICI), equity funds for the four years from 2008 to 2011 experienced net withdrawals each year. Net withdrawals from all types of mutual funds including equity funds totaled $100 billion in 2011. See ICI, *2012 Investment Company Fact Book*, 52nd ed., chap. 2, "Recent Mutual Fund Trends," esp. p. 24, accessed May 14, 2012, www.ici.org/pdf/2012_factbook.pdf.

7. See Edgar L. Smith, *Common Stocks as Long Term Investments* (New York: Macmillan, 1928). Also see Chelcie Bosland, *The Common Stock Theory of Investment: Its Development and Significance* (New York: Ronald Press, 1937).

8. The phrase "cult of equity" is widely used. See, for instance, Tony Keller, "The Cult of Equity," *Financial Post Magazine*, September 13, 2011, accessed May 15, 2012, http://business.financialpost.com/2011/09/13/the-cult-of-equity/.

9. While other exchanges exist in the United States, in this book, "the Exchange" refers solely to the NYSE. The organization has undergone numerous changes in recent years, and in 2007, the NYSE Group, Inc., and Euronext N.V. combined to form NYSE Euronext.

10. For a discussion of some early twentieth-century criticisms of Wall Street, see Sereno S. Pratt, *The Work of Wall Street: An Account of the Functions, Methods and History of the New York Money and Stock Markets* (New York: Arno Press, 1975; first published 1903), see esp. 380–94. Also, Thomas Lawson, *Frenzied Finance* (New York: Greenwood Press, 1968; first published 1905). The rhetoric of "easy" versus "earned" money pervaded the media in the immediate aftermath of the 1929 Crash. See, for instance, *Saturday Evening Post*, Advertisement, *NY Sun*, October 25, 1929, 30; "Back to Work," *NYT*, October 24, 1929, 38. Reporter Edwin Lefevre noted, "Stock speculation always has seemed the cleanest way of making easy money. It is legalized gambling masquerading as a legitimate business." Lefevre, "The Little Fellow in Wall Street," *Saturday Evening Post*, January 4, 1930, 7. On the notion of "speculation" versus "investing," also see Edward Chancellor, *Devil Takes the Hindmost: A History of Financial Speculation* (New York: Plume, 1999), esp. x–xiii.

11. A common and somewhat justified fear was that insiders often manipulated the market at the expense of outsiders.

12. Frederick Lewis Allen, *Only Yesterday* (New York: Harper and Row, 1959; first published 1931), 261, 281. In a similar vein, Professor Amos Dice of The Ohio State University had heralded, "Truly this is the day of the small investor." Charles Amos Dice, *New Levels in the Stock Market* (New York: McGraw-Hill, 1929), 184.

13. Gardiner Means, "Diffusion of Stock Ownership," *Quarterly Journal of Economics* 44, no. 4 (August 1930): 585. See also B. Mark Smith, *Toward Rational Exuberance: The Evolution of the Modern Stock Market* (New York: Farrar, Straus and Giroux, 2001), 66.

14. In the summer of 1929, John J. Raskob, senior executive at General Motors (GM), advised average Americans not just to invest regularly in "good common stocks," but also to consider borrowing to do so. John J. Raskob, "Everybody Ought to Be Rich," *Ladies Home Journal*, August 1929, 9, 36.

15. According to some estimates, four to six million Americans out of a population of roughly 126 million adults owned stock at the height of the 1920s bull market. Most, however, owned only a handful of shares of one company, typically acquired through employee or customer stock purchase plans, and fewer than 1.5 million Americans maintained active brokerage accounts. Estimates of shareownership in the 1920s vary widely. See, for instance, U.S. Senate, Committee on Banking and Currency, *Report of the Committee on Banking and Currency*, hereafter referred to as the "Fletcher Report" (Washington, DC: GPO, 1934), 9; Gardiner Means, "Diffusion of Stock Ownership," 561–600; Means, "The Separation of Ownership and Control in American Industry," *Quarterly Journal of Economics* 46, no. 1 (December 1931): 68–100; H. T. Warshow, "The Distribution of Corporate Ownership in the United States, *Quarterly Journal of Economics* 39 (November 1924), 15–38.

16. Lawrence H. Sloan, *Everyman and His Common Stocks: A Study of Long Term Investment Policy* (New York: Whittlesby House, 1931), 298. Defending the common stock theory, Sloan viewed the "anti-equity obsession" as unreasonable. He encouraged his readers to continue buying stock, as he assumed that the Dow soon would reach its low point and then would begin recovery. He was right. Yet the Dow's recovery was painfully slow, with significant periodic retrenchments, including during the Recession of 1937. Stocks did not approach mid-1929 highs until November 23, 1954. Some, like Wharton professor Jeremy Siegel, however, have taken issue with this characterization, contending that if the total return index of the U.S. stock market is adjusted for inflation, the market recovered in only approximately eight years, not twenty-five. See Mark Hulbert, "Dispelling Myths about Stocks in the 1930s," March 6, 2009, accessed May 10, 2012, http://online.barrons.com/article/SB123637914471857307.html.

17. Robert A. Margo, "Employment and Unemployment in the 1930s," *Journal of Economic Perspectives* 7, no. 2 (Spring 1993): 41–59. Also see Alan Brinkley, *The Unfinished Nation*, 2nd ed. (New York: McGraw Hill, 1997), 684–85.

18. George Gallup and Claude Robinson, "American Institute of Public Opinion-Surveys, 1935–38," *The Public Opinion Quarterly* 2, no. 3 (July, 1938): 373–98, esp. 384.

19. Howard J. Carswell, "Business News Coverage," *Public Opinion Quarterly* 2, no. 4 (October 1938): 614, 616. Italics in original.

20. For a discussion of the Merrill Lynch polls (conducted in part by Braun & Associates), see Winthrop Smith, Conference of Bank Managers Transcript, Merrill Lynch Meeting, April 3–4, 1940, Waldorf-Astoria Hotel, New York City. My sincere thanks to Edwin Perkins for sharing this document with me. For more analysis of these polls indicating the public's continued disenchantment with Wall Street, see Edwin P. Hoyt, *The Supersalesmen* (Cleveland: World Publishing, 1962), 97.

21. Ruddick C. Lawrence (hereafter abbreviated RCL), Oral History, Interview by Deborah Gardiner, 1984, Box 4, RCL Papers, New York Stock Exchange Archive (hereafter abbreviated "NYSEA").

22. Organizational theorists Blake Ashforth and Barrie Gibbs describe a legitimate enter-

prise as one that is deemed to pursue "socially acceptable goals in a socially acceptable manner." Blake E. Ashforth and Barrie W. Gibbs, "The Double-Edge of Organizational Legitimation," *Organization Science* 1, no. 2 (1990): 177–94. According to cultural historian Roland Marchand, the extent of an organization's legitimacy is affected in part by its perceived "size, power, scope of responsibility, and freedom of action" in relation "to such other institutions as the family, the community, and the state." Marchand further defines legitimacy "not as an attribute that an entity either possesses or entirely lacks but rather as an unstable, shifting, and contested quality—always susceptible to enhancement or depletion." Marchand, *Creating the Corporate Soul*, 8n, p. 370. Also see J. Dowling and J. Pfeffer, "Organizational Legitimacy: Social Values and Organizational Behavior," *Pacific Sociological Review* 18 (1975): 122–36.

23. On disposable personal income levels, see Donald Kemmerer, "American Financial Institutions: The Marketing of Securities, 1930–1952," *Journal of Economic History* 12, no. 4 (Autumn 1952): 454–68, esp. 455. Disposable personal income in 1929 was $82.5 billion.

24. The personal savings rate in 1950 was 7.1%; 1951, 8.4%; 1952, 8.4%. Earlier, in the 1941–1945 period when America was at war, personal savings had been double-digit, ranging from 12.2 to 26%. In more recent years, the personal savings rate has been much lower; from 1999 to 2007, the rate ranged from only 1.4% (in 2005) to 3.5% (in 2002 and 2003). In the wake of the subprime debacle, savings rates have been growing again, rising to 5.9% in 2009 and 5.8% in 2010. On personal savings rates, see U.S. Department of Commerce, Bureau of Economic Analysis, *National Income and Product Accounts of the United States*, table 2.1, "Personal Income and Its Dispositions." The personal savings rate is the percentage of disposable income not consumed or spent.

25. Lewis Kimmel, *Share Ownership in the United States* ("The Brookings Report") (Washington, DC, 1952), 91, 95, 124–28, NYSEA.

26. Some other examples include the establishment of 403(b) in 1958, which enabled employees in tax-exempt organizations to open retirement savings accounts, as well as the creation of another type of 401(k) plan in 2006, the Roth 401(k).

27. For simplicity, I will refer to the NYSE's ruling body as the "Board" or "Board of Governors" even though in the pre-1938 period, the technical term was the "Governing Committee."

28. The word "seat" to connote a membership derives from the time before continuous trading of stocks, when members sat in assigned chairs during periodic calls of stocks. James E. Buck, ed., *The New York Stock Exchange: The First 200 Years* (Essex: Greenwich, 1992), 57.

29. On the NYSE's public relations efforts in the early 1900s before the Crash, see Part One of Janice Traflet, "Spinning the NYSE: Power and Public Relations at the Big Board" (PhD diss., Columbia University, 2004). Also see Julia Ott, *When Main Street Met Wall Street: The Quest for an Investors' Democracy* (Cambridge, MA: Harvard University Press, 2011), as well as her articles: "The 'Free and Open' People's Market: Public Relations at the NYSE, 1913–1929," *Business History Conference* 2 (2004): 1–43; "When Wall Street Met Main Street: The Quest for an Investors' Democracy and the Emergence of the Retail Investor in the United States, 1890–1930," *Enterprise and Society* (2008): 619–30; "'The Free and Open People's Market': Political Ideology and Retail Brokerage at the New York Stock Exchange, 1913–1933," *Journal of American History* 96, no. 1 (June 2009).

30. While critics have complained that some organizations use public relations to promote,

sometimes covertly, their own agendas, defenders of public relations emphasize that it can be a positive societal force when properly conducted, with the public interest in mind. See Nugent Wedding, "Advertising and Public Relations," *Journal of Business of the University of Chicago* 23, no. 3 (July 1950): 173; also see Richard Tedlow, "Advertising," *Readers Companion to American History*, ed. Eric Foner and John A. Garraty (Boston: Houghton Mifflin, 1991), 12–15.

31. See Susan Strasser, *Satisfaction Guaranteed: The Making of the American Mass Market* (New York: Pantheon, 1989); Emily Fogg-Meade, "The Place of Advertising in Modern Business," *Journal of Political Economy* 9, no. 2 (March 1901): 218–42; Daniel Pope, *The Making of Modern Advertising* (New York: Basic Books, 1983), esp. 45–46; Stephen Fox, *The Mirror Makers: A History of American Advertising and Its Creators* (New York: William Morrow, 1984); Earnest Elmo Calkins, *The Business of Advertising* (New York: Appleton, 1915); Jackson Lears, *Fables of Abundance: A Cultural History of Advertising in America* (New York: Basic Books, 1994); Stuart Ewen, *Captains of Consciousness: Advertising and the Social Roots of Consumer Culture* (New York: McGraw Hill, 1976).

32. Robert Sobel, *N.Y.S.E.: A History of the New York Stock Exchange, 1935–1975* (New York: Weybright and Talley, 1975), 70–71. The attitude that it was unbecoming for professionals to advertise changed only in the second half of the twentieth century. On the rising use of advertising by physicians in the past few decades, see John A. Rizzo and Richard J. Zeckhauser, "Advertising and Entry: The Case of Physician Services," *Journal of Political Economy* 98, no. 3 (June 1990): 476–500.

33. Carl Spielvogel, "Advertising: Leaving the Tombstone Behind," *NYT*, August 20, 1957, F10.

34. As Sereno Pratt, an editor at the *Wall Street Journal*, explained in 1903, the NYSE, like the London Stock Exchange, strictly limited advertising because financial advertising was "the line of separation between legitimate and illegitimate brokers." Pratt, *Work of Wall Street*, 383.

35. Likewise, bucket shops advertised. Bucket shops were gambling places where customers bet against the house on the direction of a stock's price without actually owning or taking delivery of the stock. According to Pratt, these shops were "filled with clerks and other persons, women as well as men, of small salaries or incomes, all eager to double their money in the Street, and all inflamed by the stories told of the immense fortunes that have been made there." These individuals, said Pratt, "are the very people we should keep out of the stock market. They have not the means and the knowledge for successful operations there." Pratt, *Work of Wall Street*, 381–82. Pratt emphasized that in a bucket shop "there is no actual transfer of stock or 'intent to deliver.'" On bucket shops, also see David Hochfelder, "'Where the Common People Could Speculate': The Ticker, Bucket Shops, and the Origin of Popular Participation in Financial Markets, 1880–1920," *Journal of American History* 93, no. 2 (September 2006), 335–58; Ann Fabian, *Card Sharps, Dream Books and Bucket Shops: Gambling in 19th-Century America* (Ithaca: Cornell University Press, 1990); "Bucket Shops," accessed June 28, 2011, http://en.wikipedia .org/wiki/Bucket_shop_(stock_market).

36. As Henry Clews, a NYSE member contended, only disreputable brokers operating outside the Exchange's purview "establish themselves . . . by extensive advertising in the newspapers and by sending out vast quantities of circulars through the mails." Clews, qtd. in Pratt, *Work of Wall Street*, 380.

37. U.S. Congress, House Committee on Banking and Currency, Arsène Paulin Pujo, Everis Anson Hayes, Henry McMorran, *Money Trust Investigation: Investigation of Financial and Monetary Conditions in the United States under House Resolutions Nos. 429 and 504, before a Subcommittee of the Committee on Banking and Currency* (Washington, DC: GPO, 1913).

38. In 1905, Ivy Lee, who liked to describe himself as a "physician to corporate bodies," had opened one of the first public relations firms in the United States. Among his clients were Pennsylvania Railroad, Bethlehem Steel, the House of Morgan, and oil titan John D. Rockefeller Sr. According to Lee, public relations should be more about actions than words; concrete behavioral change was the ideal way to cultivate a good image. See "Ivy Lee Dies at 57 of Brain Ailment," *NYT*, November 10, 1934. See Ray E. Hiebert's biography of Lee, *Courtier to the Crowd* (Ames: Iowa State University Press, 1966). Several solid books on public relations include Richard S. Tedlow, *Keeping the Corporate Image: Public Relations and Business, 1900–1950* (Greenwich: JAI Press, 1979), esp. 19–21; Eric Goldman, *Two-Way Street: The Emergence of the Public Relations Counsel* (Boston: Bellman Publishing, 1948); John E. Marston, *The Nature of Public Relations* (New York: McGraw Hill, 1963); and Scott M. Cutlip, *The Unseen Power: Public Relations, A History* (Hillsdale: Lawrence Erlbaum, 1994). See also Robert Heilbroner, "Public Relations— The Invisible Sell," *Harper's*, June 1957, 31–34.

39. Edward Bernays, another pioneer in the field, agreed with Lee that the ideal way to burnish an image was by implementing concrete reforms, but he was more cynical about how public relations professionals in practice often successfully redefined their clients' images. As he contended, public relations often consisted of more artful propaganda than honest communication of truly reformed behavior. Some of Edward L. Bernays's many writings include *Crystallizing Public Opinion* (New York: Liveright, 1923); *Your Future in Public Relations* (New York: Richard Rosen, 1961); *Propaganda* (New York: Liveright, 1928); *The Engineering of Consent* (Norman: University of Oklahoma Press, 1955); *The Later Years: Public Relations Insights, 1956–1986* (New York: H&M Publishers, 1986). See also Marvin N. Olasky, "Retrospective: Bernays' Doctrine of Public Opinion," *Public Relations Review* 10, no. 3 (1984): 3–12.

40. Worried about the trend toward mammoth-size corporations, some Progressive reformers like President Theodore Roosevelt contended that large corporations needed to be better regulated. Other reformers, like associate Supreme Court Justice Louis Brandeis, argued that bigness itself was something to be avoided; they maintained that large corporations inherently posed a danger to citizens, employees, and competitors. Companies in the early 1900s produced many publications to refute the charge of "no soul," such as *Heart of a Soulless Corporation* (1908), *Corporations and Souls* (1912), *United States Steel: A Corporation with a Soul* (1921), and *Humanizing a Soulless Corporation* (1937). See Roland Marchand, *Creating the Corporate Soul: The Rise of Public Relations and Corporate Imagery in American Big Business* (Berkeley: University of California Press, 1998), 4–5.

41. The NYSE did not incorporate until 1971.

42. See Traflet, "Spinning the NYSE"; also, Ott, *When Main Street Met Wall Street*; Ott, "The 'Free and Open' People's Market: Public Relations at the NYSE."

43. Cromwell continued, "The Stock Exchange has played a prominent and vital part in this tremendous widening of the shareholding class in this country, by providing at all times a free and open market where such shares can be bought and sold." He concluded that the

Exchange was "assisting in a genuine public ownership of American companies." In stressing "genuine public ownership," Cromwell was implicitly criticizing reformers' calls for the government to nationalize the NYSE. Cromwell made his speech not long after the first Red Scare in the United States (1919–1920), as fears of anarchist violence and mayhem at home mounted in the wake of the 1917 Bolshevik Revolution in Russia. Wall Street felt these fears, particularly after the bombing of J. P. Morgan & Company at 23 Wall Street in September 1920. Cromwell, qtd. in Charles W. Wood, "The Other Side of Wall Street: An Interview with Seymour L. Cromwell, President New York Stock Exchange," 8–9, reprinted from *Collier's National Weekly* (NYSE: Committee on Library, 1923), Folder 17, Box 1, Speeches, Seymour L. Cromwell, 1922–1923, NYSEA.

44. E. H. H. Simmons, "Credit as a National Asset: Before the Credit Men's Association of Milwaukee," April 9, 1925, 9, Committee on Library, NYSEA. He added, "The accumulated money of the small investor makes possible the great investments of the country."

45. Simmons further noted, "We are, therefore, apparently coming into a period when the average American will be a capitalist and security owner as well as an employee, and will in consequence have an especial incentive to become rapidly acquainted with the sound and basic principles of banking and business." E. H. H. Simmons, "Free Markets and Popular Ownership," Speech before the 41st Annual Convention of the Texas Bankers Association at Houston, Texas, May 20, 1925, 3, 4, Committee on Library, NYSEA.

46. Colleen A. Dunlavy, "Social Conceptions of the Corporation: Insights from the History of Shareholder Voting Rights," *Washington and Lee Law Review* 63, no. 4 (Fall 2006): 1349, 1354–56.

47. While the Exchange escaped Pujo's call for incorporation and thus achieved success in that sense, the Big Board still struggled with its public image, even after tightening rules on member conduct and listing securities. In 1924, as Publicity Director Jason Westerfield lamented, "In general the relations between the public and the NYSE are not just what they should be. I am reminded of the gentleman who stated he would make no Christmas gifts, as his relations were 'either dead or strained.' Now, whatever may be said of our relations with the public, they are not 'dead,' though they are sometimes 'strained.'" Westerfield uttered these words on a visit to the NYSE Institute, which recently had been formed to conduct classes for Exchange employees and employees of member firms, to inculcate them in the ways of the Exchange as well as the fundamentals of finance. Jason Westerfield, Director of Publicity, "The Stock Exchange in Relation to the Public: An Address before the NYSE Institute," January 17, 1924, Committee on Library, NYSEA.

48. The term "merchant banking" is loosely defined as "negotiated private equity investment by financial institutions in the . . . securities of either privately or publicly held companies." Valentine V. Craig, "Merchant Banking Past and Present," 29–35, accessed July 16, 2011, www.fdic.gov/bank/analytical/banking/2001sep/br2001v14n1art2.pdf.

49. The Reformers tried to campaign for measures that would stimulate the confidence of retail investors, and for other actions that would enhance their own profitability, like an increase in the minimum commission rate they could charge customers on order executions.

50. Originally, the independent broker used to receive $2 per 100 shares of execution from the second broker for this service, hence the name "two-dollar broker."

51. For a basic discussion of specialists, traders, and commission brokers, see Sobel, *N.Y.S.E.*,

16–20; Kenneth M. Morris and Virginia M. Morris, *The Wall Street Journal Guide to Understanding Money & Investing* (New York: Lightbulb Press, 1999), 63; David L. Scott, *Wall Street Words: An A to Z Guide to Investment Terms for Today's Investor* (Boston: Houghton Mifflin, 2003).

52. Sobel, *N.Y.S.E.*, 17–18. On the deeply split NYSE, also see Robert Bremner, *Chairman of the Fed: William McChesney Martin Jr. and the Creation of the Modern American Financial System* (New Haven: Yale University Press, 2004), 37.

53. Minutes, Committee on Business Conduct [CBC], 1, see esp. minutes of May 11, 1916; June 5, 1916; June 14, 1916; and September 13, 1917, NYSEA. Also see Edwin P. Hoyt, *The Supersalesmen* (Cleveland: World Publishing, 1962), esp. 83–85, 96–98; Edwin Perkins, *Wall Street to Main Street: Charles Merrill and Middle-Class Investors* (Cambridge: Cambridge University Press, 1999).

54. This line of thinking, connecting shareownership to heightened national and company loyalty, was not new to Wall Street in the 1950s; it also had prevailed in earlier years, especially the 1920s. For example Seymour Cromwell, NYSE president, 1921–1924, had emphasized that common stock ownership could ease tensions between labor and management. He claimed that "this wider distribution of American stocks and this tremendous broadening of the American investing class may prove of primary importance as a solvent to the perennial quarrels of capital and labor themselves." Cromwell, qtd. in Wood, "The Other Side of Wall Street," 9. The notion that widespread shareholding enhanced political stability harkened back to the Lockean idea that citizens who owned property possessed a more robust and permanent interest in their country than those who did not. As Alexis De Tocqueville observed in 1841, "All revolutions more or less threaten the tenure of property: but most of those who live in democratic countries are possessed of property. . . . Hence, in democratic communities, the majority of the people do not clearly see what they have to gain by a revolution, but they continually and in a thousand ways feel that they might lose by one." Alexis De Tocqueville, *Democracy in America*, vol. 2, 3rd ed. (Cambridge: Sever and Francis, 1863), 310–11. Cromwell and others viewed it as important for Americans to have ownership stakes (and hence vested interests) in securities, much like they did home ownership. Eager to promote economic citizenship, they perceived "popular proprietorship" in every form as beneficial. On popular proprietorship, see, for instance, William L. Ransom, "Property Ownership as a Social Force," *Proceedings of the Academy of Political Science in the City of New York* 11, no. 3 (April 1925): 164–98.

55. B. C. Forbes, "'Share Owner' Better than 'Stockholder,'" *Forbes*, December 1, 1950, 12, 13.

56. As historian Pamela Walker Laird notes, "Societies do not produce advertisements— specific people within societies produce advertisements." Laird, *Advertising Progress: American Business and the Rise of Consumer Marketing* (Baltimore: Johns Hopkins University Press, 1998), 38.

57. As Roland Marchand explained, advertisers strove to convey "not a true mirror but a *Zerrspiegel*, a distorting mirror that would enhance certain images." He emphasized, however, that a *Zerrspiegel* "nevertheless provides some image of everything within its vision. Advertising's mirror not only distorted, it also selected. Some social realities hardly appeared at all." Roland Marchand, *Advertising the American Dream: Making Way for Modernity* (Berkeley: University of California Press, 1985), xvii.

58. In the 1950s, the middle class indeed was growing.

59. See John Kenneth Galbraith, *American Capitalism: The Concept of Countervailing Power* (Boston: Houghton Mifflin, 1952).

60. GKF, *NYSE 1951 Annual Report* (New York: NYSE, 1951), 12.

61. The term "individual" investors refers to people who own corporate stock and/or mutual funds directly. Exchange officials often used the terms "individual" investor, "retail" investor, and "direct" investor interchangeably. "Indirect" stock ownership (which Exchange leaders sometimes conflated with "institutional" investing) included individuals' "stock investments . . . held by such institutions as life insurance companies and mutual savings banks" as well as pension plans. Notably, when the OYS program began, the pension fund revolution was still two decades away, and mutual funds were not yet very popular. While the terms "direct" and "indirect" shareownership are vague, this book nevertheless uses them as they were then widely deployed. To be sure, some "individual" investors were high net worth large investors. Nevertheless, the NYSE in both its internal and external correspondence predominantly used the term "individual" investors to connote small shareholders. In the early 1950s, individual investors accounted for the vast majority (some 80%) of overall trading volume on all the stock exchanges in the United States. See Jonathan A. Brown, "Memorandum to George Bookman on Indirect Ownership," October 8, 1963, NYSEA; George Keith Funston (hereafter, abbreviated GKF), "Institutional Investors: How Is Their Growth Affecting the Stock Market?" Remarks before the American Life Convention, Chicago, Illinois, October 14, 1955, 8, 10–11, Speeches, President Funston, NYSEA.

62. On the public's growing acceptance of large firms in the early twentieth century, see Louis Galambos, *The Public Image of Big Business in America, 1880–1940: A Quantitative Study in Social Change* (Baltimore: Johns Hopkins University Press, 1975). See also Tedlow, *Keeping the Corporate Image*.

63. GKF, Interim Report, February 15, 1951, NYSEA.

64. On the soft side of anticommunism, see Elaine Tyler May, *Homeward Bound: American Families in the Cold War* (New York: Basic Books, 1988). Also see Richard Fried, *The Russians Are Coming! The Russians Are Coming! Pageantry and Patriotism in Cold-War America* (New York: Oxford University Press, 1998).

65. While the Cold War lasted until 1991, a "soft" brand of anticommunism was most evident at the NYSE in the period from the late 1940s through the 1960s.

CHAPTER ONE: **Reeling from the Great Crash**
Epigraph. London: Hamish Hamilton, 1955, 11.

1. Ruddick C. Lawrence, Oral History, Interview by Deborah Gardiner, 1984, Box 4, RCL Papers, NYSEA.

2. Paul T. Cherington Papers, Harvard Business School Archives, Baker Library Historical Collections, Harvard Business School. See his speech, "Securities Liquidation: Office Speech [at JWT]," October 29, 1929, Box 2, Cherington, Speeches and Articles, 1929–1931, Clippings, 1937–1941.

3. For various opinions on the causes of the Crash, see Harold Bierman Jr., *The Causes of the 1929 Stock Market Crash: A Speculative Orgy or a New Era?* (Westport: Greenwood Press, 1998); Michael A. Bernstein, *The Great Depression: Delayed Recovery and Economic Change in*

America, 1929–1930 (Cambridge: Cambridge University Press, 1987), Bierman, *The Great Myths of 1929 and the Lessons to Be Learned* (New York: Greenwood Press, 1991). Some scholars contend that the Federal Reserve provided a major trigger for the Crash when it tightened credit in 1929. See Eugene White, ed., *Crashes and Panics* (Homewood, IL: Business One Irwin, 1990). On the Exchange's early ideas about the Crash's causes, see NYSE President E. H. H. Simmons, "The Principle Causes of the Stock Market Crisis of Nineteen Twenty Nine," January 25, 1930, Folder 38, Box 2, NYSEA.

4. Survey, qtd. in "Crash Not Due to Adverse Business: Guaranty Trust Survey Sees Psychological Factors," *NY Sun*, October 28, 1929, 46. Ironically, only a short time earlier, an official at that same bank had preached the benefits of diffuse share ownership, predicting that mass investing would "decrease class-conscious antagonism by bringing about a partial identification of interests as between laborers and capitalists," and would "discourage the propagation of dangerous and violent social theories." Guaranty Trust, qtd. in Sumner H. Slichter, "The Current Labor Policies of American Industries," *Quarterly Journal of Economics* 43, no. 3 (May 1929): 408.

5. Lefevre, "The Little Fellow in Wall Street," *Saturday Evening Post*, January 4, 1930, 6.

6. Gustave LeBon, *The Crowd: A Study of the Popular Mind* (London: Unwin Hyman, 1977; first published 1895), 23–34. Italics in original.

7. Thomas W. Lamont Papers, Mss 783, 1894–1948, Baker Library Historical Collections, Harvard Business School. Hereafter abbreviated TWL Papers, BL. See TWL, Memo, July 12, 1932, Box 116, Folder 8; TWL, undated memo, ca. 1932, Box 116, Folder 7, TWL Papers, BL. Lamont also said, "I think it preferable that these born gamblers should do their speculating in a local way rather than through any agencies of the NYSE."

8. John Kenneth Galbraith, *The Great Crash: 1929* (London: Hamish Hamilton, 1955), 78.

9. For dark humor on the Crash and the plight of the margin investor, see Eddie Cantor, *Caught Short!* (New York: Greenwood Press, 1929).

10. Unsigned letter to the editor, *NYT*, October 24, 1929, 28. For more on Fisher's views, see Irving Fisher, *Booms and Depressions: The Stock Market Crash—And After*, vol. 10 in *The Works of Irving Fisher*, ed. William J. Barber (London: Pickering and Chatto, 1997; first published 1932). President Theodore Roosevelt popularized the phrase "lunatic fringe" a quarter of a century earlier, using it to describe extreme segments of popular movements, like feminism. Fisher thus appropriated "lunatic fringe" to refer to the "extreme" segment of the investor base: emotional and heavily margined small shareholders.

11. Richard Whitney was no relation to the New York Whitneys associated with the Whitney Museum of American Art.

12. Whitney recollected his own and his colleagues' responses to the Crash in his speech, "The Work of the NYSE in the Panic of 1929," June 10, 1930, Folder 1, Box 3, NYSEA.

13. On Whitney's bid for U.S. Steel, see Ron Chernow, *The House of Morgan* (New York: Atlantic Monthly Press, 1990), 316. More than a quarter of a century earlier, in 1901, J. P. Morgan had played a critical role in the formation of U.S. Steel, which instantly became the largest business enterprise in U.S. history to that point.

14. Whitney resolution, qtd. in Matthew Josephson, "Profiles: Groton, Harvard, Wall Street," *New Yorker*, March 3, 1932, 19, 29.

15. Josephson, "Profiles," 19, 29. Josephson also quoted Whitney.

16. Ibid.

17. Rockefeller, qtd. in Chernow, *House of Morgan*, 319.

18. "President Hoover Issues a Statement of Reassurance on Continued Prosperity of Fundamental Business," *NYT*, October 26, 1929, 1. Hoover, qtd. in Galbraith, *Great Crash*, 109. For other words of confidence, see "Brokers in Meeting Predict Recovery," *NYT*, October 25, 1929, 2; "Stocks Gain as Market Is Steadied; Bankers Pledge Continued Support; Hoover Says Business Basis Is Sound," *NYT*, October 26, 1929, 1; "Schwab Optimistic on Business Future," *NYT*, October 26, 1929, 3; "Brokers Believe Worst Is Over: Many Houses Optimistic in Market Letters," *NY Sun*, October 25, 1929, 52; "Business IS Sound," Ad for Commercial National Bank Trust Company of New York, *NYT*, November 4, 1929, F41. For a discussion of Hoover's public relations failings, see Joan Hoff Wilson, *Herbert Hoover: Forgotten Progressive* (Prospect Heights: Waveland Press, 1975), 139–40, 142.

19. Richard Whitney, "Business Honesty," *The Functions of Stock Exchanges: A Collection of Addresses by Richard Whitney, President NYSE, 1930–1935* (New York: NYSE, 1935), 115–34. The same speech also appears in other forms. See Whitney, "Business Honesty," March 24, 1931, Folder 1, Box 3, Speeches of Presidents, Chairmen, and Officers, NYSEA.

20. Richard Whitney, "Public Opinion and the Stock Market," Address before the Boston Chamber of Commerce, Boston, MA, January 29, 1931, repr. in Whitney, *The Functions of Stock Exchanges*.

21. Richard Whitney, "The Investor and Security Markets," Address over the NBC-WEAF Network of the National Broadcasting Co., January 30, 1935, repr. in *The Investor and Security Markets, Industry and Security Markets, Security Markets and the People: Three Addresses by Richard Whitney* (New York, 1935), 2, NYSEA.

22. Cricuolo Letter to TWL, October 15, 1930, Box 116, Folder 7, TWL Papers, BL.

23. For more on Whitney's speeches, see Folder 1, Box 3, Speeches of Presidents, Chairmen, and Officers, NYSEA.

24. Criscuolo's first name is not mentioned in the memorandum to Lamont—only the initial "L." The stationary says 40 Wall Street.

25. Criscuolo, Letter to TWL, October 15, 1930, Box 116, Folder 7, TWL Papers, BL.

26. Ibid.

27. Richard Whitney (RW) to George Whitney (GW), October 27, 1930, Box 116, Folder 7, TWL Papers, BL.

28. On short selling, see Galbraith, *Great Crash*, 126, 143, 144; Whitney, "Short Selling," October 16, 1931; and Whitney, "Short Selling and Liquidation," December 15, 1931, both in Folder 1, Box 3, NYSE President Speeches, NYSEA.

29. Whitney, "Public Opinion and the Stock Market," 108–9.

30. TWL Memo for GW, October 8, 1931, Box 137, Folder 12, TWL Papers, BL.

31. Whitney, "Public Opinion and the Stock Market," 98, 99, 102–3, 108–9.

32. On the Great Bear Hunt, see Chernow, *House of Morgan*, 351–52.

33. Matthew Josephson, "Sell 'em Ben," Profiles, *New Yorker*, May 14, 1932, 22–25. Also see Josephson, "Jolly Bear II," Profiles, *New Yorker*, May 21, 1932, 21–23. Wall Street's bulls and bears, Josephson explained, all believed they were "true patriots (not anarchists), for whom the

desirability of quick profits won by lawful means is the first article of patriotism." He quoted the well-known bear Bernard E. Smith as saying, "It's still legal in this country to speculate in the hope of a profit, isn't it?" (23)

34. See John Brooks, *Once in Golconda: A True Drama of Wall Street, 1920–1938* (New York: John Wiley and Sons, 1999), 198.

35. See Robert A. Margo, "Employment and Unemployment in the 1930s," *Journal of Economic Perspectives* 7, no. 2 (Spring 1993): 41–59.

36. William O. Douglas, Commissioner SEC, "Your Securities: Their Future Protection," A Speech Before Graduate School of Public Affairs of American University and Department of Agriculture, Washington, DC, April 17, 1937, *Vital Speeches*, 436–42.

37. FDR, Inaugural Address, March 4, 1933.

38. The NYSE Board appointed a special committee to address policy and procedure questions while the Exchange was closed during the bank holiday. See box on Special Committee of Seven, NYSEA.

39. FDR, Inaugural Address.

40. See Ferdinand Pecora, *Wall Street under Oath: The Story of Our Modern Money Changers*, Reprints of Economic Classics (New York: Augustus M. Kelley, 1968; first published 1939). Some recent scholars, however, question the extent to which National City and its President acted improperly. See George Benston, *The Separation of Commercial and Investment Banking: The Glass-Steagall Act Revisited and Reconsidered* (London: Macmillan, 1990); also, Thomas F. Huertas and Joan L. Silverman, "Charles E. Mitchell: Scapegoat of the Crash?" *Business History Review* (Spring 1986): 81–103. The "short-selling" charge against Wiggins reflected societal ambivalence about the practice. While the extent to which these episodes constituted scandals has been debated, the fact remains that they were then popularly deemed so. Charles Geisst, *100 Years of Wall Street* (New York: McGraw-Hill, 2000), 41.

41. See John Flynn, *Investment Trusts Gone Wrong!* (New York: Arno Press, 1975; first published 1930).

42. Diana Henriques, *Fidelity's World: The Secret Life and Public Power of the Mutual Fund Giant* (New York: Touchstone, 1997), 57–58.

43. Ron Chernow, *The Death of the Banker: The Decline and Fall of the Great Financial Dynasties and the Triumph of the Small Investor* (New York: Vintage Books, 1997), 44.

44. Roosevelt, qtd. in "National Affairs: Caveat Venditor," *Time*, April 10, 1933, accessed August 25, 2011, www.time.com/time/magazine/article/0,9171,929518,00.html. On the Securities Act of 1933, see William Leuchtenburg, *Franklin D. Roosevelt and the New Deal* (New York: Harper and Row, 1963), 59, 90–91, 149. For more discussion on the New Deal's effort to regulate Wall Street, see Leuchtenburg, 11, 33, 36, 58–69, 148–49, 335–36. On the SEC Act, see Leuchtenburg, 90–91, 155–57.

45. William O. Douglas, Commissioner SEC, "Your Securities: Their Future Protection," A Speech before the Graduate School of Public Affairs of American University and Department of Agriculture, Washington, DC, April 17, 1937, *Vital Speeches*, 436–42, esp. 436 and 437. For the Exchange's reaction to the SEC, see Brooks, *Golconda*, 203–5.

46. Committee on Business Conduct [CBC], Minute Book, February 2, 1933, to June 14, 1934, NYSEA, my italics. After much debate, the Committee finally permitted Brown Bros.

to use the illustrations, but only because they deemed the founders' picture "of a dignified character."

47. John B. Newman, Letter to Perry D. Bogue, December 7, 1933, Committee on Customers' Men Box, NYSEA.

48. Whitney, qtd. in Brooks, *Golconda*, 198.

49. See Richard Whitney, "Economic Freedom," December 10, 1934, *Vital Speeches*, 212.

50. Qtd. in Chris Welles, *The Last Days of the Club* (New York: E. P. Dutton, 1975), 13.

51. See chap. 5, "Landis and the Statecraft of the SEC," in Thomas McGraw, *Prophets of Regulation: Charles Francis Adams, Louis D. Brandeis, James M. Landis, Alfred E. Kahn* (Cambridge, MA: Harvard University Press, 1984), 153–209.

52. Landis, "Address before the New York Stock Exchange Institute," June 19, 1935. Returning to the Institute a few months later, Landis again said, "It has always been my thesis that self-government is the most desirable form of government, and whether it be self-government by the exchange or self-government by any other institution, the thesis still holds." Landis, "Speech to the New York Exchange Institute," October 10, 1935; "Speech to the Swarthmore Club of Philadelphia," February 27, 1937. Both addresses qtd. in McGraw, *Prophets of Regulation*, 192–93. See also SEC, *First Annual Report* (Washington, DC: GPO, 1935), 38.

53. Douglas, qtd. in Welles, *Last Days*, 12.

54. On Whitney's opposition to the proposed National Securities Act of 1934, see Richard Whitney, "Statement in Regard to HR 7852," February 22–23, 1934; "Statement in Regard to Senate Bill 2693," February 29, 1934; "Statement in Regard to the 'National Securities Exchange Act of 1934' as Amended (HR 8720)," March 22, 1934, both in Whitney Speeches Box, NYSEA. Brooks, *Golconda*, 222. On the SEC, see Joel Seligman, *The Transformation of Wall Street: A History of the Securities and Exchange Commission and Modern Corporate Finance* (Boston: Northeastern University Press, 1995); Louis Kohlmeier, *The Regulators: Watchdog Agencies and the Public Interests* (New York: Harper and Row, 1969); Ralph F. De Bedts, *The New Deal's SEC: The Formative Years* (New York: Columbia University Press, 1964).

55. Joseph Kennedy, Address to Boston Chamber of Commerce, November 15, 1934 (Washington, DC: GPO, 1934), 10, BL. Also see Kennedy, "Shielding the Sheep," *Saturday Evening Post*, January 18, 1936, which he wrote after he departed the SEC.

56. Robert Sobel, *N.Y.S.E.: A History of the New York Stock Exchange, 1935–1975* (New York: Weybright and Talley, 1975), 18.

57. The NYSE suffered from what organizational management theorists Blake Ashforth and Barrie Gibbs have termed "the double-edged sword of organizational legitimization." See Blake E. Ashforth and Barrie W. Gibbs, "The Double-Edged Sword of Organizational Legitimacy," *Organization Science* 1, no. 2 (1990): 177. Also see Sobel, *N.Y.S.E.*, 18–19.

58. Richard Whitney to NYSE Members, Partners, Branch Office Managers and Correspondents, October 30, 1934, Box 116, Folder 8, TWL Papers, BL. Martin Egan to TWL, October 31, 1934, Box 116, Folder 8, TWL Papers, BL.

59. Martin Egan to TWL, October 31, 1934, Box 116, Folder 8, TWL Papers, BL.

60. Richard Whitney, "Economic Freedom," December 10, 1934, *Vital Speeches*, 212. Whitney displays tremendous self-pity and an acute sense of personal persecution in this speech. The tone and content support Seymour Lipset's and William Schneider's observation, "One

effect of declining confidence in leaders is status insecurity. An elite that is not esteemed by the public will probably feel anxious about its own authority. In fact, many institutional leaders in this country feel that they are disliked, or at least not sufficiently respected, by the public. The leaders' response . . . is a sometimes obsessive concern with their public image." Seymour Lipset and William Schneider, *The Confidence Gap: Business, Labor, and the Government in the Public Mind* (New York: Free Press, 1983), 376. Whitney's speech also evokes what Richard Hofstadter termed "the paranoid style in American politics." While feeling persecuted, the paranoid spokesman in politics views the conspiracy as directed not so much against him personally, but "against a nation, a culture, a way of life whose fate affects not himself alone, but millions of others." As Hofstadter explains, the paranoid spokesman possesses a "sense that his political passions are unselfish and patriotic." Hofstadter, *The Paranoid Style in American Politics and Other Essays* (New York: Vintage Books, 1964), 4.

61. Richard Whitney, "Economic Freedom," December 10, 1934, *Vital Speeches*, 212.

62. "Three Suggested as Exchange Head," *NYT*, March 5, 1935, 34. Brooks, *Golconda*, 226. On Gay's nomination, see also TWL to GW, March 3, 1935, Box 137, Folder 13, TWL Papers, BL.

63. As Whitney stepped down from the presidency, the Board enacted several resolutions praising him. Thomas Lamont added his own words of praise in a letter to his old classmate, effusively complimenting Whitney for the "superb job" he had performed for the NYSE community. "During all those weary anxious months at Washington, in all the discussions over the SEC bill, you were the man who bore the brunt of the battle." TWL to RW, May 9, 1935, Box 137, Folder 16; see also RW to TWL, August 11, 1935, Box 137, Folder 16, and TWL, Confidential Memorandum for GW, February 10, 1934, Box 137, Folder 12. Also see TWL to GW, May 29, 35, Box 137, Folder 13. All in TWL Papers, BL.

64. Sobel, *N.Y.S.E.*, 6–7.

65. *NY Sun*, March 17, 1935, 24, also qtd. in Sobel, *N.Y.S.E.*, 6–7.

66. Baseball had suffered from the Black Sox scandal, and Hollywood had been tarnished by the Roscoe "Fatty" Arbuckle rape and murder scandal.

67. *NY Sun*, March 17, 1935, 24, also qtd. in Sobel, *N.Y.S.E.*, 6–7.

68. Ibid.

69. In his early speeches as president, Gay sounded like a moderate, refraining from attacking either the SEC or the New Deal and focusing instead on simply propounding the Exchange's worth. At the start of his tenure, Gay often made "educational" speeches such as "The Need for Stock Exchanges," September 5, 1935, Box 3, Folder 4; "The Utility of Stock Exchanges," May 22, 1936, Box 3, Folder 42; "The Stock Exchange and Its Functions," March 9, 1936, Box 3, Folder 30; "Stock Exchanges and Investors," May 18, 1936, Box 3, Folder 40; "Public Relations and the Stock Exchange," September 11, 1935, Box 3, Folder 5, Speeches of Presidents, Chairmen, and Officers, NYSEA.

70. Charles Gay, "The Stock Exchange and the Public," December 5, 1935, Folder 17, Box 3, NYSEA. Gay tempered his harsh criticism by acknowledging, "Our great client is the public and our responsibility is to the public. The public provides the nation's growing fund of capital."

71. The practice of using a company's annual report as a public relations tool was not yet widespread. See Dickson Hartwell, "Telling the Stockholders," *Public Opinion Quarterly* 4, no. 1 (March 1940): 35–47. Hartwell cites GM's Annual Report as a model in this regard (38–39).

72. Joseph Alsop and Robert Kintern discussed the 1937 Recession and the 1938 Reorganization in their two-part series, "The Battle of the Market Place," *Saturday Evening Post*, June 11, 1938, and June 25, 1938.

73. Belittling Roosevelt's concern about a "capital strike," Lamont commented, "Incidentally, the suggestion that this recession has been engineered, or is being acquiesced in philosophically, by business men is of course fantastic. Men of substance and of experience do not throw away their fortunes because they may happen to disagree with some of the philosophic tenets of the present Administration." TWL to Berle, December 28, 1937, Box 84, TWL Papers, BL.

74. Carlton Shively, Financial Notes, *NY Sun*, November 23, 1937, 35.

75. William O. Douglas met with Reformers Pierce and Shields on October 16, 1937, to discuss a proposed internal reorganization of the NYSE. See Alsop and Kinter, "Marketplace," June 25, 1938, 82.

76. Ralph M. Hower Papers, Harvard Business School Archives, Baker Library Historical Collections, Harvard Business School. See Harry L. Hanson, "Three-Hour Examination, Business History, February 1937," Box 11, F1, Modern Business Background, 1937–1942, Series V, Teaching Materials. Abbreviated as "RMH Papers, BL" henceforward.

77. For a discussion of the Conway Committee, see Alsop and Kinter, "Marketplace," June 25, 1938, 81–82. Also see Brooks, *Golconda,* 251–52. The Old Guard most objected to Maurice Farrell's appointment to the Committee, as they viewed him as the most liberal pick.

78. Ibid.

79. Hanson, "Examination," Box 11, RMH Papers, BL.

80. In his novel, *The Embezzler* (Boston: Houghton Mifflin, 1966), Louis Auchincloss provides a thinly disguised fictional account of Whitney's fall from grace.

81. See Securities and Exchange Commission, *In the Matter of Richard Whitney*, esp. vol. 1 (Washington, DC, 1938).

82. Qtd. in Alsop and Kinter, "Marketplace," June 25, 1938, 82.

83. Welles, *Last Days*, 14. Also see Brooks, *Golconda,* 248, 273, 283–86.

84. "Exchange Talks with Press Agent: E. L. Bernays Consults with Officials," *NY Sun*, March 15, 1938, 39. See also Wayne W. Parrish, "Ivy Lee, Family Physician to Big Business," *Literary Digest*, June 9, 1934, 30.

85. Andrew F. Brimmer, "William McChesney Martin," *Proceedings of the American Philosophical Society* 44, no. 2 (June 2000).

86. Douglas, qtd. in Brooks, *Golconda,* 281.

87. George Gallup and Claude Robinson, "American Institute of Public Opinion-Surveys, 1935–38," *The Public Opinion Quarterly* 2, no. 3 (July 1938): 373–98, esp. 384. Also see Winthrop Smith, Conference of Bank Managers Transcript, Merrill Lynch Meeting, April 3–4, 1940, Waldorf-Astoria Hotel, New York City, and Edwin P. Hoyt, *The Supersalesmen* (Cleveland: World Publishing, 1962), 97.

88. I borrow the term "confidence gap" from Lipset and Schneider, who used it in their book *The Confidence Gap* to describe American sentiment toward business and government during the 1970s.

CHAPTER TWO: **Experimenting with Advertising**

Epigraph. Vol. 9, Issue 2, 236.

1. For reported stock volume and annual turnover rates, see NYSE, *NYSE Factbook* (New York: NYSE, 1963), 40, NYSEA. For historical seat prices on the NYSE, 1875–1953, see NYSE, *NYSE Yearbook 1954*, 7, NYSEA. On the DJIA levels, see http://stockcharts.com/freecharts/historical/djia19201940.html, accessed June 9, 2011.

2. James W. Young, "The Advertising Council at Work," Address at Hotel Statler, Washington, DC, September 18, 1946, Folder, The Advertising Council, Misc., Box 1, SMOF, Dallas C. Halverstadt Files, Truman Library (TL).

3. Robert Sobel, *The Big Board: A History of the New York Stock Market* (New York: Free Press, 1965), 306–7.

4. "Fenner & Beane Begins Advertising Program under Stock Exchange's Liberalized Rules," *NYT*, April 27, 1939, 39. See also Robert Sobel, *N.Y.S.E.: A History of the New York Stock Exchange, 1935–1975* (New York: Weybright and Talley, 1975), 70–71.

5. Fenner & Beane, founded in 1916, was based in New Orleans, LA. Its main competitor, E. A. Pierce, was led in the 1930s by E. A. Pierce, Edmund Lynch, and Winthrop Smith. See "Business & Finance: No. 1 Wire House," *Time*, February 4, 1935, accessed July 10, 2011, www.time.com/time/magazine/article/0,9171,788558,00.html.

6. This paragraph and the previous one draw on "Fenner & Beane Begins Advertising," 39 and Robert Sobel, *Inside Wall Street: Continuity and Change in the Financial District* (New York: W. W. Norton, 1982), 70–71.

7. Russell, qtd. in "Fenner & Beane," 39.

8. Fenner & Beane did not report on the number of accounts opened in the wake of the advertisements, but that they remained wedded to such promotions indicates that they were working—or at least, that Fenner & Beane believed that they were working.

9. See www.doremus.com and http://en.wikipedia.org/wiki/Doremus_%26_Co., accessed June 23, 2011.

10. Russell, qtd. in "Advertising News and Notes," *NYT*, April 12, 1940, 44.

11. "Business: Bigger Biggest," *Time*, November 10, 1930, accessed July 10, 2011, www.time.com/time/magazine/article/0,9171,740665,00.html. When E. A. Pierce & Co. acquired Merrill Lynch & Co., it got Merrill's large wire system as well as its massive retail sales and stock commission organization. Merrill Lynch also had a sizable presence in investment banking, a business that now E. A. Pierce & Co. entered in a large way.

12. Winthrop Smith, Transcript, Conference of Bank Managers, Merrill Lynch Meeting, April 3–4, 1940, Waldorf-Astoria Hotel, New York City. My sincere thanks to Edwin Perkins for sharing this document with me. Also see Edwin P. Hoyt, *The Supersalesmen* (Cleveland: World Publishing, 1962), 97. For more on Winthrop H. Smith's role in the partnership, see Warren Bennis and David A. Heenan, *Co-Leaders: The Power of Great Partnerships* (New York: John Wiley and Sons, 1999), chap. 4, 63–80. Also see Henry Hecht, ed., *A Legacy of Leadership: Merrill Lynch, 1884–1985* (New York: Merrill Lynch, 1985), as well as Joseph Nocera, *A Piece of the Action: How the Middle Class Joined the Money Class* (New York: Simon and Schuster, 1994).

13. See Edwin Perkins, *Wall Street to Main Street: Charles Merrill and Middle-Class Investors* (Cambridge: Cambridge University Press, 1999); Perkins, *Perkins on U.S. Financial History and Related Topics* (New York: University Press of America, 2009), esp. chap. 11, "Market Research

at Merrill Lynch & Co., 1940–1945: New Direction for Stockbrokers," 149–60; Perkins, "Growth Stocks for Middle Class Investors: Merrill Lynch & Co., 1914–1941," in *Coping with Crisis: International Financial Institutions in the Interwar Period,* ed. Makoto Kasuya (Oxford: Oxford University Press, 2003).

14. "Advises Customers to Get out of Debt," *NYT,* April 1, 1928, 41. The headline of the letter that Merrill sent to his customers read: "Now Is a Good Time to Get out of Debt."

15. Merrill, qtd. in Transcript, Conference of Bank Managers, 90–91. Regarding the firm's continued use of public relations, Merrill was quick to admit, "On a number of occasions we will sit down with fellows we know that work for newspapers, and we will tell them what we are trying to do, and give them the facts, and how they interpret those facts and how they write the story, is their business, and nobody in this firm has authority to go to one reporter and complain as to how he interprets the facts we have given him. Now, let's get that straight. We will take these fellows into our confidence, we will tell them what we are doing, we will tell them our plans, and there it is."

16. Prior to its merger with Merrill Lynch, Fenner & Beane was doing so well that it was actually hiring at a time when most commission houses on Wall Street were not. By 1948, Merrill Lynch Pierce Fenner & Smith had a total of 99 offices in 33 states, the District of Columbia, and even Cuba. See J. E. McMahon, "Wall Street Attacks Seen Wide of Mark," *NYT,* August 29, 1948, F3.

17. "Chain Store Methods Aid Business of the Biggest Firm on Wall Street," *NYT,* February 11, 1943, 29. In 1942, Merrill Lynch added 27,160 new customers, bringing the total number of accounts to more than 120,000.

18. On the cost of advertising versus the benefits, see Pamela Walker Laird, *Advertising Progress: American Business and the Rise of Consumer Marketing* (Baltimore: Johns Hopkins University Press, 1998), 351, and Emily Fogg-Meade, "The Place of Advertising in Modern Business," *Journal of Political Economy* 9, no. 2 (March 1901): 218–42.

19. Paul T. Cherington [PTC] Papers, Harvard Business School Archives, Baker Library Historical Collections, Harvard Business School; PTC, "Advertising in a Period of Business Recovery," Address to Advertising Club of Boston, September 23, 1930, 1–2, Folder, PTC Speeches and Articles, Book 1, A-G, 1929–1931, Box 2, Cherington, Speeches and Articles, 1929–1931, Clippings, 1937–1941.

20. The connection between "orderliness" and liquidity continued to pervade Exchange documents in later years, such as in the *NYSE 1950 Annual Report* (New York: NYSE, 1950), 4.

21. Leonard I. Pearlin and Morris Rosenberg, "Propaganda Techniques in Institutional Advertising," *Public Opinion Quarterly* 16, no. 1 (Spring 1952): 5–26, esp. 14. On institutional advertising, see also Jackson Lears, *Fables of Abundance: A Cultural History of Advertising in America* (New York: Basic Books, 1995), 244–50; Roland Marchand, *Creating the Corporate Soul: The Rise of Public Relations and Corporate Imagery in American Big Business* (Berkeley: University of California Press, 1998), 54, 70, 80–82, 177–201.

22. The Nye Committee subpoenaed makers of warships, military airplanes, explosives, firearms, and chemicals. Richard Tedlow, *Keeping the Corporate Image: Public Relations and Business, 1900–1950* (Greenwich: JAI Press, 1979), 347. See also Martin Grams, *The History of the Cavalcade of America* (Kearney: Morris Publishing, 1998). Several companies that Nye targeted (like DuPont and Remington Arms) were Morgan clients, and so the papers of Morgan partner

Thomas Lamont provide rich insights into the hearings. In the autumn of 1935, Tom Lamont wrote his friend, publisher Joseph Knapp, that while the Nye Committee "has not produced one single shred of proof" that American munitions manufacturers and bankers had led the nation into war, nevertheless, Senator Nye and his fellow committee members "have succeeded in creating the impression which they have desired to create." Thomas W. Lamont [TWL] Papers, Baker Library Historical Collections, Harvard Business School. See TWL to Joe Knapp, September 20, 1935, 101–21, Mss 783. Also see "Report of the Special Committee on Investigation of the Munitions Industry" (The Nye Report), U.S. Senate, 74th Congress, 2nd Session, February 24, 1936, esp. 3–13.

23. In 1952, DuPont began broadcasting the show also on television. On the "Cavalcade," see Tedlow, *Keeping the Corporate Image,* 349.

24. "Exchange Pushes Its Ad Campaign," *NYT,* October 18, 1939, 42. The report noted that the present "plans call for using leading newspapers in the larger cities, those which have more than a handful of Stock Exchange member offices. Full pages would be used, spaced a week apart."

25. Ibid.

26. Ibid.

27. Martin survived the war, but never returned to the NYSE presidency. Instead, he became Chairman of the Federal Board, serving in the post from 1951 to 1970. See Charles R. Geisst, *100 Years of Wall Street* (New York: McGraw-Hill, 2000), 62, and also Robert P. Bremner, *Chairman of the Fed: William McChesney Martin Jr. and the Creation of the American Financial System* (New Haven: Yale University Press, 2004).

28. Sobel, *N.Y.S.E.,* 106–115, passim.

29. Qtd. in Sobel, *N.Y.S.E.,* 114.

30. Schram, qtd. in Sobel, *N.Y.S.E.,* 113.

31. "We are afforded," Schram, *NYSE 1942 Annual Report,* 5; "Stewardship," "deep sense of responsibility," *NYSE 1944 Annual Report,* 4; "Essentially a service organization," *NYSE 1944 Annual Report,* 1.

32. By 1944, 5,983 members of the Exchange community were in the armed forces. *NYSE 1944 Annual Report,* 4–5.

33. *NYSE 1943 Annual Report,* 5. On trading volume and shares outstanding in the war years, see *NYSE 1945 Annual Report,* 1.

34. Schram, qtd. in *NYSE 1944 Annual Report,* 4.

35. According to the *NYSE 1943 Annual Report,* the U.S. Treasury Department "promptly recognized the special usefulness of this nation-wide securities distributing organization by integrating it directly into the War Bond campaign." *NYSE 1943 Annual Report,* 2; also see *NYSE 1944 Annual Report,* 4–5.

36. On reported stock volume, see *NYSE Factbook 1963,* 40, and also *NYSE 1945 Annual Report,* 1.

37. Schram, qtd. in *NYSE 1942 Annual Report,* 1.

38. Schram, qtd. in *NYSE 1943 Annual Report,* 1–2.

39. Ibid.

40. Benjamin Graham and David L. Dodd, *Security Analysis: Principles and Technique* (New

York: McGraw-Hill, 1951; first published 1934), vii, 624. Graham and Dodd admitted, "every now and then some manipulative activities are engaged in by hardy souls," yet they contended that such individuals "generally find their schemes exposed and themselves in serious trouble." "In every major sense," they wrote in 1951, "the market has been free of manipulation since the middle 1930's." On the SEC Act, see Graham and Dodd, 624–27.

41. For a discussion of the Merrill Lynch polls (conducted in part by Braun & Associates), see Winthrop Smith, Transcript, Conference of Bank Managers. Also see Edwin P. Hoyt, *The Supersalesmen* (Cleveland: World Publishing, 1962), 97.

42. For average annual dividend yields on Barron's 50 common stock average in the period 1926–1952, see Richard W. Lambourne, "The Stock Market Situation," *The Analysts Journal* 9, no. 1 (February 1953): 106. Notably, in 1942, the dividend yield on the Barron's 50 common stock average was 8.8%. See http://stockcharts.com/charts/historical/djia19201940.html, accessed July 28, 2010.

43. On the rise of installment plans in the 1920s and the revolution in consumer credit that it engendered, see Martha Olney, *Buy Now, Pay Later: Advertising, Credit, and Consumer Durables in the 1920's* (Chapel Hill: University of North Carolina Press, 1991).

44. "New York Stock Exchange Recommends a Security," NYSE Advertisement, *NYT*, March 24, 1942, 15.

45. Gene Miller, "Background on New Advertising and Public Relations Plan," 5, ca. 1969, NYSEA.

46. Schram, *NYSE 1946 Annual Report*, 4.

47. N. W. Ayer & Son, *Forty Years of Advertising* (N. W. Ayer: Philadelphia, 1909), 21–24, in Box 19, Ralph M. Hower Papers, Harvard Business School Archives, Baker Library Historical Collections, Harvard Business School. Ayer was never an agency for the NYSE; the first string of agencies that the Exchange retained included Gardner, BBDO, Calkins & Holden, Reach & McClinton, and Compton & Knowles.

48. Ayer, *Forty Years of Advertising*, 22. Italics in original.

49. "Advertising and the War Effort," *Collier's*, August 26, 1944, 82.

50. Carrie McLaren, Interview with Inger Stole, "Selling Advertising: The Ad Industry's Battle against the Consumer Movement of the 1930s," *Stay Free*, no. 18, accessed June 21, 2011, www.stayfreemagazine.org/achives/18/inger.html. Also see Inger L. Stole, *Advertising on Trial: Consumer Activism and Corporate Public Relations in the 1930s* (Champaign: University of Illinois Press, 2005), 54–58, 72, 78–79, 152–58. On the Wheeler-Lea Act (esp. Section 5), also see Martin L. Lindahl, "The Federal Trade Commission Act as Amended in 1938," *Journal of Political Economy* 47, no. 4 (August 1939): 497–525. Also on the Tugwell Bill, see Robert Griffith, "The Selling of America: The Advertising Council and American Politics, 1942–1960," *Business History Review* 57 (Autumn 1983): 389–412. See also Otis Pease, *The Responsibilities of American Advertising* (New Haven: Yale University Press, 1958).

51. William Enright, "Batt Bids Ad Men Get into Defense," *NYT*, November 14, 1941, 25. See also James Webb Young, "What Shall We Do about It?," November 14, 1941, Series 13/2/300, Box No. 1, War Advertising Council File, 1941–1945, University of Illinois Archives of the Advertising Council (hereafter abbreviated UIAAC). Also please see Griffith, "The Selling of America," 390.

52. Young, "What Shall We Do about It?" Also see Griffith, "The Selling of America," 389–90, and C. B. Larrabee, "If You Looked for a Miracle," *Printers' Ink*, November 21, 1941, 13–15, 79–80.

53. On the Advertising-Advertising campaign, see esp. Letter to Associated Advertising Clubs, January 21, 1927; William M. Armistead, Stenographic Notes, 50th Anniversary Dinner, April 4, 1919; Ayer Agency to Mr. Houstin Harte, publisher, the *San Angelo Standard*, Inc. (San Angelo, Texas), March 23, 1922; Barnes, Manager of Bristol Press Publishing Co. to N. W. Ayer & Son, Advertising Agency, Philadelphia, February 8, 1922, all in Folder 6, Advertising, Box 13, Series 7, N. W. Ayer & Son, Inc., Research Materials, ca. 1870–1938, Ralph M. Hower Papers, Arch: GA 39.5, Baker Library.

54. The conference attendees vowed to improve their image by using advertising "in other than commercial ventures, and specifically in the public interest." In fact, the federal government did not perceive advertising in quite as harsh a light as ad executives feared. Government officials who attended the A.A.A.A./A.N.A. meeting emphasized the fallacy of the idea that they were "against advertising." OPA administrator Leon Henderson asserted that the ad industry "faced no peril" from the New Deal; he and his colleagues realized that "advertising is the cheapest and most efficient method of selling goods." "Won't Curb Ads, Henderson Says," *NYT*, November 14, 1941, 35.

55. Clifford Montague, "OWI: Winning Wars with Words," *Media History Digest* 11, no. 2 (Fall/Winter 1991): 28–37, 46.

56. Chester J. LaRoche, "Advertising Role in the War Effort," in *An Appeal to Business from the Country's War Leaders: The Role of Advertising in Creating a Strong Home Front as Broadcast to a Nationwide Audience of Business Leaders, July 14, 1943, over the National Broadcasting Company Network*, Record Series 13/2/207, Folder #9083, UIAAC. Italics in original.

57. See Elmer Davis, Director, OWI, in "The Wartime Information Problem," in *An Appeal to Business*.

58. See Davis, "The Wartime Information Problem." Also see Montague, *OWI*, 28–37, 46.

59. Mark H. Leff, "The Politics of Sacrifice on the American Home Front in World War II," *Journal of American History* 74, no. 4 (March 1991): 1298.

60. Stole, *Advertising on Trial*, 185–86.

61. West further noted, "It is quite beyond me to fathom the mind of anyone who says that advertising and public relations are entirely separate in his organization. Perhaps it is sometimes wishful thinking that causes us to try to separate advertising from public relations. There are still unfortunately a few of us who would have cause for rejoicing if the public did not judge us by our advertising—if all our advertising were not inevitably and inseparably an instrumentality of public relations." Paul B. West, "The Faith that Makes Sales," Talk to the Pittsburgh Advertising Club, September 11, 1945, Advertising Council Folder (1 of 2), Box 1, SMOF, Charles W. Jackson Files, OWMR File, Papers of Harry S. Truman, Truman Library (TL).

62. "Advertising and the War Effort," 82.

63. War Advertising Council, "From War to Peace: The New Challenge to Business and Advertising" (New York: War Advertising Council, 1945), 3–7. James W. Young, "The Advertising Council at Work," September 18, 1946, and Theodore S. Repplier, "How the American Enterprise System is Being Re-sold to the American People," October 1, 1946, both speeches in

Box 1, Dallas C. Halverstadt Files, Harry S. Truman Papers, TL. Stuart Peabody, "Advertising and Total Diplomacy," March 1, 1950, Speech in Box 16, Charles W. Jackson Files, Harry S. Truman Papers, TL. See FDR and Truman quotes, Presidential Letters and Quotations, 1944–88, Record Series 13/2/282, Box 1, WAC, UIAAC. See also Griffith, "The Selling of America", 391.

64. For projections of pending depression after the war, see James Grant, *Money of the Mind: Borrowing and Lending in America from the Civil War to Michael Milken* (New York: Farrar, Straus and Giroux, 1992), 23–36.

65. Griffith, "The Selling of America," 388–89.

66. "Advertising and the War Effort," 82.

67. War Advertising Council, "From War to Peace," 8; Theodore S. Repplier, Speech at Association of National Advertisers Convention, Atlantic City, October 1, 1946, "How the American Enterprise System is Being Resold to the American People," Folder, The Advertising Council, Miscellaneous, Box 1, SMOF, Dallas C. Halverstadt Files, TL.

68. FDR and Truman quotes, Box 1, Presidential Letters Folder, WAC, UIAAC. On the creation of the postwar Ad Council, also please see Griffith, "The Selling of America," 393–94.

69. In 1950, *Sales Management Magazine* reported that the average age of members of the Association of Customers' Brokers was 54. Lawrence M. Hughes, "NYSE President to Sell Shares of American Business," *Sales Management Magazine*, 1951, 104, 36, NYSEA.

70. The "Barton" in the name referred to Bruce Barton, who had written the bestseller *The Man Nobody Knows* two decades earlier. An article in *Media/Scope* in December 1957 discussed why the NYSE preferred to use newspapers as its dominant advertising medium: the NYSE traditionally "had been close to newspapers. Newspapers print the daily stock listings." Also, quoting NYSE vice president Rud Lawrence, the magazine reported that the NYSE felt that newspapers, more than any other media outlet, would enable the Exchange "to reach the mass of the public . . . a total cross section of the population from high school students, who are the investors of tomorrow, to the corner druggist, teachers, and housewives"; "How Media Are Chosen and Used in a Public Relations Ad Campaign," *Media/Scope*, December 1957, 38–41, RCL, Box 2, NYSEA. In another article, a NYSE official remarked, "We consider the nation's newspaper frontline troops in the revolution. . . . Our industry is dependent to a large extent upon the daily press. Not only do many newspapers carry daily stock tables, but as a group they do an enormous job in reporting the news of finance and business so vital to informed citizens." Philip Schuyler, "Goal of NY Stock Exchange Ad Effort," *Editor & Publisher*, August 1, 1959, 23, 24, RCL, Box 3. The order of public relations firms retained by the NYSE in the 1940s through the 1960s was Gardner, then BBDO, followed by Calkins & Holden, and then, Reach & McClinton.

71. Keyserling, qtd. in Robert Sobel, *The Great Boom: How a Generation of Americans Created the World's Most Prosperous Society* (New York: St. Martin's Press, 2000), 29, 33–34.

72. Schram, qtd. in *NYSE 1947 Annual Report*, 1.

73. Winston Churchill, "The Sinews of Peace" [Iron Curtain Speech], delivered at Westminster College, March 5, 1946, accessed July 16, 2011, www.americanrhetoric.com/speeches/winstonchurchillsinewsofpeace.htm.

74. Harry S. Truman, "The Truman Doctrine," speech delivered to Congress, March 12, 1947, accessed July 16, 1911, www.americanrhetoric.com/speeches/harrystrumantrumandoctrine.html.

75. On the Marshall Plan, see Nicolaus Mills, *Winning the Peace: The Marshall Plan and America's Coming of Age as a Superpower* (New York: John Wiley and Sons, 2008).

76. "Stockholders' Meeting," advertisement, discussed in J. A. Livingston, *The American Stockholder* (Philadelphia: J. B. Lippincott, 1958), 22–23. At the time of that campaign in 1947, the Brookings study had not yet been conducted, so the Exchange had no real basis for asserting widespread shareownership.

77. "Working Hours . . . 9 to 5. Earnings Hours . . . Around the Clock," NYSE Advertisement, clipping in author's possession, ca. 1947.

78. Marchand notes, "Of all the themes that AT&T explored in its search for antidotes to the taint of monopoly and 'the curse of bigness,' none proved as satisfying to company executives or found such resonance in other corporate image campaigns as the concept of 'investment democracy.'" He further explains how "this theme equated the corporation with its hundreds of thousands of stockholders. A focus on 'typical' stockholders among this multitude legitimized the company's exercise of power as truly democracy. Rather than asserting a rightful, dominating power for huge corporations within the nexus of social institutions, the concept of investment denied that the corporation represented any nucleus of power distinct from the public at large." Marchand, 74, 75–82.

79. "The Investor is Almost Everybody," *Saturday Evening Post*, May 24, 1949, 32–34.

80. Some of these reporters who frequently ran favorable stories on the NYSE during this period included Sam Shulsky (*Coronet*) and Sylvia Porter (*Good Housekeeping*).

81. Livingston, *American Stockholder*, 22–23.

82. Merrill, qtd. in Sobel, *Dangerous Dreamers*, 30.

83. Merrill, qtd. in Transcript, Conference of Branch Office Managers, 9.

84. "What Keeps a Customer Happy," Merrill Lynch Advertisement, *Magazine of Wall Street*, December 13, 1952, 269.

85. Merrill Lynch, Conference of Branch Office Managers, 77.

86. "How Big a Customer," Merrill Lynch Advertisement, *NYT*, June 14, 1950, 48.

87. Sylvia F. Porter, "How About Your Lazy Money?" *Good Housekeeping* 130, February 1950, 228.

88. Raymond Trigger, "Wall Street Goes to the Fair," *Coronet*, January 1951, 41. *Coronet* enthusiastically reported that 17,000 of the 169,000 people who attended Cleveland's Flower Show visited the Prescott booth—but this represented only 10% of the attendees, and a presumably a far smaller percentage actually purchased stock.

89. Trigger, "Wall Street Goes to the Fair," 41. J. S. Bache's subway ads are discussed in "Small Investors: Wall Street Dynamite?" *Forbes*, December 15, 1950, 19.

90. "Small Investors: Wall Street Dynamite?," 19.

91. Ibid. Stock market history has proven this fear to be not entirely founded: in some downturns, small investors have largely refrained from panic selling.

92. Ibid.

93. *NYSE 1951 Annual Report*, 8. Scott later served as Chairman of the Board from May 1954 to May 1956.

94. Letter from Edward D. Jones of Edward D. Jones & Co., Members NYSE, St. Louis,

Missouri, September 19, 1950, Folder, Special Committee on the Presidency, Letters of Application and Endorsement, August 23, 1950–September 19, 1950, NYSEA.

CHAPTER THREE: **Marketing the "Own Your Share" Program**

Epigraph. GKF Memo to the Board, Establishment of a Market Development Program, June 12, 1953, R. C. Lawrence, Presentations to Board of Governors, June 12, 1953–December 19, 1957, Folder, RCL Box 1, NYSEA.

1. The Berlin Blockade lasted from June 24, 1948, to May 12, 1949.

2. Richard M. Fried explores the "soft side" of anticommunism in *The Russians Are Coming! The Russians Are Coming! Pageantry and Patriotism in Cold-War America* (New York: Oxford University Press, 1998). Also see Elaine Tyler May, *Homeward Bound: American Families in the Cold War* (New York: Basic Books, 1988).

3. Folder on Special Committee on the Presidency, Letter of Application and Endorsement, August 23, 1950–September 19, 1950, NYSEA. See especially Charles F. Ros, Letter from the Econometric Institute, Inc., to Robert P. Boylan, August 25, 1950. Ros endorsed Hardenbrook.

4. Folder on Special Committee on the Presidency, NYSEA.

5. Lawrence M. Hughes, "NYSE President to Sell Shares of American Business," *Sales Management Magazine*, 1951, 36, NYSEA.

6. Folder on Special Committee on the Presidency, NYSEA.

7. Ros, Letter to Boylan, August 25, 1950.

8. Ibid.

9. "Young Turk on Wall Street," *Forbes*, December 5, 1951, 21–22.

10. RCL, Oral History, Interview with Deborah Gardiner, 1984, Box 4, RCL Papers, NYSEA.

11. Funston, qtd. in Robert Sobel, *N.Y.S.E.: A History of the New York Stock Exchange, 1935–1975* (New York: Weybright and Talley, 1975), 189. On the search for a successor to Schram and more on the selection of Funston, see also Sobel, N.Y.S.E., 186–92. See also "Young Turk on Wall Street," 21–22; Lawrence M. Hughes, "NYSE President to Sell Shares of American Business," *Sales Management Magazine* (1951), NYSEA; *NYSE Annual Reports*, 1952 and 1953; RCL, Oral History.

12. Sobel, N.Y.S.E., 191. During Funston's long presidency, the chairmanship position rotated among a series of individuals: Richard Crooks, Harold Scott, James Kellogg, Edward Werle, J. Truman Bidwell, Henry Watts, and Walter Frank. Many past chairmen such as Coleman, Stott, and Boylan remained on the Board, and continued to influence policy making.

13. On the new Public Reception Room and the 1950 Advisory Committee objectives, see *NYSE 1951 Annual Report*, 8. The Public Reception Room opened in December 1950, several months before Funston was hired in May 1951.

14. Funston, qtd. in Sobel, N.Y.S.E., 192.

15. "Young Turk in Wall Street," 21–22. To help the Exchange recover from the Depression, Funston had to convince many in the financial community to discard their old ideas about public relations, which were buried in the "dark mahogany ways of the past," as *Forbes* described it.

16. On the history of market research in the financial services sector, see Edwin Perkins,

"Market Research at Merrill Lynch & Co., 1940–1945: New Direction for Stockbrokers," chap. 2 in Perkins, *U.S. Financial History and Related Topics* (Lanham, MD: University Press of America, 2009), 149–60. On the broader origins of market research, see Douglas B. Ward, *A New Brand of Business: Charles Coolidge Parlin, Curtis Publishing Company, and the Origins of Market Research* (Philadelphia: Temple University Press, 2009).

17. "100,000 Stockowners Club," *Fortune*, 1952.

18. RCL, in his oral history, attributes part of the problem of no shareowner census to the small size of most brokerage firms at midcentury, Merrill Lynch notwithstanding.

19. Lewis Kimmel, *Shareownership in the United States*, Brookings Report (Washington, DC, July 1952), hereafter cited as the "Brookings Report." For a detailed discussion of the procedures and the survey methods, see 132–36, also, iii, 4–5. On the problem of shares registered in the names of brokers and dealers, see esp. 55. Donald Kemmerer also discusses the Brookings results in "American Financial Institutions: The Marketing of Securities, 1930–1952," *Journal of Economic History* 12, no. 4 (Autumn 1952): 466–67.

20. Kimmel, *Shareownership in the United States*, 128.

21. For a detailed breakdown of nine forms of investments and the percent of family units with one or more owners of them, see Brookings Report, 116.

22. "Young Turk in Wall Street," 21.

23. Funston, *NYSE 1951 Annual Report*, 12.

24. RCL, "Speech to Members of the N.Y. Chapter of the Special Libraries Association," October 26, 1954, NYSEA.

25. "Capitalists among the 'Poor,'" *Chicago Sun-Times*, July 6, 1952, Business Section, 1; Harold Wincott, "Who Owns American Industry?" *Financial Times*, July 8, 1952, 1; Harry Schwartz, "Soviet Hate Campaign Stirs Wide Speculation," *NYT*, July 6, 1952, E7.

26. Ferdinand Lundberg, *America's Sixty Families* (New York: Vanguard Press, 1960; first published 1934). A notable exception to the decrease in criticism regarding "who owns America" in the 1940s was the 1946 pamphlet of that title by American communist historian James S. Allen. Allen contended that communism was the best alternative for the country, since a capitalist society allegedly could not exist without monopoly. James S. Allen, *Who Owns America?* (New York: New Century, 1946).

27. "6,500,000 Capitalists," *New York Daily News*, July 2, 1952, 24.

28. "Who Owns Our Corporations?" *NYT*, July 6, 1952, 8E.

29. "Looks Like WE Are the 'American Capitalists,'" Cartoon, *San Francisco Chronicle*, July 1, 1952, 14. The capitalization, bolding, and underlining are the *Chronicle's*.

30. In the early 1950s, the NYSE often deemed as "middle class" those families with incomes of more than $5,000 a year. By the mid-1950s, the NYSE was no longer speaking as much of the middle class as it was of a larger group that it deemed the "Middle Majority," which the NYSE loosely considered to include members of the "upper lower class" through the "lower upper class."

31. Statistics are from the Brookings Report. On Funston's interpretations of those statistics, see, for instance, his comments in *NYSE 1953 Annual Report*.

32. Brookings Report, 81, 89.

33. "Who Owns Business," *Fortune*, September 1952, 87.

34. Joseph A. Livingston, *The American Stockholder* (Philadelphia: J. B. Lippincott, 1958), 23.

35. The *Magazine of Wall Street*, founded in 1907 by financial writer Richard Wyckoff, was edited and published for many years by his wife, Cecilia Gertrude ("C. G.") Wyckoff. See "The Press: Owners," *Time*, March 21, 1927, accessed July 10, 2011, www.time.com/time/magazine/article/0,9171,730203,00.html.

36. C. G. Wyckoff, "The Trend of Events," *Magazine of Wall Street*, September 9, 1952, 512.

37. Ibid.

38. "The NYSE Faces a Problem," *Magazine of Wall Street*, November 1, 1952, 104.

39. Stewart, Dougall & Associates, Inc., "Digest of Recommended Program for Merchandising Equity Securities Listed on the New York Stock Exchange," June 1953, see esp. p. 6, NYSEA. Hereafter abbreviated as "Digest."

40. For a discussion of the Brookings findings regarding average holding patterns, see "The NYSE Faces a Problem," *Magazine of Wall Street*, November 1, 1952, 104. As the *Magazine* reported, "This means that they are not as much interested in active trading as in the accumulation of savings in investments of one kind or another." On the percentage of Americans holding fewer than four issues, see Brookings, 128. Notably, 92% of all shareowners held less than ten issues, and 46% owned just one issue.

41. "Digest."

42. Ibid.

43. By 1975, the situation had almost reversed: institutions comprised a staggering 75% of all trading volume, as compared to only 20% 25 years earlier. In the late 1970s and 1980s, institutional trading volume continued to skyrocket, due to several pivotal events, especially the passage of the Employment Retirement Income Security Act (ERISA) in 1974, commission rate deregulation in 1975, and the introduction of 401(k) plans in 1978. See Marshall E. Blume and Irwin Friend, *The Changing Role of the Individual Investor* (New York: John Wiley and Sons, 1978), 105. Also on the rise of institutions in the market, see Charles Ellis, *Institutional Investing* (Homewood, IL: Dow Jones-Irwin, 1971), and James J. Needham, *The Threat to Corporate Growth* (Philadelphia: Girard Bank, 1974), 13.

44. Raymond W. Goldsmith, "The Historical Background: Financial Institutions as Investors in Corporate Stock before 1952," in *Institutional Investors and Corporate Stock: A Background Study*, ed. Goldsmith (New York: National Bureau of Economic Research, 1973), 34–90, esp. 52–53, 55, 57. For a discussion of the mutual savings bank idea and the historically high level of fiduciary standard applied to the decisions of savings bank trustees, see R. Daniel Wadhwani, "Protecting Small Savers: The Political Economy of Economic Security," *Journal of Policy History* 18, no. 1 (2006): 126–45, and Wadhwani, "Citizen Savers: Family Economy, Financial Institutions, and Public Policy in the Nineteenth-Century Northeast," Business History Conference 2004, *Enterprise & Society* 5, no. 4 (December 2004): 617–24.

45. Goldsmith, "Historical Background," 65. According to the NYSE, in 1950, pension funds had invested only 500 million of common stock in pension funds. *NYSE 1950 Annual Report*, 5.

46. Notable exceptions were property and casualty companies, which always had the right

to own common stock. Robert Sobel, *Dangerous Dreamers: The Financial Innovators from Charles Merrill to Michael Milken* (New York: John Wiley and Sons, 1993), 32.

47. Supreme Court justice Louis Brandeis popularized the phrase with his book *Other People's Money and How the Bankers Use It* (New York: Harper and Row, 1914).

48. *Harvard College v. Armory*, 26 Mass (9 Pick), 446, 461 (1830). On the evolution of prudent man thought, see John Brooks, *The Go-Go Years: The Drama and Crashing Finale of Wall Street's Bullish 60s* (New York: John Wiley and Sons, 1999), 129.

49. Sobel, *Dangerous Dreamers*, 32. See also Wilford J. Eiteman, "Trends in Investment Policies of Individuals: Discussion," *Journal of Finance* 4, no. 2 (June 1949): 176–79.

50. G. Keith Funston, "Institutional Investors: How Is Their Growth Affecting the Stock Market?" Remarks before the American Life Convention, Chicago, Illinois, October 14, 1955, 5, Speeches, President Funston, Folder 31, Box 7, RG 2.2, NYSEA.

51. See Chelcie C. Bosland, *The Common Stock Theory of Investment* (New York: Ronald Press, 1937), and Clark Belden, *Common Stocks and Uncommon Sense* (New York: Coward McCann Inc., 1939).

52. See Harry Markowitz, "Portfolio Selection," *Journal of Finance* 7, no. 1 (March 1952): 77–91. Also see Mark Rubinstein, "Portfolio Selection: A Fifty-Year Retrospective," *Journal of Finance* 57, no. 3 (June 2002): 1041–45.

53. Notably, New York liberalized its prudent man laws three years before Markowitz had written his theory of portfolio diversification (1949 versus 1952).

54. *NYSE 1950 Annual Report*, 5.

55. On the birth of the GM pension fund, see Peter Drucker, *The Unseen Revolution: How Pension Fund Socialism Came to America* (New York: HarperCollins, 1976), 5–7, and Sobel, *Dangerous Dreamers*, 32. See also Nelson Lichtenstein, *Walter Reuther: The Most Dangerous Man in Detroit* (Champaign: University of Illinois Press, 1997).

56. Sobel notes, "By 1955, life insurance companies owned more than $3.6 billion in common stock, while the property and casualty companies . . . held another $5.4 billion." *Dangerous Dreamers*, 32–33.

57. *NYSE 1951 Annual Report*, 12–13. Also see Brooks, *Go-Go Years*, 129; *NYSE 1950 Annual Report*, 5–6.

58. Funston downplayed these concerns, noting "the specter of sizable institutional holdings need not haunt us." Funston, "Institutional Investing," 8.

59. In the United States and Canada today, a "block trade" is usually defined as 10,000 shares of stock or $200,000 worth of bonds. In the mid-twentieth century, a block trade was less strictly defined, but it did involve thousands of shares of stock. See Robert Sobel, *Inside Wall Street: Continuity and Change in the Financial District* (New York: W. W. Norton, 1982), 54.

60. Kenneth M. Morris and Virginia M. Morris, *The Wall Street Journal Guide to Understanding Money & Investing* (New York: Lightbulb Press, 1999), 42.

61. In the first half of 1952, the daily averages dropped approximately 25% to 1,168,000 shares from 1,650,000 shares in the comparable period the prior year. Wyckoff, "Trend of Events," 512.

62. Needham relates this viewpoint and juxtaposes it to the other perspective that institutions had seriously undermined the market. Needham contended, "I believe the time has come

to abandon the fiction that there must be an inherent, unavoidable conflict between the interests of institutional and individual investors." Needham, *Threat to Corporate Growth*, 30.

63. Only members (i.e., companies or individuals who own seats on the trading floor) are permitted to buy and sell stocks on the Exchange trading floor. In 1953, the number of seats on the NYSE was 1,366. The NYSE maintained elaborate rules regarding eligibility, in part to ensure the continued character and professionalism of "the Club," as it was often known.

64. For more on the rate deregulation controversy, see Janice Traflet and Michael Coyne, "Ending a NYSE Tradition: The 1975 Unraveling of Brokers' Fixed Commissions and Its Long Term Impact on Financial Advertising," *Essays in Economic and Business History* 25 (2007): 131–41. For a good overview of the events leading to negotiated rates, see Marshall E. Blume, Jeremy Siegel, and Dan Rottenburg, *Revolution on Wall Street: The Rise and Decline of the NYSE* (New York: W. W. Norton, 1993), 14–17, 23–24, 50–52, 68, 107–9, 115, 128–42, 161–63. The principle of fixed commission rates is contained in the 1792 Buttonwood Agreement that led to the founding of what would become the precursor to the New York Stock Exchange. In the Buttonwood Agreement, 24 brokers pledged: "we will not buy or sell from this date for any person whatsoever any kind of public stocks at a less rate than one-quarter of one percent commission on the specie value." Buttonwood Agreement, NYSEA.

65. Sobel, *Inside Wall Street*, 73.

66. The 1960s and 1970s would witness the growth of this "Third Market," but in the early 1950s, the Third Market was not yet a major presence.

67. Sobel presents a different interpretation, claiming it was a mistake for the NYSE to focus so much on little investors while letting the OTC dealers expand. See Sobel, *Inside Wall Street*, 73–74.

68. Digest of Recommended Program for Merchandising Equity Securities on the New York Stock Exchange (New York: Stewart, Dougall and Associates, 1953), 7. In June 1953, the first memos circulated suggesting a Market Development Department; by November, the department was established, with a head. GKF Memo, Establishment of a Market Development Department, June 12, 1953, NYSEA. Keith Funston also encouraged the department's expansion. See also Memo, GKF to Board, Recommendation for Establishing a National Speakers Bureau, December 15, 1953, and December 17, 1953; Memo, GKF to Board, Recommended Market Research Program for 1954, May 6, 1954; Memo, GKF to Board, Recommendation for Employing an Advertising and Sales Manager, October 19, 1954; Memo, GKF to Board, Recommendation for Employing an Education Director, October 19, 1954; all in R. C. Lawrence, Presentations to Board of Governors, June 12, 1953–December 19, 1957 Folder, RCL Box 1, NYSEA.

69. GKF Memo, Establishment of a Market Development Program, June 12, 1953.

70. Ibid. Funston explained to the Board how the Program would function. Essentially repeating Stewart Dougall's recommendations, Funston wrote, "It would work closely with the other departments of the Exchange, esp. Public Relations, Member Firms, and Stock List but would in no way duplicate their work. . . . Public Relations would continue its customary work of an educational and institutional nature with the press and general public, and administer Exchange advertising, consulting with Market Development on themes and media on advertising of a merchandising nature. Stock List and Member Firms would continue to carry out their basic responsibilities for administering the listing and regulatory rules and policies of

the Board. Stock List would continue the operation of the listed company cooperation program for widening share ownership and soliciting new listings; and Member Firms would carry on its program for obtaining new member firms."

71. Ward Howell, qtd. in Richard Ruter, "Along the Highways and Byways of Finance," *NYT*, April 17, 1955.

72. Boyd Burchard, "Exchange Promoter Builds Investor Roll," *Seattle Times*, October 7, 1964, 22, in RCL Box 2, NYSEA. "Exchange promoter" was an interesting word choice considering the once derogatory meaning popularly accorded promotion.

73. RCL, Oral History.

74. Bleiberg, qtd. in Martin S. Fridson, *It Was a Very Good Year: Extraordinary Moments in Stock Market History* (New York: John Wiley and Sons, 1998), 140. Fridson also discusses the low share volume in 1953 as compared to 1925.

CHAPTER FOUR: **Courting Retail Investors during the Cold War**

Epigraphs. George K. Funston, "Wanted—More Owners of American Business," Dickinson Lectures, Harvard Business School, April 20–21, 1954, Harvard Business School Archives Vertical File, Baker Library Historical Collections, Harvard Business School, hereafter abbreviated as GKF, "Wanted—More Owners of American Business"; Talk by RCL to American Institute of Accountants, April 20, 1954, NYSEA.

1. Martin S. Fridson, *It Was a Very Good Year: Extraordinary Moments in Stock Market History* (New York: John Wiley and Sons, 1998), 140.

2. RCL discusses Merrill Lynch's reactions to OYS in his Oral History, Interview by Deborah Gardiner, 1984, Box 4, RCL Papers, NYSEA.

3. RCL, interview with the author, September 1999; also see RCL, Oral History, NYSEA.

4. Janet Wolff, *What Makes Women Buy: A Guide to Understanding and Influencing the New Woman of Today* (New York: McGraw-Hill, 1958), 109. On the use of the second person ("you") in ad copy, also see Roland Marchand, *Advertising the American Dream: Making Way for Modernity* (Berkeley: University of California Press, 1985).

5. B. C. Forbes, " 'Share Owner' Better than 'Stockholder,' " *Forbes*, December 1, 1950, 12, 13.

6. See Elaine Tyler May, *Homeward Bound: American Families in the Cold War* (New York: Basic Books, 1988), and Richard M. Fried, *The Russians Are Coming! The Russians Are Coming! Pageantry and Patriotism in Cold-War America* (New York: Oxford University Press, 1998).

7. President Truman, Text of Freedom Train Radio Address, August 28, 1947, Forbes-Freedom Train, Folder 2, Box 37, Papers of Tom C. Clark, Attorney General Files, TL.

8. See discussion of Freedom Train in Michael Kammen, *Mystic Chords of Memory: The Transformation of Tradition in American Culture* (New York: Knopf, 1991), 576–79; Stuart J. Little, "The Freedom Train: Citizenship and Postwar Political Culture 1946–1949," *American Studies* 34 (Spring 1993): 35–67. See also Lynn B. Hinds and Theodore O. Windt Jr., *The Cold War as Rhetoric: The Beginnings, 1945–1950* (New York: Praeger, 1991), 89–94.

9. In the OYS years, the NYSE periodically reenacted the Buttonwood signing.

10. "Own a Share in America," ARC Identifier 515161, Local Identifier 44-PA-1496, Item from RG 44: Records of the Office of Government Reports, 1932–1947, NARA.

11. Also, in the 1940s, the Federal Housing Administration (FHA) coined the slogan "Own

Your Home," and now, the Big Board wanted to make equity investing something as common—and as socially legitimate—as purchasing a home.

12. John Kenneth Galbraith, *The Great Crash* (Boston: Houghton Mifflin, 1955), 174.

13. Talk by RCL to American Institute of Accountants, April 20, 1954, NYSEA.

14. GKF, "Wanted—More Owners of American Business."

15. Ibid.

16. "Own Your Share of American Business Is Theme of New NYSE Campaign," Leaflet, 1954 Campaign Folder, Box 1, Press Relations, Public Information Advertising Campaigns, 1954–1964, NYSEA. Three successive ad agencies—BBDO, Calkins & Holden, and Compton—worked on the Own Your Share account. Morton Silverstein, "Balladeer in a Bull Market," *Printers' Ink*, 44–48, in NYSE Articles, March 1954–December 1961 Folder, RCL Box 2, NYSEA.

17. "How Media Are Chosen and Used in a Public Relations Ad Campaign," *Media/Scope*, December 1957, 38–41. The magazine's assertion that "many of its member firms" had advertised prior to 1954 is debatable.

18. Elizabeth Fones Wolf, *Selling Free Enterprise: The Business Assault on Labor and Liberalism, 1945–60* (Champaign: University of Illinois Press, 1994). Also see Robert Griffith, "The Selling of America: The Advertising Council and American Policies, 1942–1960," *Business History Review* 57 (Autumn 1983): 389–412.

19. See NAM's official website, accessed July 10, 2011, www.nam.org/About-Us/History/Landing-Page.aspx.

20. See Richard S. Tedlow, "The National Association of Manufacturers and Public Relations during the New Deal," *Business History Review* 50, no. 1 (Spring 1976): 25–45, and Jonathan Soffer, "The National Association of Manufacturers and the Militarization of American Conservatism," *Business History Review* 75, no. 4 (Winter 2001): 775–805.

21. Committee on Economic Development, Mission Statement, accessed July 10, 2011, www.ced.org/about/mission-statement.

22. Judging this local pilot campaign a success, the NYSE featured it in its Annual Report that year. See *NYSE 1954 Annual Report*, 6. Goerke's Department Store was founded by Rudolph Goerke, and the Elizabeth store was located at 100 Broad Street.

23. The idea of management social responsibility was not new; in fact, it had been popular in the 1920s, but in the 1950s it enjoyed a resurgence, perhaps because the heightened Cold War emphasis on individual citizenship provoked a similar outpouring of corporate citizenship. See Morrell Heald, "Management's Responsibility to Society: The Growth of an Idea," *Business History Review* 31 (Winter 1957): 375–84, and also see Morrell Heald, "Business Thought in the Twenties: Social Responsibility," *American Quarterly* 13 (Summer 1961): 127.

24. "Talk at Goerke's Department Store, Elizabeth, New Jersey," January 4, 1955, RCL Talks 1954–1955 Folder, RCL Box 1, NYSEA. The storeowner's belief that promoting the NYSE would not harm his business suggests that attitudes about equity investing had softened from the Depression days, though ill-will toward Wall Street still existed.

25. "Department Store Sponsors Own Your Share of American Business Drive," May 1954, RCL Box 1, NYSEA.

26. Etana M. Kelley, "Window Displays Find New Buyers for Brokers," *Sales Management*, 112, Folder, NYSE Articles, etc., March 1954–December 1961, RCL Box 3, NYSEA.

27. "What Every Russian Ought to Know about Owning Stocks in America," OYS Advertisement, *Life* 38, no. 25, June 20, 1955.

28. Merrill executives only mildly complained that the NYSE was "stealing [their] thunder" because they realized that Merrill Lynch benefited from the new Exchange program. Merrill Lynch liberally augmented its in-house advertisements with Own Your Share ads. RCL, Oral History, 1984.

29. Own Your Share advertising tear sheets, NYSEA. In contrast to the NYSE and member firms, listed companies unabashedly used the anticommunism theme in their advertisements promoting shareownership. See the General Telephone advertisement "Joe Citizen Capitalist," the Con Ed advertisement "Communists Would 'Liquidate' all American Stockholders as Capitalists," and more examples in Listed Company Tie-In Ads Folder Press Relations / Public Information Advertising Campaigns, RCL Box 2, 1965–1973, NYSEA.

30. RCL, Oral History.

31. Alfred Politz, Transcribed Notes of Politz' Verbal Report, October 25, 1954, 31, NYSE Department of Research, NYSEA.

32. Comments by RCL, December 16, 1954, Regarding Advertising Copy for 1955, R. C. Lawrence, Presentations to Board of Governors, June 12, 1953–December 19, 1957 Folder, RCL Box 1, NYSEA.

33. "NY Stock Exchange Likes Advertising, Will Do More of It, but with Proper Restraint," September 20, 1954, RCL Collection, NYSEA.

34. Comments by RCL, December 16, 1954, Regarding Advertising Copy for 1955.

35. "Earnest Elmo Calkins (1868–1965)," *Ad Age*, September 15, 2003, accessed June 30, 2011, http://adage.com/article/adage-encyclopedia/calkins-earnest-elmo-1868-1964/98555/.

36. "The Care and Feeding of People's Capitalism," *Editor & Publisher*, March 14, 1959, 36, 38. Folder, NYSE Articles, etc. March 1954–December 1961, RCL Box 3, NYSEA.

37. Ibid.

38. D. Kirk Davidson, *Selling Sin: The Marketing of Socially Unacceptable Products* (Westport: Quorum, 1996), 2, 163.

39. See Camille P. Schuster and Christine Pacelli Powell, "Comparison of Cigarette and Alcohol Advertising Controversies," *Journal of Advertising* 16, no. 2 (1987): 26–27.

40. Radio Reports, Inc., Manuscript Services, "Stock Exchange Offers Advice on Investment in Stocks," Don Gardiner at 11:30 A.M. over WABC (NY), NYSEA.

41. Ibid.

42. Hooper, qtd. in Fridson, *It Was a Very Good Year,* 150.

43. Fridson, *It Was a Very Good Year,* 143–45, 150.

44. On the 65% increase in the S&P index and the ensuing Fulbright study, see Burton Crane, "Fulbright Study is Still Friendly," *NYT*, March 27, 1955, F1.

45. On the implications of a baby boom, see Michael Kourday, "Investing in the Younger Generation," *Forbes*, June 1, 1954.

46. See Milton Friedman and Anna Schwartz, *A Monetary History of the United States 1867–1960* (Princeton: Princeton University Press, 1963).

47. "Text of the Senate Banking Committee's Report on Its Stock Market Survey," *NYT*, May 27, 1955, 8.

48. Louis M. Kohlmeier Jr., *The Regulators: Watchdog Agencies and the Public Interest* (New York: Harper and Row, 1969), 237.

49. "Text of the Senate Banking Committee's Report," 8.

50. Rud Lawrence poked fun at the study's nickname: "The Stock Exchange is the subject now of a great deal of friendly interest. However, one difference between the 'friendly' study in Washington and our friendly meeting today is that I feel sure we don't have to put quotation marks around the friendly." RCL, Talk to Association of Corporate Secretaries at Harvard Club, March 15, 1955, NYSEA.

51. "The 'Friendly Findings,'" *Time*, June 6, 1955. As *Time* noted, the most recent margin increase (to 70%) seemed to have been effective in dampening trading volume. *Time* reported that prior to the margin increase, in the winter of 1954, "sales were averaging 3,000,000 shares a day, but during May daily volume averaged about 2,000,000 shares." The Federal Reserve Board during this period was headed by former NYSE president William McChesney Martin.

52. "Wall Street Finds Fulbright Report Has Both Good and Bad Points," *NYT*, May 28, 1955, 18.

53. Ibid.

54. Ibid.

55. "Text of the Senate Banking Committee's Report," 8.

56. Livingston, qtd. in "Text of the Senate Banking Committee's Report," 8.

57. As *Time* reported, "Capehart accused the Democrats of bringing forth a gloom-and-doom report, aimed at damaging the Republican Administration." "The Friendly Findings."

58. "Text of the Senate Banking Committee's Report," 9.

59. Ibid.

60. *NYSE 1955 Annual Report*, 1–2.

61. Investment Company Institute (ICI), *2008 Investment Company Fact Book: A Review of Trends and Activity in the Investment Company Industry*, 4th ed., 70, 110, accessed June 24, 2008, www.icifactbook.org. (The ICI is the national association of U.S. investment companies.) By 1965, AUM had skyrocketed to $35.22 billion, and the number of shareholder accounts in the United States had jumped to 6.7 million. Unlike pension funds and life insurance companies, mutual funds (formerly known as "investment companies") had always been able to invest significantly in common stocks.

62. Matthew P. Fink, "Political Horse-Trading Produces a Miracle: The 70th Anniversary of the Investment Company Act," *Financial History* (Spring 2010): 33, also 32–34, 37; see also Fink, "The Revenue Act of 1936: The Most Important Event in the History of the Mutual Fund History," *Financial History* (Fall 2005): 16–19.

63. Support for the Investment Company Act was not unanimous. Some predicted that the legislation would confer a "death sentence" upon the industry. In fact, the opposite happened. See Jackson Goodwin, "Address before the Sixth Annual Mutual Fund Sales Convention," The Palmer House, Chicago, Illinois, December 22, 1954, 2, accessed December 16, 2007, www.sec.gov/news/speech/1954/092254goodwin.pdf.

64. "Many Investment Trust Firms Feel Regulation is a Constructive Move," *WSJ*, August 24, 1940, 3. In a formal statement, MIT emphasized that both the SEC and the investment company industry wanted to ensure "honest and competent management" of the industry and

to regulate it in such a way as to prevent the recurrence of "isolated instances of wrongdoing and practices contrary to the best interests of investors."

65. Fink, "Horse-Trading," 34.

66. Gene Smith, "Mutual Funds: Everyman's Investing Media," *NYT*, October 6, 1958, 51; Elizabeth Fowler, "Broker Preaches Gospel of Mutuals," *NYT*, July 7, 1957, 1, 6; Gene Smith, "The Funds Are Mutual: A Glance at the Spectacular Growth of Open-End Investment Companies," *NYT*, September 7, 1955, 41. See also "Gain in Popularity for Mutual Funds," *NYT*, January 2, 1952, 64. For a discussion of the range of marketing strategies employed by mutual fund promoters in the 1950s and 1960s, see Janice Traflet, "Never Bought, Always Sold: Salesmanship, the Small Investor, and the Early Postwar Surge in Mutual Fund Participation," *Essays in Economic and Business History* 27 (2009): 5–14, esp. 8. Also see Emily Martz, " 'Relationships, Relationships, Relationships': The Mutual Fund Industry's Mantra for Success from the 1940s through the 1960s," *Essays in Economic and Business History* 28 (2010): 57–69.

67. Fink, *Rise of Mutual Funds*, 56–58. Notably, despite the rise of bond funds and other types of funds, the industry's tremendous concentration in equities (more than 90%) still remained as late as 1960.

68. Fink, *Rise of Mutual Funds*, 101.

69. Ibid., 100–101.

70. Ibid., 101, 103–4. These prohibitions remained in effect until the late 1970s. As Fink notes, the SEC's adoption in August 1979 of rule 434d proved beneficial to funds in helping them market directly to the public and investors.

71. "Mutual Fund Head Criticizes Ad Curb," *NYT*, October 6, 1955, 43.

72. Goldman Sachs earns the dubious distinction of being the largest promoter of closed-end funds in the year leading up to the Great Crash of 1929. See George Spritzer, "1929's Closed End Fund Craze: Lessons for Today," February 5, 2007, accessed July 7, 2010, http://seekingalpha.com/article/26041-1929-s-closed-end-fund-craze-lessons-for-today.

73. Fink, *Rise of Mutual Funds*, 58.

74. Ibid., 134.

75. Paul Hefernan, "Wall Street Turns to Working Profitable Field of Fast Growing Mutual Investment Funds," *NYT*, March 3, 1949, F1.

76. Ibid.

77. Fink, *Rise of Mutual Funds*, 134.

78. Edwin Perkins, *Wall Street to Main Street: Charles Merrill and Middle-Class Investors* (Cambridge: Cambridge University Press, 1999), 226–29.

79. Ibid.

80. Fink, *Rise of Mutual Funds*, 135–36. See also Terry Robards, "Merrill Lynch to Acquire Edie," *NYT*, March 30, 1969.

CHAPTER FIVE: **Selling Stocks on the Monthly Plan**

Epigraph. Sydney Mirkin, "Joe Doakes Goes to Wall Street with 40 Bucks in Hand," *Daily News*, December 14, 1954.

1. This is known as the "odd lot differential."

2. Sylvia Porter, "The MIP? It's Alive and Well," *New York Post*, February 12, 1969, MIP

Folder, Box 22, NYSEA. Also see Intro. MIP 1953 Folder, RCL Box 3, NYSEA. Rob Aitken, *Performing Capital: Towards a Cultural Economy of Popular and Global Finance* (New York: Palgrave, 2007), 130–32; Robert Sobel, *Inside Wall Street: Continuity and Change in the Financial District* (New York: W. W. Norton, 1982), 105–7; Edwin Perkins, *Wall Street to Main Street: Charles Merrill and Middle-Class Investors* (Cambridge: Cambridge University Press, 1999), 234–36; and Lou Engel, *How to Buy Stocks* (Boston: Little, Brown, 1953), 106–10. The degree to which MIP was truly innovative briefly became a matter of legal contention in the late 1950s. One broker, who had already been offering a product similar in concept to MIP (the "Quinby Plan"), unsuccessfully sued the NYSE for allegedly falsely advertising MIP as something new. John S. Tompkins, "A Puff Is No Lie, Court Declares," *NYT*, September 14, 1958, F1.

3. Sobel, *Inside Wall Street*, 69.

4. See Lendol Calder, *Financing the American Dream: A Cultural History of Consumer Credit* (Princeton: Princeton University Press, 2001).

5. Stewart, Dougall & Associates, Inc., *Digest of Recommended Program for Merchandising Equity Securities Listed on the New York Stock Exchange*, Pamphlet, June 1953, 15–16, NYSEA. Interestingly, the Stewart Dougall report made no mention whatsoever of mutual funds.

6. RCL, "Talk before Association of Customers' Brokers," NYC, January 5, 1954, NYSEA.

7. Qtd. in ibid.

8. *The Daily News, Boston Herald,* and *Chicago Sun-Time* excerpts are all noted by RCL in RCL, "Talk before Association of Customers' Brokers," January 5, 1954.

9. RCL, "Talk Before Governors-Association of Stock Exchange Firms," Washington, DC, February 15, 1954, 1–11, NYSEA.

10. Ibid. Cost to Merrill Lynch was $39,000.

11. www.westegg.com/inflation/infl.cgi, accessed August 5, 2010.

12. "At Last You Can Be an Investor for Only $40 a Month," Merrill Lynch Advertisement, *NYT*, January 20, 1954, 40. See also "Now You Can Be an Investor for Only $40 a Month," Merrill Lynch Advertisement, *NYT*, May 26, 1954, 46. "Class of '74 . . . Maybe!," Merrill Lynch Advertisement, *NYT*, September 3, 1958, 51; "Your Choice—for $40!," Merrill Lynch Advertisement, *NYT*, May 31, 1961, 43.

13. RCL, "Talk before Governors-Association of Stock Exchange Firms," 10. Lawrence noted that Merrill Lynch expected to convert somewhere between 15 to 20% of the inquiries into actual MIP accounts.

14. Engel, *How to Buy Stocks*, 106–10.

15. 1954 statistic is from J. E. McMahon, "Market Break Fails to Dampen Interest in Monthly Investment Plan," *NYT*, January 23, 1955, F1; 1966 statistic is from "No Get-Rich-Quick Scheme," *Barron's*, ca. 1966, Box 22, Alpha Files, NYSEA.

16. On Bache's efforts, see, for instance, McMahon, "Market Break Fails to Dampen," F1.

17. RCL, "Talk Before Governors-Association of Stock Exchange Firms," 1–11.

18. Sydney Mirkin, "Joe Doakes Goes To Wall Street with 40 Bucks in Hand," *Daily News*, December 14, 1954.

19. "Exchange's Monthly Investment Plans Top 19,000 in Six Months," *Barron's*, July 26, 1954, 34, 30.

20. The author expresses gratitude to Edwin Perkins for highlighting this point.

21. NYSE, *How to Invest on a Budget*, Pamphlet, January 1967, Publications Box, NYSEA.

22. Ibid.

23. RCL, "Talk Before Governors-Association of Stock Exchange Firms," 5–6. Lawrence added, "I think it is important for all of us to understand, however, that we have been given no authority and no budget and no personnel to develop any marketing activities for the Exchange. Demand for such activities must come from you and our other members and we must have the specific approval of our Governors before we can launch upon any major project of this kind."

24. Engel, *How to Buy Stocks*, 106.

25. Ibid., 106–7.

26. Ibid.

27. MIP Purchase Order in *How to Invest on a Budget*, 17.

28. Author expresses appreciation to Edwin Perkins for this point.

29. MIP Purchase Order in *How to Invest on a Budget*, 17. In the waning days of the MIP program in the 1970s, this exit clause was invoked by brokers as they cancelled their plans.

30. On the diversification of many listed companies offering MIPs, see "Suggestions for Merchandising the New Monthly Investment Plan," NYSE Memo [unsigned] to Members, Allied Members, and Branch Office Managers, December 31, 1953, Intro. MIP Folder, RCL Box 3, NYSEA.

31. Engel, *How to Buy Stocks*, 108–9. Yet Engel noted, "Of course, if he discontinues buying in a downtrend and sells out when the value of his accumulated shares is less than their purchase cost, he will incur a loss." Precisely because the MIP contract was not binding, some investors who opened MIPs eventually closed their accounts when market conditions soured.

32. Ibid.

33. NYSE, *How to Invest on a Budget*, 6.

34. Engel, *How to Buy Stocks*, 108.

35. "Exchange's Monthly Investment Plans Top 19,000 in Six Months," *Barron's*, July 26, 1954, 34, 30.

36. "Exchange's Monthly Investment Plans Top 19,000," 34. AT&T grew to be the most popular MIP account.

37. RCL, "Talk Before Governors-Association of Stock Exchange Firms," 11.

38. RCL, "Talk to American Institute of Accountants," April 20, 1954, NYSEA.

39. Radio Interview with RCL, moderator Martin Weldome, and Herb Kamm of the *World-Telegram and Sun* on *Let's Find Out* at 1:35 PM over WCBS (NY), December 26, 1954, Transcript, Radio Reports, Inc., NYSEA.

40. Benson & Benson Survey, Part 3, in *The Public Speaks to the Exchange Community: Highlights of Three Consumer Surveys Conducted for the New York Stock Exchange on Behalf of Its Members and Member Firms*, Prepared by the Department of Public Relations and Market Development of the New York Stock Exchange (February 1955), NYSEA.

41. Another two hundred interviews were with "next-door neighbors" of the MIP investors. "The sample of 'next-door neighbors' was selected merely to provide comparisons between MIP investors and non-MIP investors within the same general socio-economic status." Ibid.

42. Qtd. in Benson, *Public Speaks to the Exchange Community,* 56.

43. Ibid., 57.

44. Ibid., 58.

45. Ibid., 60. Other responses as to why they would continue their periodic investments included "confidence in corporations, industry, [the] economy" (15%); "long-term investment objective" (9%), miscellaneous other reasons (11%), and "don't know" (4%).

46. 3% gave no response. Benson, *Public Speaks to the Exchange Community,* 61.

47. Ibid.

48. Ibid., 62–63, 65. The Benson survey concluded, "Broader share ownership, greater familiarity with stocks, and more widespread contact with the Exchange Community go hand in hand. The public is anxious to get better acquainted—it is up to all of us to tell them our story."

49. "Every Man a Capitalist," *Time,* November 21, 1955.

50. *NYSE 1954 Annual Report,* 9–10.

51. Ibid., 9.

52. "Every Man a Capitalist."

53. *NYSE 1955 Annual Report,* 13.

54. In 1955, one MIP kit in fact won the "Advertising in Action" Merit Award (*NYSE 1955 Annual Report,* 13). Also see *How to Use Direct Mail to Advertise the Monthly Investment Plan,* NYSE Pamphlet, ca. 1954, Intro. MIP 1953 Folder, RCL Box 3, NYSEA. See also "Suggestions for Merchandising the New Monthly Investment Plan," NYSE Memo [unsigned] to Members, Allied Members, and Branch Office Managers, December 31, 1953, RCL Box 3, Intro. MIP Folder, NYSEA.

55. Many more accounts had been opened in three years than 54,000, but some had been closed for various reasons. *NYSE 1956 Annual Report,* 3. The *Report* also notes that in 1956, "40 percent more plans were started . . . than in the previous year." (3).

56. The millionth share episode is discussed in the *NYSE 1954 Annual Report,* 3, and also "Wall Street Honors a Small Investor," *NYT,* September 11, 1956, 47, 49.

57. Smith, qtd. in "Wall Street Honors," 49.

58. Stuck, qtd. in "Wall Street Honors," 49. The *Times* report on Stuck and the millionth MIP share concluded, "There are now about 53,000 monthly investment plans in effect. Merrill Lynch handles about 51 per cent of them."

59. On Romney's leadership of AMC, see "Changes of the Week," *Time,* October 25, 1954; *Time* later featured him in a cover story on April 6, 1959. Mitt Romney, presidential candidate and former governor of Massachusetts, is the son of George W. Romney. George Romney served as Governor of Michigan from 1963 to 1969.

60. Nicholas L. A. Martucci, "Helping Employees to Buy Common Stock," *Management Record,* March 1959, Reprint, Box 22, NYSEA.

61. George Romney, "A Motor-Maker Embraces MIP," Pamphlet, ca. 1957, Box 22, NYSEA.

62. Ibid., 1–2.

63. While the benefits of diversification had long been recognized, modern portfolio theory barely was in its infancy, though the subject soon would gain steam with the work of Harry Markowitz, William Sharpe, and others. On the birth of the GM pension fund, see Peter

Drucker, *The Unseen Revolution: How Pension Fund Socialism Came to America* (New York: HarperCollins, 1976; first published 1972), 5–7, and Robert Sobel, *Dangerous Dreamers: The Financial Innovators from Charles Merrill to Michael Milken* (New York: John Wiley and Sons, 1993), 32.

64. Romney, "A Motor-Maker Embraces MIP," 3.

65. Ibid., 4.

66. Ibid.

67. Martucci, "Helping Employees," 4. As Martucci reported, the ten companies that offered employees MIPs in 1959 were American Motors, Canada Dry, Carborumdum Company, Consolidated Food Corporation, De Vilbiss Company, General Finance Corporation, Motor Wheel Corporation, National Fuel Gas Company, Nehl Corporation, and Hiram Walker-Gooderham & Worts, Ltd.

68. Engel, *How to Buy Stocks,* 109.

69. Ibid. As Engel noted, "At least three or four times as many plans had been opened—and closed—over the years as were in operation at the end of 1965."

70. By mid-1969, 313,456 MIP accounts were in force and roughly 15 million shares had been purchased through MIP. But far more MIP accounts had been opened since the program debuted in 1954 (a total of 846,361 accounts). Statistics on MIP accounts are from the Investment Research Department, "Monthly Investment Plan Quarterly Report," July 1969, MIP Folder, Box 22, NYSEA. Statistics on mutual fund accounts and AUM are from the Investment Company Institute (ICI), *2008 Investment Company Fact Book: A Review of Trends and Activity in the Investment Company Industry,* 4th ed., accessed June 24, 2008, www.icifactbook.org, 70, 110. By 1965, AUM in the mutual fund industry had skyrocketed to $35.22 billion from $450 million in 1940, and the number of mutual fund accounts in the United States had risen to 6.7 million from 296,000 accounts a quarter of a century earlier.

CHAPTER SIX: **Creating a Nation of "Sound" Investors**

1. Seymour Cromwell, "The Basis of Cooperation Is Understanding," October 18, 1923, Folder 14, Box 1, RG 2.2, NYSEA; see also Jason Westerfield, Various Speeches, 1923–1925, Folder 41, Box 18, NYSEA.

2. Charles Gay, "The Stock Exchange and the Public," Stock Exchange Public Speeches, December 5, 1935, Folder 17, Box 3, RG 2.2, NYSEA.

3. On these earlier forms of economic education as part of the NYSE's public relations efforts, see Janice Traflet, "Spreading the Ideal of Mass Shareownership: Public Relations and the NYSE," *Essays in Economic and Business History* 22 (2004), 257–73. Also see Julia Ott, "The 'Free and Open' People's Market: Public Relations at the NYSE, 1913–1929," *Business History Conference* 2 (2004): 1–43; Ott, "When Wall Street Met Main Street: The Quest for an Investors' Democracy and the Emergence of the Retail Investor in the United States, 1890–1930," *Enterprise and Society* 9, no. 4 (2008): 619–30; Ott, "'The Free and Open People's Market': Political Ideology and Retail Brokerage at the New York Stock Exchange, 1913–1933," *Journal of American History* 96, no. 1 (June 2009): 44–71.

4. The Politz Group conducted the interviews in June 1954, and the interviews formed the basis for its report, *The Public Speaks to the Exchange* (February 1955), NYSEA.

5. On the business' free enterprise campaign during this period, see Robert Griffith, "The Selling of America: The Advertising Council and American Policies, 1942–1960," *Business History Review* 57 (Autumn 1983): 389–412, and Elizabeth Fones Wolf, *Selling Free Enterprise: The Business Assault on Labor and Liberalism, 1945–60* (Champaign: University of Illinois Press, 1994).

6. Burton Crane, "Wall Street Saga Told in Series of Films," *NYT*, May 18, 1952, F7.

7. Ibid. Much to Merrill Lynch's surprise, there really was a company named Supersonic Washing Machine Company, a small organization with stock traded over-the-counter. Learning from the episode, in future movies Merrill Lynch was careful to pick fictional names.

8. Ibid. While most viewers commented favorably on "Fair Exchange," some did note that the homes of investors depicted in the movie "were a little pretentious." In subsequent films, Merrill Lynch made investors seem more like average Americans of modest means.

9. "Country's First 'How to Invest' Show to Open Tomorrow at Armory Here," *NYT*, May 23, 1955, 34, 36.

10. See obituary by Elaine Woo, "John Sutherland: Acclaimed for Artistry of His Industrial Films," *LA Times*, February 27, 2001, accessed June 26, 2011, http://articles.latimes.com/2001/feb/27/local/me-30915.

11. The NYSE's Investor Education Department endeavored to make "Working Dollars" widely available, with some movie houses running it prior to their feature film. Brokerage houses, too, held open houses where people could see the movie and then ask questions of their neighborhood brokers.

12. See President Franklin D. Roosevelt, Annual Message to Congress, January 6, 1941.

13. On Rockefeller's depiction of the four freedoms, accessed July 8, 2011, www.best-norman-rockwell-art.com/four-freedoms.html.

14. In the late 1940s and early 1950s, a few groups within the Exchange community besides Merrill Lynch were developing their own films about the stock market. For instance, odd-lot dealer Carlisle & Jacquelin debuted "We're an Odd Lot" and the Investment Bankers of America, "Opportunity, USA." Crane, "Wall Street Saga Told in Series of Films," F7.

15. G. Keith Funston, Memorandum to the Board of Governors, October 19, 1954, Subject: Recommendation for Employing an Education Director, RCL Box 1, NYSEA.

16. Ibid.

17. See "Allen O. Felix, 72, Ex-Stock Exchange Aide," *NYT*, October 7, 1988, 24A.

18. Walter Williams, CED Chairman and President of Continental, Inc., August 17, 1949, "Achieving a Sound Economy," August 17, 1949, Folder, CED, 1 of 2, February–October, 1949, Committee for Economic Development, Asst. to the Asst. to the President File, 1948–1952, Box 22, Charles W. Jackson Files, Truman Library. For more on the Committee for Economic Development, see especially Robert M. Collins, *The Business Response to Keynes, 1929–1964* (New York: Columbia University Press, 1981). On business ideology in the 1950s, see also Frances X. Sutton, Seymour Harris, Carl Kaysen, et.al., *The American Business Creed* (Cambridge, MA, Harvard University Press, 1956).

19. RCL, "Remarks at Seton Hall University," November 19, 1957, Transcript, NYSEA.

20. "Teachers Get a 'Down to Earth' View of Finance," *NYT*, August 20, 1958, 37, 43.

21. Ibid.

22. David Dworsky, "6th Graders Check Their Investment," *NYT*, April 18, 1967. At the

stockholder meeting, two of the eleven-year-old students, Patricia O'Brien and Pamela Hall, asked Scovill's president why the company split its stock that year and why officers of the company had been granted stock options. After responding, Scovill president Malcolm Baldrige added jokingly, "I don't know whether I'd trade you two for Wilma Soss," a reference to the feisty and sharp president of the Federation of Women Shareholders in American Business. After initially dipping slightly, the Scovill stock, purchased at 37 1/8 a share, gradually began to rise. When the stock reached 45 1/8, students greeted the teacher that morning with shouts of "Sell, Sell!"

23. The Beardstown Ladies Investment Club, founded in 1983 in Beardstown, Illinois, gained national attention when the members claimed they earned spectacular returns, averaging 23% a year, in the eleven-year period from 1983 to 1994. The investment returns later were questioned as being possibly inflated (accidentally) by club members not professionally trained in computing returns. Leslie Whitaker and the Beardstown Ladies Investment Club, *The Beardstown Ladies' Common-Sense Investment Guide: How We Beat the Stock Market—And How You Can Too* (New York: Hyperion, 1995). Two classics dealing with the perceived rise in conformity among postwar Americans living in suburbs and working in large corporations include William Whyte's *The Organization Man* (New York: Simon and Schuster, 1956), and Sloan Wilson's *The Man in the Grey Flannel Suit* (New York: Pocket Books, 1956).

24. RCL, "Investment Clubs: A New Educational Tool for People's Capitalism," Remarks at the Annual Convention of the National Association of Securities Administrators, Rockland, Maine, September 10, 1956, NYSEA. While Lawrence proclaimed that investment clubs "have become a significant and measurable part of our market," in truth, the volume statistics were not that high. On a monthly basis in 1956, investment clubs together conducted approximately four thousand stock transactions, but the total number of monthly shares traded was under 180,000 and the total value only approximately six million dollars.

25. Ibid.

26. Ibid.

27. *Individual Shareownership around the World*, 2nd ed. (New York: NYSE, 1963), Publications Box, NYSEA.

28. Robert J. Cole, "Investment Seminar Is a Simple Way to Learn How Stock Market Works," *NYT*, April 4, 1968, 67, 69.

29. Cole, 69. Cole added, "Keep in mind that, if you join a seminar, you're there to learn about investing—not to pick up market tips. In fact, speakers generally caution you that if stocks are mentioned—and they often are—this is not to be taken as a recommendation to rush out and buy. Obviously no stock meets the needs or goals of everyone."

30. Ibid.

31. See, for instance, Francis Eames, *The New York Stock Exchange* (New York: T. G. Hall, 1894), and Sereno S. Pratt, *The Work of Wall Street: An Account of the Functions, Methods and History of the New York Money and Stock Markets* (New York: D. Appleton, 1903).

32. Robert H. Fetridge, "Along the Highways and Byways of Finance," *NYT*, August 1, 1948, F3.

33. Lou Engel, *How to Buy Stocks* (Boston: Little, Brown, 1953).

34. Burton Crane, "The Business Bookshelf," *NYT*, April 20, 1953, 34.

35. Ibid.

36. NYSE, "Investment Facts about Common Stocks and Cash Dividends," pamphlet, NYSEA, ca. 1960.

37. NYSE, *Individual Shareownership around the World*.

38. NYSE, "How to Invest for Growing Income and Family Security," Pamphlet, 1960, Fall 1960 Campaign Folder, Publications Box, NYSEA.

39. Robert Dietsch, "Minors Play Big Role in Stockholder Rise," *New York World*, June 24, 1965. The NYSE during these years sometimes referred to minors as under 21 and other times, as less than 19 years of age.

40. Louis Engel, *How To Buy Stocks* (Boston: Little, Brown, 1967), 151. See also "Recent Legislation to Facilitate Gifts of Securities to Minors," *Harvard Law Review* 69, no. 8 (June 1956): 1476–90. Also see G. Keith Funston, "Stock Gifts to Children," September 29, 1954, Folder 23, and Funston, "Stock Gifts to Children," January 26, 1956, Folder 36, both in Box 7, RG 2.2, NYSEA.

41. Letter from Philip Keuper (Department of Public Information, Press Relations) to John Cuniff (Associated Press), November 30, 1967, Stock Gifts to Minors Folder, Box 22, NYSEA.

42. Elizabeth Fowler, "Personal Finance: Paying College Tuition," *NYT*, June 29, 1964, BF 42.

43. Engel, *How to Buy Stocks,* 151.

44. Ibid.

45. Alaska and Georgia for a time were holdouts, still using the old Model Law. Fowler, "Personal Finance: Paying College Tuition," BF 42.

46. Letter from Keuper, November 30, 1967, Stock Gifts to Minors Folder, Box 22, NYSEA.

47. Ibid. Keuper also noted, "Of course, a growing phenomenon of minors' owning stock is not without its grave problems." He explained: "Consider the young girl shareowner of a food stock tagging along at the supermarket to insist on her mother buying the right products. Or the boy with the oil stock pressuring his father to 'fill 'er up' every time they roll into a gas station. Some years ago a grammar school class in upstate New York bought a share of stock collectively to learn about the investment process. When the 10-cent quarterly dividend arrived, no one knew how to split it among 40 equal investors until a financial genius thought of buying jellybeans and dividing the candy. Such are the perils of putting stock in your Christmas stocking."

48. NYSE Annual Reports in the 1950s made periodic references to the status of the Securities Gifts to Minor legislation, noting which states had passed laws in this regard. See, for instance, *NYSE 1954 Annual Report*, 16; *NYSE 1955 Annual Report*, inside cover; *NYSE 1956 Annual Report*, inside cover. Also RCL in his Oral History, 1984, NYSEA, discussed the Gifts to Minors program.

49. Dietsch, "Minors Play Big Role in Stockholder Rise"; Betty Yarmon, "Number of Minors Owning Stock Has Tripled in Last Three Years," *Pensacola News-Journal*, October 31, 1965. See also John Cunniff, "Stock Share as Gift to Youth Urged," *Tulsa Tribune*, December 8, 1966. All in Stock Gifts to Minors Folder, Box 22, NYSEA.

50. Letter from Keuper, November 30, 1967.

51. "Reverse" stock splits also can occur, although this was rare in the OYS years.

52. Fowler BF 42.

53. Qtd. in Fowler BF 42.

54. Fowler BF 42.

55. NYSE, "How to Invest for Growing Income and Family Security," October 1960, Publications Box, NYSEA. GKF, Letter to Managing Partners, "Advertising Program for Fall 1965."

56. OYS commercial on gift-giving, Stock Gifts to Minors Folder, Box 22, NYSEA.

57. "How to Make Young People PARTNERS IN PROGRESS," Stock Gifts to Minors Folder, Box 22, NYSEA.

58. Dietsch, "Minors Play Big Role in Stockholder Rise."

59. To be precise, 3.14 million women translated to 49.45% of the total adult shareowner base, versus 3.21 million men who constituted the remaining 50.55%. This author took the additional step of considering the degree to which a gender imbalance in the overall population could have skewed these results. Yet this seems not to be the case. 3.14 million women shareowners translates to 3.98% of the total female population in 1952; 3.21 million male shareowners translates to 4.11% of the total male shareowner population. An even finer analysis would take the total female adult shareowners and divide it by the total female adults in the population, and then would do the same for the male statistics. (This author looked at total females of all ages). The total number of shareholders in 1952 (male and female of all ages, including minors) was approximately 6,490,000. For statistics on women in the market in 1952, see Lewis Kimmel, *Share Ownership in the United States* ("The Brookings Report") (Washington, DC, 1952), esp. pp. 15 and 69, NYSEA. As highlighted in the Brookings Report, in 1952, the number of common and preferred stock owned by men was 1,264 million versus the total for women, which was 34% less, at 947 million (Brookings, 69). Lewis Kimmel noted "Men own far more shares in common stock of publicly owned corporations than women" (Brookings, 75).

60. In the period 1949–1951, the average life expectancy for men was 65.5 years and for women it was 71 years. Laura Shres, "Life Expectancy in the United States," CRS Report for Congress (Library of Congress Research Service), updated August 16, 2006, accessed August 8, 2008, www.policyarchive.org. See esp. table 1, U.S. Life Expectancy at Birth, by Sex, in Selected Years.

61. To clarify, the Brookings Report found 3.14 million women in the shareholding ranks in 1952, but obviously, not all of these women were new shareowners. Therefore, in searching for reasons for the gender parity, one must look also to longer-term answers, not just to new developments that may have affected the level of female shareownership.

62. The Equal Pay Act was not enacted until 1963, and in 1951, full-time women in the workplace earned only roughly 64% of what men earned. For women's earnings as a percentage of men in selected years, please see U.S. Women's Bureau and the National Committee on Pay Equity.

63. Interestingly, the Brookings Study found that half of the nation's shareowners owned stock in three or fewer companies. Brookings Report, 1952.

64. On women outnumbering men in the shareowner ranks, see Louis Engel, *How to Buy Stocks* (Boston: Little, Brown, 1967; first published 1953), 150–51, 311. On the practice of men putting stocks in their wives' names, also see "Stock," *Time*, May 18, 1925, accessed July 1, 2008, www.time.com/time/magazine/article/0,9171,720387,00.html.

65. "The NYSE Faces a Problem," *Magazine of Wall Street*, November 1, 1952, 104.

66. NYSE, *NYSE Fact Book* (New York: NYSE, 1963), 40, NYSEA. At first glance, the lower stock turnover could be attributed to decreased institutional trading, but at the time, the NYSE was still primarily an individual investor's marketplace.

67. See OYS advertisements in Own Your Share Campaign Folder, Box 1, Press Relations, Public Information Advertising Campaigns, 1954–1964, NYSEA.

68. *Reader's Digest* insert, "Family Security," 1957.

69. For a general discussion of the conflation of family and national security during the Cold War, see Elaine Tyler May, *Homeward Bound: American Families in the Cold War* (New York: Basic Books, 1988).

70. See Richard M. Fried, *The Russians Are Coming! The Russians Are Coming! Pageantry and Patriotism in Cold-War America* (New York: Oxford University Press, 1998).

71. NYSE, *Shareownership 1975, Census of Shareowners in America* (New York: NYSE, 1976), NYSEA.

72. NYSE, *Highlights of NYSE Shareowner Census Reports (1952–1990)*, accessed August 8, 2008, www.nysedata.com/factbook.

73. See Sylvia F. Porter, "How About Your Lazy Money," *Good Housekeeping* 130, no. 41, February 1950, 228. Brookings, 115.

74. "I'm Shopping for Stocks!" Merrill Lynch Advertisement, *NYT*, June 1, 1952, SM20.

75. "This Little Piggy Went to Market," Merrill Lynch Advertisement, *NYT*, June 22, 1952, SM4.

76. "Mama's Little Dividend," Merrill Lynch Advertisement, *NYT*, June 8, 1952, SM27.

77. Member Firm Tie-in Ads for Women, NYSEA, Fall 1962.

78. "Wall Street: A Man for Everyman's Capitalism," *Time*, September 23, 1966. The Funston quote is also from *Time*.

79. "Wall Street: New No. 1 Salesman," *Time*, April 28, 1967. Also see "Big Board Formally Names Robert Haack President: He Will Take Office by Fall," *WSJ*, April 26, 1967, 5; John H. Allen, "Has Big Board Found Its Man," *NYT*, April 22, 1967, 37, 47; Lee Silberman, "Haack, NASD Head, Held a Top Candidate to Succeed Funston as Big Board President," *WSJ*, April 20, 1967, 2.

80. "NASD," accessed July 8, 2011, www.investopedia.com/terms/n/nasd.asp. NASD also supervised the Nasdaq, the country's first electronic stock market, which was formed in 1971. At the time Haack headed NASD, the Nasdaq had not yet been created. Today, NASD no longer exists; the creation of the Financial Industry Regulatory Authority (FINRA) in 2007 merged NASD with the NYSE's regulatory structure.

81. For instance, while he cooperated with the SEC in helping implement several reforms such as tighter requirements for dealing in securities, Haack successfully had resisted the agency's calls for more stringent supervision of mutual-fund sales practices.

82. James J. Needham, *The Threat to Corporate Growth* (Philadelphia: Girard Bank, 1974), 20. See also Hurd Baruch, *Wall Street: Security Risk; A Report to the Investing Public on the Unsafe and Unsound Practices in the Securities Industry* (Washington, DC: Acropolis, 1971); and G. Keith Funston, "Managing Automation," March 11, 1964, Folder 42, Box 8, Speeches of NYSE Presidents, NYSEA.

83. John Brooks, *The Go-Go Years: The Drama and Crashing Finale of Wall Street's Bullish 60s* (New York: John Wiley and Sons, 1999), 184.

84. Haack, qtd. in Brooks, *Go-Go*, 189.

85. Lawrence, qtd. in "Ruddick C. Lawrence Will Quit as Big Board Public Relations Chief," *WSJ*, March 19, 1968, 24.

86. "Ruddick C. Lawrence Will Quit."

87. "Monthly Stock Plan for Investors Goes to the Graveyard," *WSJ*, March 26, 1976, 17.

88. From January 11, 1973, to December 6, 1974, the Dow dropped more than 45%. This was caused in part by the shock of the United States going off the gold standard in 1971, followed in October 1973 by a major oil crisis that unfolded when the members of the Organization of Arab Petroleum Exporting Countries (OAPEC) declared an oil embargo. OPAEC included OPEC countries in addition to Egypt, Syria, and Tunisia. Investors in the 1970s also had to contend with skyrocketing inflation. Inflation rose well into the double-digits in the Carter years, and this inflation, combined with low economic growth, created a situation that became known as "stagflation." To fight inflation, in 1979 Federal Reserve chairman Paul Volcker would champion a series of sharp interest rate increases.

89. On the need for balance, see G. Keith Funston, "Institutional Investors: How Is Their Growth Affecting the Stock Market?" Remarks before the American Life Convention, Chicago, Illinois, October 14, 1955, 10–11, Speeches, President Funston, Folder 31, Box 7, RG 2.2, NYSEA.

90. Charles J. Rolo, "The Case of the Vanishing Investor," *NYT*, June 9, 1974, 248.

91. G. Bradford Cook, chairman of the SEC, remarked in 1974, "Like the curator of the National Zoo . . . I feel constrained to warn: The individual investor has acquired the status of an endangered species." Cook, qtd. in Rolo, "The Case of the Vanishing Investor," 248. See also Vartanig Vartan, "Shareholders' Ranks Down," *NYT*, March 26, 1973, 63.

92. In the confusing growth years of the 1960s, even the NYSE had started to lose an understanding of what they meant by the term. Sometimes they began to use the label "individual investors" to refer only to investors who owned stock through a retail broker, but sometimes they adopted a wider usage of the term to refer also to investors in mutual funds.

93. "Monthly Stock Plan for Investors Goes to the Graveyard," 17.

94. MIP Purchase Order in NYSE, *How to Invest on a Budget*, Pamphlet, January 1967, 17, Publications Box, NYSEA.

95. "Monthly Stock Plan for Investors Goes to the Graveyard," 17.

96. R. John Cunningham, Memorandum to Board, "New Plan for Advertising and Public Relations, July 3, 1968, 1954 to 1971 Advertising Presentations Folder, NYSEA.

97. Cunningham, Memorandum, July 3, 1968. See also Eugene Miller, Memorandum to Board, "Advertising Program for 1969," January 7, 1969, 1954 to 1971 Advertising Presentations Folder, NYSEA.

98. D. H. Woodward, "Advertising Presentation to Board of Governors," 1954 to 1971 Advertising Presentations Folder, NYSEA.

99. "The Death of Equities: How Inflation Is Destroying the Stock Market," *Business Week*, August 13, 1979, 54.

100. Cohn and Coleman, qtd. in "The Death of Equities."

101. James J. Needham, *The Threat to Corporate Growth* (Philadelphia: Girard Bank, 1974),

10–11, 13. Also see Stan West, "Weep Not for the Little Man," *Institutional Investor* (June 1972): 76–77, 107, 109, 111–12.

102. In just the period from August 1982 to August 1987 alone, the Dow rose from 776 to 2,722. Briefly interrupting the upward trend, on Black Monday, October 19th, 1987, the Dow plummeted 508 points, a staggering 22.6% of its value in just one day. Immediately, on the day after the Crash, the stock market strongly rallied. In fact, on Tuesday, October 20th, the Dow rose 102.27 points, a record one-day gain. Two days later, on Thursday, October 22nd, the market rose 186.64 points. Two years later, by September 1989, the Dow had recovered to its pre-Crash value.

103. John Kador, *Charles Schwab: How One Company Beat Wall Street and Reinvented the Brokerage Industry* (New York: John Wiley and Sons, 2002), 211.

104. Andy Serwer, "A Nation of Traders," *Fortune* 140, no. 7, October 11, 1999, 116–20.

105. On the nature of brokerage firm advertising pitches in the dot.com period and earlier, see Michael P. Coyne and Janice M. Traflet, "Ethical Issues Related to the Mass Marketing of Securities," *Journal of Business Ethics* 78, nos. 1–2 (2007): 193–98.

106. Ibid. Also see Hal Lux, "Keeping On Line Ads in Line," *Institutional Investor* 33, no. 6 (1999): 9. Brad Barber and Terrance Odeon, "On-Line Investors: Do the Slow Die First?," *The Review of Financial Studies* 15, no. 2 (2002): 455–87.

107. Lux, "Keeping On Line Ads," 9.

108. In 2007, according to some estimates, the average holding period for stocks and ETFs was less than four months. Ilan Moscovitz, "The Coming Financial Time Bomb," September 19, 2009, accessed July 31, 2010, www.fool.com/investing/value/2009/09/19/the-coming-financial-time-bomb.aspx. See also Robert Reich, *Supercapitalism: The Transformation of Business, Democracy, and Everyday Life* (New York: Vintage Books, 2007), 71.

109. Serwer, "A Nation of Traders," 116–20. For an in-depth discussion of investors' results with online investing, see Barber and Odean, "On-Line Investors," 455–87.

110. Joseph Nocera, "Power to the People," *Fortune* 140, no. 7, October 11, 1999, 124–39.

EPILOGUE: **Own Your Share in Retrospect**

Epigraph. Ruddick C. Lawrence, Oral History, Interview by Deborah Gardiner, 1984, Box 4, RCL Papers, NYSEA.

1. The author expresses appreciation to Kraighton Stack for discussion of these points.

2. George Gallop Jr., *The Gallup Poll, 2002* (Lanham, MD: Rowman and Littlefield, 2003), 222.

3. Ibid.

4. Bush, qtd. in *Fact Sheet: America's Ownership Society; Expanding Opportunities*, White House Press Release, August 9, 2004, accessed July 3, 2010, www.whitehouse.gov/news/releases/2004/08/20040809-9.html.

5. On criticisms of the Bush privatization plan, see, for instance, Jonathan Weisman, "Skepticism of Bush's Social Security Plan Is Growing," *Washington Post*, March 15, 2005, A01.

6. Gretchen Morgenson, "How the Thundering Herd Faltered and Fell," *NYT*, November 9, 2008.

7. Ibid.

8. "Bank of America in Talks to Acquire Merrill Lynch," *NYT*, September 14, 2008.

9. For the full text of Smith's speech, see Amarendra Bushan, "Winthrop H. Smith Speech: Bye Bye Merrill Lynch!" *CEOWORLD Magazine*, December 8, 2008, accessed July 28, 2010, http://ceoworld.biz/ceo/2008/12/08/winthrop-h-smith-speech-bye-bye-merrill-lynch.

10. Ibid.

11. Graham Bowley, "In Striking Shift, Small Investors Flee Stock Market," *NYT*, August 21, 2010.

12. Ibid.

13. Ibid.

14. See William H. Whyte Jr., *Is Anybody Listening?* (New York: Simon and Schuster, 1952).

15. In 1957, Robert Heilbroner commented, "Business has sold itself the bill of goods it originally intended to sell the public." Heilbroner, "Public Relations—The Invisible Sell," *Harper's*, June 1957, 31–34.

16. Meyers continued, "Perhaps the employer came to believe some of the rhetoric of industrial harmony and 'adjustment' which his own public relations men were composing for the consumption of others." Marvin Meyers, *The Jacksonian Persuasion* (Stanford: Stanford University Press, 1960), ix.

17. Ruddick C. Lawrence, Oral History, Interview by Deborah Gardiner, 1984, Box 4, RCL Papers, NYSEA.

18. Alfred Fuller, *A Foot in the Door: The Life Appraisal of the Original Fuller Brush Man* (New York: McGraw Hill, 1960).

19. "Young Turk in Wall Street," *Forbes*, December 1, 1951, 21–22.

20. RCL, Oral History, NYSEA.

Essay on Sources

This book project began with my pondering how, why, and when did average middle-class Americans, seared by the memory of the 1929 Great Crash, come again to trust and participate in the stock market. As I delved into my research, I became increasingly interested in the NYSE's side of the story—the transformational process by which the NYSE Board of Governors and retail member brokerage houses came to *want* to court small investors. To arrive at my conclusions, I consulted a multitude of materials. The following discussion of sources, while not all encompassing, should provide a path for other researchers interested in how the NYSE during the height of the Cold War sought to democratize the stock market and thus create a "nation of small shareowners."

Primary Sources

Extensive research at the New York Stock Exchange Archive (NYSEA) in New York City proved pivotal to my understanding the Board of Governors' evolving marketing practices as well as their thoughts regarding the proper scale and scope of equity investing. The Own Your Share of American Business (OYS) promotional campaign, inaugurated in 1954, was a major turning point in the NYSE's marketing relationship with small investors, and an abundance of files on this campaign proliferate at the NYSEA. To grasp the trajectory in Exchange attitudes, I explored many files from before, during, and after the OYS era.

Particularly illuminating were the papers of Ruddick C. Lawrence (RCL). The charismatic Lawrence served as vice president of Market Development at the NYSE during the entire OYS campaign. Rud Lawrence kept copious notes and scrapbooks of his years at the NYSE, and it was my real pleasure to be able to interview him in 1999. Years earlier, in 1984, Lawrence generously gave of his time to provide the Exchange with a detailed oral history, which we also discussed. The transcript of the 1984 oral history interview (conducted by Exchange archivist Deborah Gardner) is preserved in Box 4 of Lawrence's papers at the NYSEA. Three other boxes of his papers at the NYSEA also are rich in information. The announcement of the debut of OYS can be found in the 1954 Campaign Folder, Box 1, Press Relations, Public Information Advertising Campaigns, 1954–1964. Listed company tie-in advertisements can be located in the folder for Press Relations / Public Information Advertising Campaigns, 1965–1973, in RCL Box 2. In RCL Box 3 as well as in Box 22, Alpha Files, information may be found on the NYSE's Monthly Investment Plan (MIP), among other topics.

Lawrence worked closely with G. Keith Funston (NYSE president, 1951–1967). At the NYSEA, Boxes 7 and 8, Record Group 2.2, contain many of Funston's noteworthy speeches on the theme of spreading shareownership, such as "America Embraces a People's Capitalism," "Broader Share Ownership," "A Nation of Share Owners," "Who Owns America," and "Paging Joe Public." At Harvard Business School's Baker Library Historical Collections Department (BL), I found more useful information, including the Dickinson Lecture Funston gave on April 20, 1954, entitled "Wanted—More Shareowners." See Folder, Funston, George, Keith, "Wanted—More Shareowners," CFL 18.13A, Archives Vertical File, CC2.13.5C-CFL 49, Box 14, BL.

NYSE Annual Reports helped give me a flavor for how the NYSE Board was communicating its shareownership goals, methods, and results to both the Exchange community and the outside public. In the late 1930s, the Exchange's Annual Reports began to expand in content, including, for instance, an annual letter from the president prefacing the Report. By the 1950s, the Reports began to include more information on the NYSE's public relations activities. For historical trading volume, stock turnover, and other statistics, I relied in part on the NYSE's annual Fact Books.

Various "how to invest" pamphlets, published by the NYSE in the 1950s and 1960s and available at the NYSEA, help demonstrate ways in which the Big Board tried to educate the public about the stock market's virtues. At the same time, the Exchange endeavored to educate member firms and themselves about what Main Street thought of Wall Street. To that end, the NYSE's Public Relations and Market Development compiled for internal use various studies of the stock market, and the Research and Statistics Department periodically assembled public transaction studies that depicted the investor composition of the stock market. As well, outside consultants and advertising agencies conducted reports on public attitudes about the stock market. See Alfred Politz Research, Inc., *A Survey of Attitudes toward Stock Ownership* (August 1954), and Benson & Benson, Inc., *Survey of Monthly Investment Plan for New York Stock Exchange* (September 1954). The Department of Public Relations and Market Development collated a series of public opinion polls in their book, *The Public Speaks to the Exchange Community* (February 1955). These are all preserved at the NYSEA.

These polls from the 1950s and 1960s enabled me to compare how public sentiment toward Wall Street had changed since the 1940s. In the 1940s, Merrill Lynch commissioned consultants such as Braun & Associates to take polls to gauge investors' attitudes toward the stock market and Wall Street. The Merrill Lynch polls are discussed in the Conference of Bank Managers Transcript, Merrill Lynch Meeting, April 3–4, 1940, Waldorf-Astoria Hotel, New York City. My sincere thanks to Edwin Perkins for sharing with me this outstanding primary source. To find more polls on attitudes toward Wall Street prior to the OYS years, I combed through *Public Opinion Quarterly* as well as other material. One revealing Gallup poll from 1938 asked the public questions about the extent of NYSE market reforms. See George Gallup and Claude Robinson, "American Institute of Public Opinion-Surveys, 1935–38," *The Public Opinion Quarterly* 2, no. 3 (July 1938): 373–98. Also in 1938, statistics on declining readership of stock tables and business news helped me to understand the extent to which the NYSE had fallen off the radar screen of average Americans. See Howard J. Carswell, "Business News Coverage," *The Public Opinion Quarterly* 2, no. 4 (October 1938): 613–21.

To put into perspective the NYSE's mid-twentieth century quest to enlarge shareownership, I needed to find data on the extent of shareownership before, during, and after the Own Your Share campaign. Prior to 1952, the NYSE unfortunately did not engage in any shareholder census taking, and the reliability of estimates of shareownership from other sources is questionable. Berle and Means' estimate of four to six million investors in the market in 1929 is now considered low. For early analyses of shareownership, I probed such sources as Gardiner Means, "Diffusion of Stock Ownership," *Quarterly Journal of Economics* 44, no. 4 (August 1930): 561–600; Means, "The Separation of Ownership and Control in American Industry," *Quarterly Journal of Economics* 46, no. 1 (December 1931): 68–100; H. T. Warshow, "The Distribution of Corporate Ownership in the United States, *Quarterly Journal of Economics* 39, no. 1 (November 1924): 15–38; and U.S. Congress, Senate Committee on Banking and Currency, *Report of the Committee on Banking and Currency*, known as the "Fletcher Report" (Washington, DC: GPO, 1934).

To gauge the extent of participation in the stock market in 1952, I relied upon the well-regarded Brookings Institute study of shareownership, commissioned by the NYSE and spearheaded by Lewis Kimmel. A copy of Lewis Kimmel's *Share Ownership in the United States*, also known as the "Brookings Report" (Washington, DC, 1952) is on file at the NYSEA. From 1952 until the late 1970s, the NYSE undertook periodic shareowner censuses, and I carefully reviewed each of them. Most important to my study, however, were the censuses that roughly coincided with the beginning and ending of the Own Your Share years. While the complete reports of shareowner censuses are available at the NYSEA in Manhattan, the NYX website now features summaries of the censuses taken between 1952 and 1990. See "Highlights of NYSE Shareowner Census Reports," accessed July 28, 2010, www.nyxdata.com/nysedata/asp/factbook/viewer_edition.asp?mode=table&key=2312&category=11. Likewise, historical trading volume and other statistics are also available online at the NYX website. See, for example, "Major Sources of NYSE Volume," accessed August 11, 2010, www.nyxdata.com/nysedata/NYSE/FactsFigures/tabid/115/Default.aspx.

While the main focus of my research was on the period after the Great Crash of 1929, I also explored material at the NYSEA from earlier in the twentieth century. I especially wanted to find information that would help me establish Exchange executives' early attitudes toward public participation in the stock market, to see to what extent attitudes had evolved later in the century. In the 1920s, due to the Exchange restricting member firm advertising, little marketing occurred that invited the general public to come to Wall Street. Yet perusing speeches by Big Board presidents and public relations personnel in the 1920s, I found plentiful rhetoric about the NYSE being the "people's market." I also discovered evidence of considerable public relations activity at a time of scant advertising. NYSE President Seymour Cromwell contended that "The Stock Exchange is the People's Market" in a speech on November 21, 1922 (Folder 9, Box 1, RG 2.2, NYSEA). Cromwell's successor, E. H. H. Simmons, and then Richard Whitney, also were vocal on the subject of mass investing. See, for instance, E. H. H. Simmons, "Credit as a National Asset," Speech before the Credit Men's Association of Milwaukee, April 9, 1925, Committee on Library; Simmons, "Free Markets and Popular Ownership," Speech before the 41st Annual Convention of the Texas Bankers Association at Houston, Texas, May 20, 1925, Committee on Library; Richard Whitney, "Public Opinion and the Stock Market," Address before the Boston Chamber of Commerce, Boston, Massachusetts, January 29, 1931, repr. in Whitney, *Functions of Stock Exchanges: A Collection of Essays* (New York: NYSE, 1935), NYSEA. The text of Whitney's radio broadcast, "The Investor and Security Markets," of January 30, 1935, is preserved in *The Investor and Security Markets: Industry and Security Markets, Security Markets and the People; Three Addresses by Richard Whitney over the NBC-WEAF Network of the National Broadcasting Company, Inc., Jan. 30, Feb. 6, and Feb. 13, 1935*, NYSEA.

To compare the NYSE's Own Your Share (OYS) campaign with earlier NYSE public relations initiatives, I studied the files of the NYSE's first public relations department. Established in 1913, it was originally called the Library Committee and later renamed the Committee on Publicity (COP). Exchange publicists in the pre-World War II days resorted to a variety of tactics, such as press releases, films, speeches, books, and other promotional pieces. See Special Committee of Five on Publicity, Special Committee on Public Relations, Minutes, vols. 1–3; also Letter Books, Committee on Public Relations, Minutes, vols. 4–6. The NYSE's Minutes of Committee on Business Conduct, vol. 1, covering the period March 17, 1913–June 4, 1921, illustrate how the NYSE monitored member firm advertising in the pre-New Deal era. The Committee Secretary recorded occasional disapproval of Merrill's advertisements. Seeing evidence of a young Charles Merrill in the 1920s being reprimanded by the Exchange for engaging in aggressive advertising helped me appreciate the extent to which Merrill's marketing to the middle class constituted a real risk and a revolutionary undertaking.

At Baker Library Historical Collections Department at Harvard Business School in Cambridge, Massachusetts, material from three collections gave me unusual insights into Wall Street and the advertising field before and after the 1929 Crash: the Paul T. Cherington Papers, Harvard Business School Archives, Baker Library Historical Collections, Harvard Business School; Ralph M. Hower Papers, Harvard Business School Archives, Baker Library Historical Collections, Harvard Business School; and the Thomas W. Lamont Papers, Baker Library Historical Collections, Harvard Business School. In the Thomas W. Lamont Papers, 1894–1948, Mss. 783, some of his correspondence helps illustrate Wall Street's reaction to the 1929 Crash and also shows the divisions within the NYSE about an appropriate image recovery strategy. Lamont was a high-ranking Morgan partner, and his papers show how involved he and the firm were with Exchange policy making. The Paul T. Cherington Papers, Arch GA 13, Box 2, contain fascinating speeches and articles from the 1929–1931 period and also clippings from 1937–1941. As an advertising executive at the J. Walter Thompson agency, Cherington admittedly had a vested stake in encouraging advertising. But he seemed to genuinely believe in the wisdom of continuing advertising, even during a depression. In Ralph M. Hower Papers, 1870–1940, Arch GA 39.5, are wonderful materials on N. W. Ayer & Son, Inc., the country's first advertising agency. As I started doing more research on the Ad Council in the 1940s and 1950s, I found it interesting to peruse the industry's earlier campaign to "advertise advertising." Information about this campaign is spread across several boxes in Series 7, such as Boxes 13, 14–17, 19, 20, 22, 24–25, etc.

Beginning in the late 1930s, the NYSE began substantially overhauling member firm advertising rules. I tracked member firm advertisements in the pre–Own Your Share period (1938–1954) by reviewing advertisements in the *New York Times* and *Wall Street Journal*, as well as other newspapers. I began to connect the rise of institutional advertisements of the stock market in the late 1940s to a general postwar surge in belief by American corporate leaders in the usefulness and legitimacy of institutional advertising. In my research at the NYSEA, I also began noticing that several Exchange members had been affiliated during World War II with the War Advertising Council and then with its postwar incarnation, the Advertising Council. I delved into the records of the Archives of the Advertising Council at the University of Illinois (Urbana), paying special attention to certain Ad Council campaigns in the 1950s like Democratic Capitalism, which tied into campaign themes that the Exchange simultaneously was promoting.

At the Harry S. Truman Library in Independence, Missouri, I conducted more research on the Advertising Council and studied the work of the Committee for Economic Development (CED) as well as efforts to promote U.S. Savings bonds. In particular, I examined the Charles W. Jackson Files, Office of War Mobilization and Reconversion (*OWMR*) File, Papers of Harry S. Truman, especially Boxes 1, 6, and 22; Dallas C. Halverstadt Files, especially Box 1; Spencer R. Quick Files, Papers of Harry S. Truman, especially Box 4; as well as Tom C. Clark Papers, Attorney General (AG) Files, Box 37. Folder 1 in Box 37 of Clark's papers contained information on the Advertising Council and the Freedom Train.

During my time at the Archives of the Advertising Council at the University of Illinois at Urbana I examined Ad Council material, enabling me to see the strong parallels and overlap between the NYSE's efforts to promote "democratic capitalism" and the endeavors of the Ad Council. Box 1 in Series 13/2/202 contains Ad Council Annual Reports; Box 1 in Series 13/2/226 holds Industry Advisory Committee Minutes for various years in the 1950s and 1960s; Box 6 in Series 13/2/310 contains Advertising Council Washington Campaign Material from 1942 to 1951. Also useful were Boxes 1 and 2 in Series 13/2/300, which had valuable information on the War Advertising Council (WAC).

In analyzing Own Your Share, I became curious as to the degree the stock ownership campaign was influenced by the Ad Council, and also by the government's war bond campaign in the 1940s. Probing Record Group 44, Records of the Office of Government Reports, 1932–1947, at the National Archives Record Administration (NARA) in College Park, Maryland, I found a stunning resemblance between the NYSE's Own Your Share slogan in the 1950s and war bond advertisements from the 1940s.

In writing this book, I consulted countless articles in the trade, technical, and general press, general periodicals, as well as scholarly journals. Trade journals covered various aspects of the Own Your Share campaign, and I found relevant material in these journals: *Printers' Ink*, *Media/Scope*, *Sales Management Magazine*, as well as *Editor & Publisher*. A great source was the *Magazine of Wall Street*, founded in 1907 by financial writer Richard Wyckoff and edited and published for many years by his wife, Cecilia Gertrude ("C. G.") Wyckoff. The *Magazine* gives an excellent big picture of what was happening in the country at the time and also a fine, smaller picture of events on Wall Street. It helped me understand how long the Depression on Wall Street lasted, and hence the necessity of the Board of Governors intervening with a mass marketing campaign directed to Main Street. I also reviewed material from other business periodicals such as *Advertising Age*, *Advertising and Selling*, *Barron's*, *Business Week*, *Fortune*, *Forbes*, as well as the *Wall Street Journal*. I consulted general periodicals such as *Reader's Digest*, *Atlantic*, *Colliers*, *Harper's*, *Literary Digest*, *McClure's*, *North American Review*, *New York Sun*, *New York Times*, *Time*, and *Vital Speeches*.

Secondary Sources

Public Relations and the NYSE

This book is based upon my dissertation "Spinning the NYSE: Power and Public Relations at the Big Board" (Columbia University, 2004), which was the first major exploration of the history of NYSE public relations, dealing with the period from 1900 to the early 1970s. Portions of this book also are drawn from my various articles on this subject, such as "Spreading the Ideal of Mass Shareownership: Public Relations and the NYSE," *Essays in Economic and Business History* 22 (2004): 257–73; "'Own Your Share of American Business': Public Relations at the NYSE during the Cold War," *Business and Economic History On-line* 1 (2003); and "Lessons in Crisis Mismanagement from the 1929 Crash," *Essays in Economic and Business History* 24 (2006): 89–101.

For further analysis of public relations at the NYSE in the period up to 1933, see Julia Ott's *When Main Street Met Wall Street: The Quest for an Investors' Democracy* (Cambridge, MA: Harvard University Press, 2011), as well as her articles "The 'Free and Open' People's Market: Public Relations at the NYSE, 1913–1929," *Business History Conference* 2 (2004): 1–43; "When Wall Street Met Main Street: The Quest for an Investors' Democracy and the Emergence of the Retail Investor in the United States, 1890–1930," *Enterprise and Society* 9, no. 4 (2008): 619–30; and "'The Free and Open People's Market': Political Ideology and Retail Brokerage at the New York Stock Exchange, 1913–1933," *Journal of American History* 96, no. 1 (June 2009): 44–71.

On the Exchange's public information and educational activities in the post-World War II period, Rob Aitken provides an informative discussion in his article "'A Direct Personal Stake': Cultural Economy, Mass Investment, and the New York Stock Exchange," *Review of International Political Economy* 12, no. 2 (May 2005): 334–66.

Advertising, Public Relations, and Marketing

Unpacking the meaning of Own Your Share advertisements required my thinking about what advertisements convey and the limitations of what can be discovered through an analysis of these complex messages. Historian Pamela Laird's cogent thoughts on the agency underlying the production of advertisements helped prevent me from making the mistake of reading too much into OYS advertisements as a perfect reflection of American society at the time. Laird notes that specific people, not societies, construct advertisements. As she convincingly argues, commercial advertisements are much more accurate reflections of their creators than either their targeted audiences or the broader population. I likewise noted cultural historian Roland Marchand's notion of advertising as a distorting mirror—one that selectively chooses and enhances certain images while downplaying or ignoring others. Assuming that advertisements do not simply mirror society but can shape it, this opens the door to envisioning Own Your Share as a truly transformational marketing campaign that helped change the public's investing practices. See Pamela Walker Laird, *Advertising Progress: American Business and the Rise of Consumer Marketing* (Baltimore: Johns Hopkins University Press, 1998), and John Staudenmaier and Pamela Walker Lurito Laird, "Advertising History," *Technology and Culture* 30, no. 4 (October 1989): 1031–36; Roland Marchand, *Advertising the American Dream: Making Way for Modernity* (Berkeley: University of California Press, 1985). For a different view of advertising as a mirror of society, see Stephen Fox, *The Mirror Makers: A History of American Advertising and Its Creators* (New York: William Morrow, 1984). To understand perceptions of advertising and public relations at the time of the OYS campaign, I found relevant Nugent Wedding, "Advertising and Public Relations," *Journal of Business at the University of Chicago* 23 (July 1950): 168–81. For a more dubious view of the power of advertising, see William H. Whyte Jr., *Is Anybody Listening?* (New York: Simon and Schuster, 1952).

In the late 1930s and 1940s, after the Big Board liberalized advertising, many small- to midsize member retail brokerage houses debated whether or not advertising was "worth it." The difficulties of measuring the return on investment have long troubled corporations wanting to maximize their dollars. For a classic defense of advertising's worth, see Emily Fogg-Meade, "The Place of Advertising in Modern Business," *Journal of Political Economy* 9, no. 2 (March 1901): 218–42. See also Neil H. Borden, *The Economic Effects of Advertising* (Chicago: Richard D. Irwin, 1944).

The scholarly literature on advertising is vast, but several excellent books (besides those aforementioned) include Daniel Pope, *The Making of Modern Advertising* (New York: Basic Books, 1983); Stuart Ewen, *Captains of Consciousness: Advertising and the Social Roots of Consumer Culture* (New York: McGraw Hill, 1976); William Leach, *Land of Desire: Merchants, Power, and the Rise of a New American Culture* (New York: Vintage Books, 1994); and Jackson Lears, *Fables of Abundance: A Cultural History of Advertising in America* (New York: Basic Books, 1994). For an outstanding analysis of the challenges faced by advertisers during the Great Depression and their efforts to overcome critics see Inger L. Stole, *Advertising on Trial: Consumer Activism and Corporate Public Relations in the 1930s* (Champaign: University of Illinois Press, 2005).

The Own Your Share campaign at heart was a mass marketing campaign, and the Exchange's first. On the general rise of mass marketing, see especially Susan Strasser, *Satisfaction Guaranteed: The Making of the American Mass Market* (New York: Pantheon, 1989), and Richard Tedlow, *New and Improved: The Story of Mass Marketing in America* (Boston: Harvard Business School, 1996).

Besides interpreting the messages underlying OYS advertisements, I was interested in how the Exchange increasingly employed institutional advertising. On the rise of institutional advertising in the post-World War II era, I found particularly helpful Leonard Pearlin and Morris Rosenberg, "Propaganda Techniques in Institutional Advertising," *Public Opinion Quarterly* 16, no. 1 (Spring 1952): 5–26. Roland Marchand's *Creating the Corporate Soul: The Rise of Public Relations and Corporate Imagery in American Big Business* (Berkeley: University of California Press, 1998), provoked me to think about how the NYSE's institutional advertisements in the OYS era drew upon earlier institutional advertisements pioneered by corporations such as AT&T; AT&T's "investment democracy" advertisements in the early 1900s, highlighted in Marchand's book, are quite similar to some of the NYSE's advertisements in the late 1940s.

Properly telling the OYS story also involved understanding the history of public relations (in part, because the story involved a pronounced midcentury shift from public relations toward more advertising). In recent years, marketers in the United States have tended to shift in the other direction—toward more public relations, as Al Ries and Laura Ries contend in their book, *The Fall of Advertising and the Rise of PR* (New York: HarperCollins, 2002). Some enriching studies of corporate image and public relations include Richard S. Tedlow, *Keeping the Corporate Image: Public Relations and Business, 1900–1950* (Greenwich: JAI Press, 1979); David E. Nye, *Image Worlds: Corporate Identities at General Electric, 1890–1930* (Cambridge, MA: MIT Press, 1985); John E. Marston, *The Nature of Public Relations* (New York: McGraw Hill, 1963); Eric Goldman, *Two-Way Street: The Emergence of the Public Relations Counsel* (Boston: Bellman Publishing, 1948); Scott M. Cutlip, *The Unseen Power: Public Relations, A History* (Hillsdale: Lawrence Erlbaum, 1994); as well as Robert Heilbroner, "Public Relations—The Invisible Sell," *Harper's*, June 1957, 31–34. To understand the public's growing acceptance of large firms in the early twentieth century, I consulted Louis Galambos' *The Public Image of Big Business in America, 1880–1940: A Quantitative Study in Social Change* (Baltimore: Johns Hopkins University Press, 1975).

I began to see a strong connection between the way the NYSE was trying to regain legitimacy and the ways corporations in the Depression and war years had endeavored to enhance their own images. In conceptualizing legitimacy, I was guided by Marchand's book *Creating the Corporate Soul*, in which he holds that a legitimate organization is widely seen to possess an "appropriate" relationship—"in size, power, scope of responsibility, and freedom of action—to such other institutions as the family, the community, and the state" (8n, p. 37). I also considered the notion of legitimacy put forth by Blake E. Ashforth and Barrie W. Gibbs in "The Double-Edge of Organizational Legitimation," *Organization Science* 1, no. 2 (1990): 177–94. The Own Your Share campaign was a key part of the Exchange's intense (and ultimately successful) efforts to regain the legitimacy they had lost in the Great Crash of 1929 and the scandals in its wake.

While not explicitly discussing securities, D. Kirk Davidson's *Selling Sin: The Marketing of Socially Unacceptable Products* (Westport: Quorum, 1996) stimulated me to think of stocks as products that require particularly careful marketing tactics. In 1971, just after Own Your Share concluded, Philip Kotler and Sidney Levy promoted the idea of demarketing in their *Harvard Business Review* article "Demarketing, Yes, Demarketing," *Harvard Business Review* 49 (1971): 74–80. Stocks were not mentioned by Kotler and Levy as needing to be demarketed, but my colleague Michael Coyne and I posited that idea in our article, "Ethical Issues Related to the Mass Marketing of Securities," *Journal of Business Ethics* 78 (2008): 193–98. The thought that stocks needed to be demarketed flowed through to my analysis of the "four cautions" embedded in OYS advertisements.

Charles Merrill

It is impossible to tell the story of NYSE public relations and advertising without paying homage to the role played by Charles Merrill. Besides pioneering marketing work at his own firm, Merrill was a catalyst for change in the Big Board's marketing practices. With an early vision of spreading shareownership, Merrill inspired Exchange leaders to broaden the composition of the stock market, as told in Edwin Perkins' authoritative biography *Wall Street to Main Street: Charles Merrill and Middle-Class Investors* (Cambridge: Cambridge University Press, 1999). Several articles on Merrill Lynch by Perkins also informed my research, especially "Market Research at Merrill Lynch & Co., 1940–1945: New Directions for Stockbrokers," in *Perkins on U.S. Financial History and Related Topics* (Lanham, MD: University Press of America, 2009),

149–60, and Perkins, "Growth Stocks for Middle-Class Investors: Merrill Lynch & Co., 1914–1941," in *Coping with Crisis: International Financial Institutions in the Interwar Period*, ed. Makoto Kasuya (Oxford: Oxford University Press, 2003). Edwin P. Hoyt devotes a chapter to Charles Merrill in his book *The Supersalesmen* (Cleveland: World Publishing, 1962), and Robert Sobel discusses Merrill in his book *Dangerous Dreamers: The Financial Innovators from Charles Merrill to Michael Milken* (New York: John Wiley and Sons, 1993). Merrill Lynch also commissioned a history of its company; see Henry Hecht, ed., *A Legacy of Leadership: Merrill Lynch, 1884–1985* (New York: Merrill Lynch, 1985). For a good exploration of Winthrop H. Smith's pivotal role in leading Merrill Lynch Pierce Fenner & Smith, see Warren Bennis and David A. Heenan, *Co-Leaders: The Power of Great Partnerships* (New York: John Wiley and Sons, 1999), chap. 4, 63–80. See also Joseph Nocera, *A Piece of the Action: How the Middle Class Joined the Money Class* (New York: Simon and Schuster, 1994).

MIP and Mutual Funds

The NYSE's Monthly Investment Plan (MIP), which Merrill Lynch supported wholeheartedly, has received little scholarly attention. The plan is briefly mentioned in Rob Aitken's *Performing Capital: Towards a Cultural Economy of Popular and Global Finance* (New York: Palgrave, 2007), 130–32; Robert Sobel, *Inside Wall Street: Continuity and Change in the Financial District* (New York: W. W. Norton, 1982), 105–7; Perkins, *Wall Street to Main Street*, 234–36; and Lou Engel, *How to Buy Stocks* (Boston: Little, Brown, 1953), 106–10. In addition to newspaper and magazine articles, the files on MIP at the NYSEA help provide a fuller explanation of what the NYSE, participating member firms, and listed corporations were trying to achieve with MIP. The introduction of MIP in 1954 is evidence of the Exchange's efforts to reduce the appeal of mutual funds by offering another product geared especially to small investors.

However, as historical statistics from the Investment Company Institute show, the popularity of mutual funds eventually far exceeded the allure of MIP. In addition to mutual fund coverage in newspapers and articles from the era, I found Matthew Fink's recent articles and book detailing the evolution of the mutual fund industry helpful, especially his *The Rise of Mutual Funds: An Insider's View* (New York: Oxford University Press, 2008), and his "Political Horse-Trading Produces a Miracle: The 70th Anniversary of the Investment Company Act," *Financial History* 97 (Spring 2010): 32–34, 37. Other books providing historical information about mutual funds include Diana B. Henriques' *Fidelity's World: The Secret Life and Public Power of the Mutual Fund Giant* (New York: Touchstone, 1997); William Steiner, *Investment Trusts: American Experience* (New York: Adelphi, 1929); Hugh Bullock, *The Story of Investment Companies* (New York: Columbia University Press, 1959); Natalie R. Groh, "The 'Boston-Type Open-End Fund'—Development of a National Financial Institution: 1924–1940" (PhD diss., Harvard University, 1977). For a discussion of the range of marketing strategies employed by mutual fund promoters in the 1950s and 1960s, see Janice Traflet, "Never Bought, Always Sold: Salesmanship, the Small Investor, and the Early Postwar Surge in Mutual Fund Participation," *Essays in Economic and Business History* 27 (2009): 5–14, and Emily Martz's "'Relationships, Relationships, Relationships': The Mutual Fund Industry's Mantra for Success from the 1940s through the 1960s," *Essays in Economic and Business History* 28 (2010): 57–69. In investigating the Exchange's quest to create an installment buying plan for stocks, I examined the general rise of installment plans for consumer goods in the 1920s. See Martha Olney, *Buy Now, Pay Later: Advertising, Credit, and Consumer Durables in the 1920's* (Chapel Hill: University of North Carolina Press, 1991).

Democratic Capitalism, the NYSE, and the Cold War

In the 1950s and 1960s, promoters of both stocks and equity mutual funds emphasized the importance of widespread stock ownership as a matter of national, not just individual, security. To a significant extent, the deepening Cold War influenced the tone and content of the Own Your Share campaign. I began to see the activities of the NYSE as part of a soft side of anti-communism. This soft side is discussed by Elaine Tyler May in *Homeward Bound: American Families in the Cold War* (New York: Basic Books, 1988). Also see Richard Fried, *The Russians Are Coming! The Russians Are Coming! Pageantry and Patriotism in Cold-War America* (New York: Oxford University Press, 1998). While neither Fried nor May explicitly discuss the NYSE, the Own Your Share campaign is better understood when framed in light of Cold War culture as well as the effort to promote economic citizenship. Mark H. Leff's article, "The Politics of Sacrifice on the American Home Front in World War II," *Journal of American History* 77, no. 4 (March 1991), suggested to me how the Exchange was using a similar strategy in marketing stocks to the American public during the Cold War, although Leff does not mention the NYSE's archives.

Exchange rhetoric at the time was filled with the language of "democratizing" the market and "free enterprise." To understand what was meant by these phrases, I tapped into sources such as *People's Capitalism? Part I: The American Round Table* (New York: The American Advertising Council, 1957); David W. Raudenbush, *Democratic Capitalism* (New York: John Day, 1946); Robert V. Eagly, "American Capitalism: A Transformation?" *The Business History Review* 33, no. 4 (Winter 1959): 549–68; as well as Adolph A. Berle, "Corporations and the Modern State," in Thurman W. Arnold, Morris L. Ernst, Adolph A. Berle Jr., Lloyd K. Garrison, and Sir Alfred Simmern, *The Future of Democratic Capitalism* (Philadelphia: University of Pennsylvania Press, 1950), 35–62. Also, I found useful Elizabeth Fones Wolf's *Selling Free Enterprise: The Business Assault on Labor and Liberalism, 1945–60* (Champaign: University of Illinois Press, 1994), as well as Robert Griffith's "The Selling of America: The Advertising Council and American Policies, 1942–1960," *Business History Review* 57 (Autumn 1983): 389–412.

Colleen Dunlavy's work exploring the different types of shareholder voting rights that proliferated earlier in history reveals the inaccuracy of the phrase "democratic capitalism" in describing today's shareownership voting rights, which are, as she points out, more of a plutocratic, than democratic, arrangement. See Colleen A. Dunlavy, "Social Conceptions of the Corporation: Insights from the History of Shareholder Voting Rights," *Washington and Lee Law Review* 63, no. 4 (Fall 2006): 1347–88. For criticisms of "people's capitalism" and "democratic capitalism," see Art Preis, "Myth of 'People's Capitalism,'" *International Socialist Review* 23, no. 1 (Winter 1962): 3–9; Joseph A. Livingston, *The American Stockholder* (Philadelphia: J. B. Lippincott, 1958); and more recently Aaron Brenner, "The Myth of the Shareholder Nation," *New Labor Forum* 13, no. 2 (Summer 2004): 20–35. See also Sylvia A. Allegretto, "The State of America's Working Wealth, 2011," Economic Policy Institute Briefing Paper No. 292, March 23, 2011.

Wall Street History

For much of Wall Street's history, the American public has debated whether stock buying represents "speculation" or true "investment," and whether or not outsiders (i.e., "average" Americans) should be in the market. Ann Fabian provides a fascinating picture of bucket shops in her book *Card Sharps, Dream Books, and Bucket Shops: Gambling in 19th-Century America* (Ithaca: Cornell University Press, 1990). For insight into historical attitudes toward speculation, see Cedric B. Cowing, *Populists, Plungers, and Progressives: A Social History of Stock and Commodity Speculation, 1890–1936* (Princeton: Princeton University Press, 1965); Edward Chancellor, *Devil Take the Hindmost: A History of Financial Speculation* (New York: Farrar, Straus and Giroux, 1999); David Hochfelder, "'Where the Common People Could Speculate': The Ticker, Bucket Shops, and the Origin of Popular Participation in Financial Markets, 1880–1920," *Journal of American History* 93 (September 2006): 335–58; as well as Paten Thomas, "Bucket Shop in Speculation," *Munsey's* (October 1900): 68–70.

Robert Sobel authored numerous general histories of Wall Street, including *Inside Wall Street: Continuity and Change in the Financial District* (New York: W. W. Norton, 1982); *N.Y.S.E.: A History of the New York Stock Exchange, 1935–1975* (New York: Weybright and Talley, 1975); and *The Great Boom: How a Generation of Americans Created the World's Most Prosperous Society* (New York: St. Martin's Press, 2000). I found useful Sobel's delineation of the distinct functions of different groups of Exchange members, such as specialists, floor traders, and commission brokers. Understanding the fractured nature of the Exchange "community" helped me appreciate why some retail-oriented NYSE members (like Charles Merrill) espoused Exchange marketing activities and the goal of widespread shareownership from the onset, while other members were slower to accept the desirability of mass marketing. While much of Sobel's *N.Y.S.E.: A History* was relevant, a couple chapters in particular resonated. Chap. 4 ("The Dead and the Dying," 66–82) gives a feel for the malaise affecting Wall Street in the late 1930s and early 1940s, and chap. 10 ("People's Capitalism," 182–97), and chap. 11 ("The New Investors," 198–216) provide an excellent analysis of the changes sweeping over the Exchange in the Funston era.

Charles Geisst's books *Wall Street: A History* (New York: Oxford University Press, 2004), and *Visionary Capitalism: Financial Markets and the American Dream in the Twentieth Century* (New York: Praeger, 1990) provided useful insights. Another solid book is Steve Fraser's *Wall Street: A Cultural History* (New York: HarperCollins, 2005), see especially chap. 16, "Shareholder Nation," 506–43. B. Mark Smith's book, *The Equity Culture: The Story of the Global Stock Market* (New York: Farrar, Straus and Giroux, 2003) provided insights into an "equity culture" and the extent to which American culture today is immersed in the stock market. Also see Robert J. Shiller, *Irrational Exuberance* (Princeton: Princeton University Press, 2000); B. Mark Smith, *Toward Rational Exuberance: The Evolution of the Modern Stock Market* (New York: Farrar, Straus and Giroux, 2000); Thomas Frank, *One Market under God: Extreme Capitalism, Market Populism, and the End of Economic Democracy* (New York: Doubleday, 2000).

For information on Wall Street during the 1920s and 1930s, in addition to primary sources, I consulted Maury Klein, *Rainbow's End: The Crash of 1929* (New York: Oxford University Press,

2001); John Brooks, *Once in Golconda: A True Drama of Wall Street, 1920–1938* (New York: John Wiley and Sons, 1999); Harold Bierman Jr., *The Causes of the 1929 Stock Market Crash: A Speculative Orgy or a New Era?* (Westport: Greenwood Press, 1998); Bierman, *The Great Myths of 1929 and the Lessons to Be Learned* (New York: Greenwood Press, 1991); and Michael A. Bernstein, *The Great Depression: Delayed Recovery and Economic Change in America, 1929–1930* (Cambridge: Cambridge University Press, 1987). On the history of the Securities and Exchange Commission (SEC), see Joel Seligman, *The Transformation of Wall Street: A History of the Securities and Exchange Commission and Modern Corporate Finance* (Boston: Northeastern University Press, 1995), and Louis Kohlmeier, *The Regulators: Watchdog Agencies and the Public Interests* (New York: Harper and Row, 1969), and Thomas McGraw, *Prophets of Regulation: Charles Francis Adams, Louis D. Brandeis, James M. Landis, Alfred E. Kahn* (Cambridge, MA: Harvard University Press, 1984), esp. 153–209.

John Brooks' *The Go-Go Years: The Drama and Crashing Finale of Wall Street's Bullish 60s* (New York: John Wiley and Sons, 1999) captures the vivacious spirit of the 1960s on Wall Street. On the growing cult of performance espoused by mutual fund managers, see Adam Smith, *The Money Game* (New York: Random House, 1967), as well as Janice Traflet and Elton McGoun, "Has Elvis Left the Building? The Rise—and Fall (?) of Celebrity Fund Managers," *Journal of Cultural Economy* 1, no. 2 (July 2008): 199–214. With regard to the Great Paperwork Crisis that unfolded in 1968, Wyatt Wells provides a comprehensive account in "Certificates and Computers: The Remaking of Wall Street, 1967 to 1971," *Business History Review* 74, no. 2 (Summer 2000): 193–235. To highlight some of the market highs that occurred in the 1950s, I consulted Martin S. Fridson's *It Was a Very Good Year: Extraordinary Moments in Stock Market History* (New York: John Wiley and Sons, 1998). I also examined classic histories of Wall Street, such as Sereno S. Pratt's *The Work of Wall Street: An Account of the Functions, Methods and History of the New York Money and Stock Markets* (New York: Arno Press, 1975; first published 1921).

Two intertwined questions underlying my research are whether most people should be in the stock market and whether stocks are the best long-term investment. For early articulations of the common stock theory, I relied upon Edgar L. Smith, *Common Stocks as Long Term Investments* (New York: Macmillan, 1928); Chelcie C. Bosland, *The Common Stock Theory of Investment* (New York: Ronald Press, 1937); and Clark Belden, *Common Stocks and Uncommon Sense* (New York: Coward McCann, 1939). Also significant are alternate investment vehicles where ordinary people historically have placed their savings, such as traditional bank accounts and life insurance policies. Perhaps the most comprehensive history of life insurance is J. Owen Stalson, *Marketing Life Insurance: Its History in America* (Cambridge, MA: Harvard University Press, 1942). In the 1950s and 1960s, the rise of modern portfolio theory affected Main Street's and Wall Street's perceptions of stock market risk. Harry Markowitz's article, "Portfolio Selection," *Journal of Finance* 7, no. 1 (March 1952): 77–91 is pivotal. Also see Mark Rubinstein, "Portfolio Selection: A Fifty-Year Retrospective," *Journal of Finance* 57, no. 3 (June 2002): 1041–45.

As the Own Your Share promotional campaign ended in the late 1960s, institutional trading volume was burgeoning at a far faster pace than individual investing. On the rise of institutions in the market, see Charles Ellis, *Institutional Investing* (Homewood, IL: Dow Jones-Irwin, 1971); James J. Needham, *The Threat to Corporate Growth* (Philadelphia: Girard Bank, 1974); Marshall E. Blume and Irwin Friend, *The Changing Role of the Individual Investor* (New York:

John Wiley and Sons, 1978); Peter Drucker, *The Unseen Revolution: How Pension Fund Socialism Came to America* (New York: HarperCollins, 1972); Chris Welles, *Last Days of the Club* (New York: E. P. Dutton, 1975). For detailed breakdowns of institutional investors' buying behavior (including in the pre-1950s period), see Raymond W. Goldsmith, ed., *Institutional Investors and Corporate Stock—A Background Study* (Ann Arbor: UMI, National Bureau of Economic Research, 1973).

Commission rate deregulation in May 1975 led to the rise of discount brokers like Charles Schwab, who is discussed in John Kandor's refreshing book, *Charles Schwab: How One Company Beat Wall Street and Reinvented the Brokerage Industry* (New York: John Wiley and Sons, 2002). Robert Reich's *Supercapitalism: The Transformation of Business, Democracy, and Everyday Life* (New York: Vintage Books, 2007) puts in perspective the changes in investing and the transformation of other areas of life in recent decades. Additionally, a worthwhile examination of the pressure today to invest wisely and its impact on notions of self-identity and worth is Randy Martin's *Financialization of Daily Life* (Philadelphia: Temple University Press, 2002).

Imagining Shareholders

Much of this book concerns how the NYSE imagined and envisioned the contours of a shareowner nation. This book also explains how many ordinary Americans in the mid-twentieth century came to see themselves as part of a shareholding community. Benedict Anderson's *Imagined Communities: Reflections on the Origin and Spread of Nationalism* (London: Verso, 1991) provides insight into the process of nation building. Also helpful was Regina Lee Blaszczyk's *Imagining Consumers: Design and Innovation from Wedgwood to Corning* (Baltimore: Johns Hopkins University Press, 2000). While Blaszczyk crisply analyzes how companies in the American ceramics and glass industries sought to understand consumers and imagine their desires to satisfy their customers, my book examines how the NYSE and the securities industry endeavored to imagine what potential investors might want and need. In the Own Your Share years, the Big Board strove to make the process of buying stocks easy and unintimidating to average Americans—men, women, and children alike. Importantly, Keith Funston, Rud Lawrence, and the fellow architects of OYS (the longest marketing campaign in Exchange history) also sought to create a nation of "sound," well-informed investors who understood the potential risks, as well as the rewards, of shareownership.

Index